C000066511

Contents

Side Dishes · · · · · · · · · · 41

Main Dishes · **55**

Snacks and Appetizers · **69**

Fish and Seafood · **83**

Poultry · **97**

Meat Recipes · **111**

Introduction

You surely know that air frying makes food crispy and appetizing without actual frying. Maybe it's too good to be true, but fried foods can be healthy. Air frying is an easy way to prepare something promptly without using oil for frying in excesses.

The question arises, what can be cooked in an air fryer apart from the French fries. We can show you as many air fryer meals, low-carb desserts, veggie options, baked goods as you have never even though of. Plenty of recipes will take care of your limited cooking time and will show you the most simple and efficient way to prepare your everyday meals for a busy self or your loved ones.

Satisfy your fried cravings from easy breakfasts to hearty nutritive main dishes. Catchy textures of your favorite fried foods are closer than you can imagine! This air fryer cookbook will be your answer to enjoying foods while being sure in their taste and health benefits. Who could have thought one kitchen appliance could do so incredibly well and cook so many?! This book knows for sure, and you are about to discover it.

Breakfast Recipes

Simple Egg Breakfast

Prep time: 4 minutes
Cooking time: 10 minutes
Servings: 2

Ingredients:

Eggs – 4	Green Onion
Yellow mustard – 1	(chopped) – 2
tsp.	Paprika – ½ tsp.
Mayonnaise – ½ cup	Salt and pepper to
	taste

Directions:

Mix eggs, yellow mustard and green onion in a bowl.
Add mayonnaise, salt and pepper with paprika. Beat well.
Add the mixture in a round baking tray.
Place it in the air fryer and let it cook for 10 minutes.
When ready, serve and enjoy!

Nutrition:

Calories:96	Carbohydrates: 10g
Fat: 9g	Protein: 35g

Mushrooms and Beef Recipe

Prep time: 5 minutes
Cooking time: 10 minutes
Servings: 3

Ingredients:

Mustard – 1 tbsp.	Mushrooms
Honey – ½ tbsp.	(chopped) – 6 large
Garlic clove – 1	Onion (chopped) – 1
minced	Cheese (shredded) –
Mayonnaise – ½ cup	1 cup
Salt and pepper to	Sandwich bread
taste	pieces
Beef (chopped) – ½	Oil – 1 tbsp.
lb.	

Directions:

Put the beef into the bowl.
Add mustard, honey, garlic, mayonnaise, onion, cheese and mushrooms. Blend well.
Grease the round baking tray with oil.
Place the bread pieces at the bottom as a layer in the tray. Pour the mixture over it.
Let it cook in the air fryer for 10 minutes.
When ready, enjoy!

Nutrition:

Calories:70	Carbohydrates: 10g
Fat: 6g	Protein: 10g

Muffin Mix Breakfast

Prep time: 6 minutes
Cooking time: 12 minutes
Servings: 2

Ingredients:

Oil – 1 tbsp.	Cheese (shredded) –
Egg – 1	1 cup
Muffin – whole wheat	Canadian bacon – 4
Black pepper to taste	slices

Directions:

Whisk egg in a bowl.
Add black pepper and mix well.
Grease the round baking tray with oil and pour the egg mixture.
Add cheese and bacon.
Place the round baking tray in air fryer with the muffin.
Let it cook for 12 minutes on 300 F.
When ready, enjoy!

Nutrition:

Calories: 90	Carbohydrates: 20g
Fat: 8g	Protein: 25g

Simple Bacon and Egg Recipe

Prep time: 4 minutes
Cooking time: 10 minutes
Servings: 2

Ingredients:

Eggs – 3	Green pepper – ½
Egg whites – 3	tbsp.
Milk – ½ cup	Bread pieces – 4
Mushrooms – 3 dices	Bacon – 2 slices
	Cheese (slices) – 3

Directions:

Whisk eggs and egg white in a bowl.
Add milk, mushrooms, green pepper and bacon. Mix well.
Pour the mixture in a round baking tray and add cheese over it.
Place the bread slices on the sides of the try in the air fryer.
Cook for 10 minutes on 300 F.
When done, serve and enjoy!

Nutrition:

Calories:95	Carbohydrates: 10g
Fat: 6g	Protein: 200g

Bacon and Avocado Mix Recipe

Prep time: 5 minutes
Cooking time: 10 minutes
Servings: 3

Ingredients:

Bun – 1 small pack
Half squash – 2 cups
Bell pepper (chopped) – 1
Bacon – 2 slices
Avocado (chopped) – 1

Humus – 1 tbsp.
Cheese – shredded – 1 cup
Any sauce you like – as desired

Directions:

Add squash, bell pepper and bacon in a bowl.
Add avocado and humus.
Stir well the ingredients.
Add cheese.
Make small round patties and turn on the air fryer to 300 F.
Place the patties on the grill and let it cook for 10 minutes.
When done, place the patty in a bun and enjoy!

Nutrition:

Calories: 90
Fat: 8g

Carbohydrates: 20g
Protein: 25g

Asparagus Air fryer Recipe

Prep time: 6 minutes
Cooking time: 15 minutes
Servings: 2

Ingredients:

Bread pieces – 2
Avocado – 3 slices
Ham (slices) – 3
Asparagus – 3 sticks

Tomato (slices) – ½
Egg – 1
Oil – 1 tbsp.

Directions:

Whisk egg in a bowl.
Add avocado, ham and asparagus. Mix well.
Get a round baking tray and grease oil.
Pour the mixture with sprinkling tomato slices. Place in the air fryer.
Place the bread pieces on the sides of the baking tray.
Cook for 15 minutes on 300 F.
When done, serve and enjoy!

Nutrition:

Calories: 125
Fat: 7g

Carbohydrates: 10g
Protein: 40g

Bacon and Ham Mix Recipe

Prep time: 5 minutes
Cooking time: 10 minutes
Servings: 2

Ingredients:

Bacon (slices) – 4
Bread slices – 6
Ham (chopped) – 1 cup

Cheddar cheese – 1 cup
Eggs – 3
Milk – ½ cup
Salt to taste

Directions:

Whisk eggs in a bowl.
Add ham, cheese, milk and salt.
Blend well and add bacon slices.
Get a round baking tray and pour the mixture in it.
Let it bake for 10 minutes in the air fryer on 300 F.
When ready, serve with the bread slices and enjoy!

Nutrition:

Calories: 115
Fat: 7g

Carbohydrates: 9g
Protein: 40g

Steak Strips Recipe

Prep time: 4 minutes
Cooking time: 15 minutes
Servings: 2

Ingredients:

Strips steak – 5
Salt and pepper to taste
Ciabatta bread – 6 slices
Garlic (chopped) – 2 tbsp.

Tomato (chopped) – 1
Basil (chopped) – ½ cup
Cheese (shredded) – ½ cup

Directions:

Mix cheese with basil in a bowl.
Add garlic and tomato in it with salt and pepper.
Pour the mixture in the round baking tray and place steak strips.
Let it bake in the air fryer for 15 minutes.
When done, serve with bread and enjoy!

Nutrition:

Calories:95
Fat: 6g

Carbohydrates: 10g
Protein: 200g

Potato Mix Breakfast Recipe

Prep time: 5 minutes
Cooking time: 10 minutes
Servings: 2

Ingredients:

Provolone Cheese –
2 cups
Steak (sliced) – 1 lb.
Onion (chopped) – 1
Potato (diced) – 1

Butter – 1 tbsp.
Salt and pepper to
taste
Oil – 1 tbsp.
Bread (slices) – 4

Directions:

Add cheese and potato in a bowl.
Mix onion, butter and salt and pepper. Blend
well.
Grease the round baking tray with oil and
pour the mixture with placing the steak on
the mixture.
Let it cook for 10 minutes on 300 F.
When ready, serve it with the bread slices
and enjoy!

Nutrition:

Calories: 90
Fat: 8g

Carbohydrates: 20g
Protein: 25g

Chicken with Salsa

Prep time: 6 minutes
Cooking time: 18 minutes
Servings: 3

Ingredients:

Salsa – 2 cups
Tomato sauce – 1
tbsp.
Chipotle sauce – 1
tbsp.

Chicken chopped – 1
lb.
Salt and pepper to
taste
Cheese (shredded)
Cilantro to garnish

Directions:

Put the chicken into the bowl.
Add salsa, tomato sauce, chipotle sauce and
cheese.
Mix well and add salt and pepper.
Make small patties out of the mixture and
place them in the air fryer.
Let it cook for 18 minutes on 300 F.
When ready, garnish with cilantro and enjoy!

Nutrition:

Calories:96
Fat: 9g

Carbohydrates: 10g
Protein: 35g

Veggie Mix Recipe

Prep time: 6 minutes
Cooking time: 14 minutes
Servings: 2

Ingredients:

Milk – 1/2 cup
Spinach – chopped
Cheese (shredded) –
1 cup
Onion (chopped) –
1/2
Bell Pepper
(chopped) – 1/2

Eggs – 4
Salt and Pepper to
taste
Mint (chopped) – ½
cup
Oil – 1 tbsp.

Directions:

Whisk eggs in a bowl.
Add milk, cheese, spinach, onion, bell
pepper, salt and pepper and mint.
Get the round baking tray. Grease with oil.
Pour the mixture in the tray.
Let it cook in the air fryer for 14 minutes on
300 F.
When done, serve and enjoy!

Nutrition:

Calories:96
Fat: 9g

Carbohydrates: 10g
Protein: 35g

Eggs with Dill

Prep time: 4 minutes
Cooking time: 18 minutes
Servings: 2

Ingredients:

Garlic cloves – 2
minced
Dill – 1 tbsp.
Vinegar – 1 tbsp.
Salt and pepper to
taste

Oil – 1 tbsp.
Oregano – 1 tbsp.
Tomato (sliced) – 1
Olives – 1 cup
Onion (chopped) – 1
Eggs – 3

Directions:

Whisk eggs in a bowl.
Add garlic, dill, vinegar, oregano, tomato,
olives and onion.
Grease the round baking tray with oil.
Pour the mixture in the baking tray.
Let it cook in the air fryer for 18 minutes on
300 F.
When ready, serve!

Nutrition:

Calories: 125
Fat: 7g

Carbohydrates: 10g
Protein: 40g

Tofu for Breakfast

Prep time: 4 minutes
Cooking time: 20 minutes
Servings: 2

Ingredients:

Peppercorns – 1 tbsp.
Oil – 1 tbsp.
Salt and pepper to taste
Buns – 4
Coriander seeds – 1 tbsp.
Paprika – 1 tbsp.
Bay leaf – 1
Tofu – 2 cups
Mayonnaise – 1 tbsp.
Lettuce (shredded) – ½ cup
Onion (sliced) – 1

Directions:

Grease the round baking tray with oil.
Add tofu, salt and pepper, coriander seeds, paprika, bay leaf, onion and mayonnaise in a bowl. Mix well.
Pour in the baking tray.
Cook in the air fryer for 20 minutes on 300 F.
When ready, cover with lettuce and serve with buns!

Nutrition:

Calories:95
Fat: 6g
Carbohydrates: 10g
Protein: 200g

Spinach and Thyme Mix Recipe

Prep time: 5 minutes
Cooking time: 14 minutes
Servings: 3

Ingredients:

Red wine vinegar – ½ tbsp.
Shallot – ½ cup
Thyme (chopped) – ½ cup
Salt and Pepper to taste
Spinach (chopped) – 2 cups
Bread pieces – 4
Basil (chopped) – ½ cup
2 tbsp. mayonnaise – 3 tbsp.
Cheddar cheese – ½ cup

Directions:

Layer the bread pieces into the round baking tray.
Add red wine vinegar, shallot, thyme with salt and pepper in a bowl.
Add spinach, basil, mayonnaise and cheese. Blend well. Cook in the air fryer for 14 minutes on 300 F.
When ready, serve and enjoy!

Nutrition:

Calories:70
Fat: 6g
Carbohydrates: 10g
Protein: 10g

Scallions Mix Eggs

Prep time: 6 minutes
Cooking time: 14 minutes
Servings: 3

Ingredients:

Beans – 1 small can
Cheddar cheese – 1 cup
Tortilla chips – 1 small pack
Scallions (chopped) – 3
Cilantro (chopped) – 1 cup
Garlic cloves – 2 minced
Stew powder – 1 tbsp.
Salt to taste
Egg white – 1
Wheat pitas – 4
Onion (chopped) – 1
Lime juice – 1 tbsp.

Directions:

Add cheese with scallions into a bowl.
Add cilantro, garlic, stew powder, salt, egg white, onion and lime juice.
Blend well and then add the mixture in the round baking tray.
Cook it in the air fryer for 14 minutes on 300 F.
When done, dress it with tortilla chips and serve with wheat pitas.

Nutrition:

Calories: 105
Fat: 9g
Carbohydrates: 10g
Protein: 30g

Squashy Breakfast Recipe

Prep time: 5 minutes
Cooking time: 10 minutes
Servings: 3

Ingredients:

Oil – 1 tbsp.
Squash – 1 cup
Onions – 2 chopped
Cheese (shredded) – 2 cups
Salt and pepper to taste
Sauce (any) – 1 tbsp.
Basil to garnish
Garlic (minced) – 2 cloves

Directions:

Add squash with cheese into a bowl.
Mix onion, salt and pepper, sauce and garlic. Blend well.
Get a round baking tray. Grease with oil.
Add the mixture in the tray and cook it in air fryer for 10 minutes on 300 F.
When done, garnish it with basil and serve!

Nutrition:

Calories: 125
Fat: 7g
Carbohydrates: 10g
Protein: 40g

Shallot Mix Recipe

Prep time: 4 minute
Cooking time: 19 minutes
Servings: 2

Ingredients:

Garlic cloves – 2 minced
Shallot – 1 small
Vegetable oil – 1 tbsp.
Cheddar cheese – 1 cup
Cream – ½ cup
Salt and pepper to taste
Olives – ½ cup
Mint (chopped) – ½ cup
Zucchini (chopped) – 1 cup
Lettuce (shredded) – 1 cup

Directions:

Grab a bowl and add shallot and garlic.
Mix cheese, cream, salt and pepper, olives and mint. Blend well.
Get the round baking tray. Grease it with oil.
Add the mixture in the tray and spread the chopped zucchini over it.
Let it cook in the air fryer for 19 minutes on 300 F.
When ready, serve with lettuce and enjoy the healthy breakfast!

Nutrition:

Calories: 90
Fat: 8g
Carbohydrates: 20g
Protein: 25g

Salsa Mix Recipe

Prep time: 4 minutes
Cooking time: 17 minutes
Servings: 2

Ingredients:

Green bell pepper (chopped) – 1
Sour Cream – 1 tbsp.
Milk – 1 cup
Salsa – 1 tbsp.
Cheese (shredded) – 1 cup
Cilantro leaves (chopped) – 1 cup
Onions (sliced) – 2

Directions:

Mix green bell pepper with sour cream.
Add milk, salsa, cheese, cilantro leaves and onion.
Pour the mixture in the baking tray. Place the onion slices on the mixture.
Let it cook in the air fryer for 17 minutes on 300 F.
When done, serve and enjoy the simple meal!

Nutrition:

Calories: 70
Fat: 6g
Carbohydrates: 10g
Protein: 10g

Chicken with Orange Taste

Prep time: 4 minutes
Cooking time: 15 minutes
Servings: 2

Ingredients:

Chicken – boneless (shredded) – 1 lb.
Carrots (sliced) – 2
Onion (sliced) – 2
Cajun seasoning
Orange juice – ¼ cup
Peas (frozen) – 1 cup
Dill – 2 tbsp.
Parsley for garnishing

Directions:

Add the chicken into the bowl.
Mix carrots, onion, orange juice, peas and dill. Blend well.
Add the mixture in the round baking tray.
Cook for 15 minutes in the air fryer on 300 F.
When done, garnish it with Cajun and parsley to serve!

Nutrition:

Calories: 96
Fat: 9g
Carbohydrates: 10g
Protein: 35g

Broccoli Mix Breakfast Recipe

Prep time: 4 minutes
Cooking time: 14 minutes
Servings: 2

Ingredients:

Butter – 1 tbsp.
Mayonnaise – 2 tbsp.
Mushroom soup – ½ cup
Salt and pepper to taste
Onion (slices) – 1
Chicken – cooked and mashed – ½ lb.
Broccoli – chopped – 1 cup

Directions:

Add the chicken into the bowl.
Mix mayonnaise, mushroom soup, onion, broccoli and salt and pepper.
Grease the round baking tray with butter.
Add the mixture in the tray.
Let it cook in air fryer for 14 minutes on 300 F.
When ready, serve and enjoy!

Nutrition:

Calories: 70
Fat: 6g
Carbohydrates: 10g
Protein: 10g

Artichokes Mix Egg

Prep time: 6 minutes
Cooking time: 15 minutes
Servings: 2

Ingredients:

Artichokes (peeled) –
2 cups
Fennel – 1 tbsp.
Cream – 2 tbsp.
Egg – 3

Garlic (cloves) – 4
minced
Nutmeg powder – 1
tbsp.
Salt and pepper to
taste

Directions:

Whisk the eggs in a bowl.
Add fennel, cream, nutmeg powder, salt and pepper.
Blend well and then add artichokes.
Add the mixture in the round baking tray.
Cook in the air fryer for 15 minutes on 300 F.
When ready, serve with bread and enjoy!

Nutrition:

Calories: 90
Fat: 8g

Carbohydrates: 20g
Protein: 25g

Tomato and Cheese Mix Breakfast

Prep time: 5 minutes
Cooking time: 10 minutes
Servings: 3

Ingredients:

Bread – slices – 4
Spinach (chopped) –
1 cup
Cheese (shredded) –
½ cup

Tomato (chopped) –
1
Salt and pepper to
taste

Directions:

Place the bread as a layer in the round baking tray.
Add spinach, tomato and cheese.
Sprinkle salt and pepper.
Let it cook in the air fryer for 10 minutes.
When done, serve and enjoy the quick meal!

Nutrition:

Calories:95
Fat: 6g

Carbohydrates: 10g
Protein: 200g

Spinach Mushroom Mix Recipe

Prep time: 4 minutes
Cooking time: 10 minutes
Servings: 2

Ingredients:

Oil – 1 tbsp.
Onion (chopped) – 1
Mushrooms
(chopped) – 6 small
Garlic cloves – 2
mined
Spinach – 1 cup
Parsley (chopped) –
½ cup

Milk – 2 cups
Salt and pepper to
taste
Chicken (shredded) –
3 cups
Almonds for
seasoning

Directions:

Put the chicken into a bowl.
Mix onion, mushrooms, garlic, spinach and parsley. Blend well.
Add milk and salt and pepper.
Get a round baking tray. Grease it with oil.
Add the mixture in it.
Cook it in the air fryer for 10 minutes on 300 F.
When ready, serve with seasoning almonds!

Nutrition:

Calories: 115
Fat: 10g

Carbohydrates: 10g
Protein: 30g

Bacon Simple Recipe

Prep time: 5 minutes
Cooking time: 20 minutes
Servings: 2

Ingredients:

Bacon – 8 strips
Paprika – ½ tsp.
Salt and pepper to
taste
Garlic powder – 1
tbsp.
Cayenne powder – 1
tbsp.

Hamburger patties –
4
Hamburger buns – 4
Tomato (chopped) –
1
Cheddar cheese – ½
cup

Directions:

Get the round baking tray and place the hamburger patties as the bottom layer.
Add paprika, salt and pepper, garlic powder, tomato, cayenne powder and cover with cheese.
Let it cook in the air fryer for 20 minutes on 300 F.
Heat the buns in the air fryer as well for 2 minutes.
When done, place the patties in bun and serve!

Nutrition:

Calories:70
Fat: 6g

Carbohydrates: 10g
Protein: 10g

Delicious Bacon Recipe

Prep time: 6 minutes
Cooking time: 15 minutes
Servings: 3

Ingredients:

Milk – 2 cups
Cream – ½ cup
Garlic – cloves – 3 minced
Bay leaf – 1
Salt and pepper to taste
Bacon – slices – 4
Spinach leaves – 1 cup
Butter – 1 tsp.
Onions (chopped) – 2
Cheese (shredded) – 1 cup
Lemon juice – 1 tbsp.

Directions:

Mix milk and cream in a bowl.
Add garlic, spinach leaves, butter, onions, and cheese and lemon juice.
Add bay leaf with salt and pepper. Mix well.
Grease the round baking tray with butter and add the mixture.
Cook it in the air fryer for 15 minutes on 300 F.
When ready, serve!

Nutrition:

Calories:96
Fat: 9g
Carbohydrates: 10g
Protein: 35g

Carrot Mixed Chicken Recipe

Prep time: 4 minutes
Cooking time: 15 minutes
Servings: 2

Ingredients:

Chicken breast (chopped) – 1 lb.
Tomatoes (chopped) – 2
Carrot (chopped) – 1
Garlic – Cloves – 2 minced
Red Chili powder – ½ tsp.
Cheese (shredded) =- 1 cup
Cilantro to garnish

Directions:

Add chicken to the bowl with tomatoes. Blend well.
Add carrot, garlic, red chili powder and cheese. Mix well.
Make small patties out of the mixture and place it in the air fryer.
Cook for 15 minutes on 300 F.
When done, garnish cilantro and serve!

Nutrition:

Calories: 90
Fat: 8g
Carbohydrates: 20g
Protein: 25g

Peanut butter Bread

Prep time: 6 minutes
Cooking time: 5 minutes
Servings: 3

Ingredients:

Oil – 1 tbsp.
Peanut butter – 2 tbsp.
Bread – 4 slices
Banana (slices) – 1

Directions:

Get the slices of bread and on one side add the peanut butter.
Place slices of banana and cover with the other slice.
Grease the air fryer with oil.
Place the bread in it and cook for 5 minutes on 300 F.
When done, enjoy the delicious breakfast!

Nutrition:

Calories:95
Fat: 6g
Carbohydrates: 10g
Protein: 200g

Bell Pepper Mix Breakfast

Prep time: 6 minutes
Cooking time: 10 minutes
Servings: 2

Ingredients:

Onion – chopped – 1
Green bell pepper – 1 chopped
Mushrooms – 5 chopped
Eggs – 2
Salt and pepper to taste

Directions:

Whisk eggs in a bowl.
Mix onion, green bell pepper, mushrooms and salt and pepper. Blend well.
Add the mixture in the round baking tray.
Let it cook in the air fryer for 10 minutes on 300 F.
When done, serve with bread or pitas to enjoy!

Nutrition:

Calories: 114
Fat: 8g
Carbohydrates: 9g
Protein: 40g

Chicken with Cheese Breakfast Recipe

Prep time: 4 minutes
Cooking time: 15 minutes
Servings: 2

Ingredients:

Chicken (chopped) – 1 lb.	Salt and pepper to taste
Parsley as needed	Oil – 1 tbsp.
Garlic cloves – 2 minced	Breadcrumbs – 1 cup
Parmesan cheese – 1 cup	Basil (chopped) – ½ cup
	Buns – 4

Directions:

Add chicken to the bowl.
Mix garlic, cheese, salt and pepper with basil and parsley.
Grease the air fryer grill.
Make small patties out of the mixture and cover it with breadcrumbs.
Place them in the air fryer to cook for 15 minutes on 300 F.
When done, serve with placing each patty in the bun and enjoy!

Nutrition:

Calories: 125	Carbohydrates: 10g
Fat: 7g	Protein: 40g

Black beans with Eggs

Prep time: 5 minutes
Cooking time: 14 minutes
Servings: 2

Ingredients:

Olive Oil – 2 tbsp.	Salsa – 3 tbsp.
Eggs – 4	Salt and pepper to taste
Black beans – 1 cup	
Avocado (sliced) – 1	

Directions:

Whisk the eggs in a bowl.
Add avocado, salsa, black beans and salt and pepper.
Pour the mixture in the round baking tray with greasing it in oil.
Let it cook in the air fryer for 14 minutes on 300 F.
When done, serve and enjoy!

Nutrition:

Calories:96	Carbohydrates: 10g
Fat: 9g	Protein: 35g

Cheese Burger Patties Recipes

Prep time: 5 minutes
Cooking time: 20 minutes
Servings: 2

Ingredients:

Cheese burger patties – 4	Hamburger buns – 4
Salt and pepper to taste	French fries (frozen) – ½ small pack
Cheddar cheese – 1 cup	Steak sauce – 1 tbsp.

Directions:

Place the burger patties in the air fryer.
Add cheese, steak sauce with salt and pepper.
Add the fries around an empty space of the air fryer.
Let it cook in the air fryer for 20 minutes on 300 F.
When done, place each patty in the bun and enjoy with the fries!

Nutrition:

Calories: 90	Carbohydrates: 20g
Fat: 8g	Protein: 25g

Meat Patties for Breakfast

Prep time: 5 minutes
Cooking time: 10 minutes
Servings: 2

Ingredients:

Ground meat – 1 lb.	Tomato sauce – 2 tbsp.
Garlic, minced – 3 cloves	Cheese (shredded) – 1 cup
Onion (chopped) – 1	Burger buns – 4
Cumin powder – 1 tbsp.	Green onions (chopped) for garnishing
Garlic powder – 1 tbsp.	

Directions:

Put grounded meat with garlic into a bowl.
Now mix onion, cumin powder, garlic powder, and cheese and tomato sauce.
Blend well.
Make small patties out of it and place them in the air fryer.
Cook it for 10 minutes on 300 F.
When done, place each patty in the bun and garnish with green onions.
Serve and enjoy when ready!

Nutrition:

Calories: 125	Carbohydrates: 10g
Fat: 7g	Protein: 40g

Spinach Mixed Eggs

Prep time: 4 minutes
Cooking time: 19 minutes
Servings: 3

Ingredients:

Oil – 1 tbsp.
Butter – 2 tbsp.
Spinach – chopped – 2 cups
Onion – chopped – 1
Cheese – any, shredded – 1 cup
Garlic – chopped, minced – 3 cloves
Potato – mashed – 2
Eggs – 2
Salt and pepper to taste
Milk – 1/2 cup

Directions:

Whisk eggs in a bowl and add butter.
Mix spinach, onion, cheese, garlic, potato, milk and salt and pepper. Blend well.
Grease the round baking tray with oil.
Pour the mixture in it and let it cook in the air fryer for 19 minutes on 300 F.
When ready, serve and enjoy!

Nutrition:

Calories:70
Fat: 6g
Carbohydrates: 10g
Protein: 10g

Fluffy Egg Recipe

Prep time: 6 minutes
Cooking time: 10 minutes
Servings: 2

Ingredients:

Milk – 1 ½ cup
Pumpkin Puree – 1 cup
Egg – 2
Oil – 2 tbsp.
Vinegar – 2 tbsp.
Flour (all-purpose) 2 cups
Baking powder – 2 tsp.
Baking soda – 1 tsp.
Brown Sugar – 1 tbsp.
Cinnamon powder – 1 tsp.

Directions:

Whisk eggs into a bowl.
Add milk, pumpkin puree, flour, baking powder, baking soda, and brown sugar and cinnamon powder.
Mix well and add milk.
Grease the baking tray with oil and pour the mixture.
Place it in the air fryer for 10 minutes on 300 F.
When ready, enjoy!

Nutrition:

Calories:95
Fat: 6g
Carbohydrates: 10g
Protein: 200g

Eggs with Onion

Prep time: 3 minutes
Cooking time: 10 minutes
Servings: 2

Ingredients:

Mayonnaise – 1 tbsp.
Mustard – 1 tbsp.
Onion (chopped) – 1
Salt and pepper to taste
Vinegar – 1/2 tsp.
Eggs – 2
Paprika – 1 tbsp.

Directions:

Whisk eggs in a bowl.
Add mayonnaise, mustard and vinegar.
After mixing it well, add onion, paprika and salt.
Pour the mixture in the round baking tray.
Let it cook for 10 minutes in the air fryer on 300 F.
When ready, serve and enjoy!

Nutrition:

Calories: 110
Fat: 7g
Carbohydrates: 10g
Protein: 20g

Chicken Mix Recipe

Prep time: 6 minutes
Cooking time: 10 minutes
Servings: 2

Ingredients:

Boneless chicken (chopped) – 1 lb.
buttermilk – ½ cup
Cayenne pepper – 1 tbsp.
For Maple Sauce
Mustard – 2 tbsp.
Maple syrup – 2 tbsp.
Salt to taste
flour (all-purpose) – 1 cup
Vegetable oil – ½ tbsp.
Salt to taste

Directions:

Mix buttermilk with cayenne pepper into a bowl.
Add salt and flour. Mix well.
Place the chicken in the baking tray and pour the mixture over it.
Cook it in the air fryer for 10 minutes on 300 F.
Meanwhile prepare the sauce: add mustard, vegetable oil, salt and maple syrup in a bowl.
Mix well.
When the cooking is done, take it out and serve with the delicious sauce.

Nutrition:

Calories:70
Fat: 6g
Carbohydrates: 10g
Protein: 10g

Avocado Mixed Eggs Recipe

Prep time: 4 minutes
Cooking time: 15 minutes
Servings: 3

Ingredients:

Buns – 4
Salt and pepper to taste
Avocado (chopped) – 1
Onion (chopped) – 1
Garlic cloves, minced – 3
Eggs – 2
Lime juice – 1 tbsp.

Directions:

Mix eggs with onion, garlic cloves and lime juice in a bowl.
Add salt and pepper and avocado.
Pour the mixture in the round baking tray.
Place it in the air fryer for 15 minutes on 300 F.
Place the buns aside it.
When ready, serve and enjoy!

Nutrition:

Calories:96
Fat: 9g
Carbohydrates: 10g
Protein: 35g

Egg Sauce Breakfast

Prep time: 5 minutes
Cooking time: 15 minutes
Servings: 2

Ingredients:

Muffins – 2
Butter – 1 tbsp.
Spinach (chopped) – 2 cups
For Sauce
Egg yolk – 2
Lemon juice – 1 tbsp.
Salt and pepper – 2 pinch
Eggs – 2
Vinegar – 1 tsp.

Water – ½ cup
Butter – 1 tbsp.

Directions:

Whisk eggs into a bowl.
Add vinegar, spinach and butter. Blend well.
Place muffins in the baking tray and pour the mixture.
Cook in the air fryer for 15 minutes on 300 F.
Prepare the sauce: mix egg yolk, lemon juice, water, butter and salt and pepper.
Whisk until smooth and fluffy.
When the baking it done, take it out and serve with the sauce!

Nutrition:

Calories: 90
Fat: 8g
Carbohydrates: 20g
Protein: 25g

Ham Breakfast Recipe

Prep time: 4 minutes
Cooking time: 15 minutes
Servings: 3

Ingredients:

Margarine – 1 tbsp.
Eggs – 2
Salt and pepper
Ham – ½ lb. chopped
Cheese (shredded) – 1 cup
Tomato (chopped) – 1

Directions:

Whisk eggs in a bowl.
Add salt and pepper, margarine, cheese and tomato.
Get a round baking tray and place ham as a layer.
Pour the mixture over it.
Let it cook in air fryer for 15 minutes on 300 F.
When done, serve and enjoy the meal!

Nutrition:

Calories:96
Fat: 9g
Carbohydrates: 10g
Protein: 35g

Fish and Bread Recipe

Prep time: 5 minutes
Cooking time: 10 minutes
Servings: 2

Ingredients:

Fish (canned) – 1 small
Salt and pepper to taste
Mayonnaise – 2 tbsp.
Bread (slices) – 4

Directions:

Add fish in a bowl with mayonnaise.
Add salt and pepper. Mix well.
Add the mixture in a round baking tray.
Place it in the air fryer for 10 minutes on 300 F.
Place the bread pieces aside from the tray.
When done, serve!

Nutrition:

Calories:95
Fat: 6g
Carbohydrates: 10g
Protein: 200g

Carrot Mix Salmon Breakfast

Prep time: 6 minutes
Cooking time: 15 minutes
Servings: 2

Ingredients:

Bread slices – 4	Feta Crumbled – 2
Salmon (chopped) –	cups
1 lb.	Pickled Red Onion –
Carrot (shredded) – 1	3 tbsp.
Cucumber (slices) –	
2	

Directions:

Put salmon with feta into a bowl.
Add carrot, cucumber and red onion. Mix
well.
Make a layer of bread in the oven safe tray
and then pour the mixture over it.
Let it cook in the air fryer for 15 minutes on
300 F.
When ready, serve and enjoy!

Nutrition:

Calories: 90	Carbohydrates: 20g
Fat: 8g	Protein: 25g

Amazing Crab Breakfast

Prep time: 4 minutes
Cooking time: 10 minutes
Servings: 2

Ingredients:

Crab meat – 1 lb.	Salt and pepper to
Garlic (minced) – 3	taste
cloves	Swiss cheddar – 1
Hot sauce to taste	cup

Directions:

Put crab meat and garlic into a bowl.
Mix with hands and add hot sauce, salt and
pepper.
Add cheese and blend well.
Make small round patties and place them in
the air fryer.
Cook the patties for 10 minutes on 300 F.
When ready, serve and enjoy!

Nutrition:

Calories: 118	Carbohydrates: 10g
Fat: 5g	Protein: 25g

Mushroom Eggs Recipe

Prep time: 5 minutes
Cooking time: 10 minutes
Servings: 3

Ingredients:

Mushrooms (sliced) –	Tomatoes
1 cup	(chopped) – 2
Eggs – 4	Basil (chopped) – 1
Salt and Pepper to	cup
taste	Butter – 1 tbsp.

Directions:

Whisk eggs into a bowl.
Add salt and pepper, tomatoes, basil and
mushrooms. Mix well.
Grease the round baking tray and pour the
mixture.
Place it in the air fryer and cook for 10
minutes on 300 F.
When done, enjoy the delicious mushroom
treat!

Nutrition:

Calories:95	Carbohydrates: 10g
Fat: 6g	Protein: 200g

Delicious Shrimp Breakfast

Prep time: 4 minutes
Cooking time: 10 minutes
Servings: 2

Ingredients:

Lettuce (chopped) –	Dill – 1 tbsp.
1 cup	Lime juice – 2 tbsp.
Tomato (chopped) –	Coriander
1	(chopped) – ½ cup
Shrimp/Prawn	Mayonnaise – 1 tbsp.
(chopped) – 1 lb.	Cajun Seasoning
White Cabbage – 1	
cup	

Directions:

Grab a bowl and add shrimp/prawn.
Mix tomato, white cabbage, dill, lime juice,
coriander and mayonnaise.
Pour mixture in an oven safe tray. Cook for
10 minutes in air fryer on 350 F.
When done, sprinkle lettuce and Cajun.
Serve and enjoy the delicious meal!

Nutrition:

Calories: 125	Carbohydrates: 10g
Fat: 7g	Protein: 40g

Tilapia Mix Recipe Egg

Prep time: 4 minutes
Cooking time: 15 minutes
Servings: 3

Ingredients:

Tilapia fillets (sliced) – 1 lb.	Mayonnaise – 2 tbsp.
Wheat buns – 4	Sweet pickle relish – 3 tbsp.
Egg yolks – 2	Hot sauce – 1 tbsp.
Fish sauce – 1 tbsp.	Nectar – 1 tbsp.

Directions:

Mix egg yolks and fish sauce into a bowl.
Mix well.
Add mayonnaise, sweet pickle relish, hot sauce and nectar.
Pour the mixture in a round baking tray.
Place it in air fryer with tilapia fillets on the sides.
Let it cook for 15 minutes on 300 F.
When done, take it out and serve with buns!

Nutrition:

Calories:70	Carbohydrates: 10g
Fat: 6g	Protein: 10g

Quick Recipe of Eggs

Prep time: 5 minutes
Cooking time: 10 minutes
Servings: 2

Ingredients:

Eggs – 2	Salt and pepper to taste
Bread – 4 slices	
Butter – 2 tbsp.	

Directions:

Whisk eggs in a bowl.
Add butter to it. Blend well.
Add salt and pepper.
Pour the mixture in the round baking tray.
Let it cook on 300 F for 10 minutes by placing the bread pieces aside.
When done, enjoy the simple and quick breakfast!

Nutrition:

Calories: 125	Carbohydrates: 10g
Fat: 7g	Protein: 40g

Eggs with Honey Mix Air Fryer Recipe

Prep time: 6 minutes
Cooking time: 15 minutes
Servings: 3

Ingredients:

Eggs – 3	Baked Ham – 3 slices
Bread – 4 slices	Cheese (shredded) – ½ cup
Mayonnaise – 2 tbsp.	Salt to taste to taste
Honey – 1 tbsp.	

Directions:

Whisk eggs in a bowl.
Add baked ham, honey and mayonnaise.
Get a round baking tray and pour the mixture in it.
Sprinkle it with cheese and salt.
Let it cook on 300F in the air fryer for 15 minutes by placing the bread pieces beside it.
When done, enjoy the delicious breakfast.

Nutrition:

Calories:70	Carbohydrates: 10g
Fat: 6g	Protein: 10g

Simple Breakfast Recipe

Prep time: 4 minutes
Cooking time: 10 minutes
Servings: 2

Ingredients:

Bell pepper (slices) – 1	Onion (slices) – 1
Steak – 1 lb.	Cheese (shredded) – 1 /2 cup

Directions:

Place steak on the baking tray.
Place bell pepper and onion slices.
Spread the cheese.
Cook in the air fryer for 10 minutes on 300 F.
When ready, serve and enjoy!

Nutrition:

Calories: 90	Carbohydrates: 20g
Fat: 8g	Protein: 25g

Lettuce Mixed Breakfast Recipe

Prep time: 6 minutes
Cooking time: 5 minutes
Servings: 2

Ingredients:

Hot Sauce – 1 tbsp.
Ranch Dressing – 2 tbsp.
Chicken Breast (chopped) – 1 lb.
Lettuce leafs – 1 cup
Mozzarella cheese (shredded) – 1 cup
Bread pieces – 4

Directions:

Mix chicken and ranch dressing in a bowl.
Add hot sauce and cheese. Mix well.
Pour it in the round baking tray.
Place the tray in the air fryer and let it cook for 5 minutes on 300 F.
Keep the bread pieces aside from the tray.
When done, take it out and serve with lettuce leafs!

Nutrition:

Calories:96
Fat: 9g
Carbohydrates: 10g
Protein: 35g

Salmon Mixed Eggs

Prep time: 6 minutes
Cooking time: 10 minutes
Servings: 2

Ingredients:

Salmon (cooked) – 1 lb.
Eggs – 2
Onion (chopped) – 1
Celery (chopped) – 1 cup
Oil – 1 tbsp.
Salt and pepper to taste

Directions:

Whisk the eggs in a bowl.
Add celery, onion, salt and pepper.
Add oil in the round baking tray and pour the mixture.
Place it in the air fryer on 300 F.
Let it cook for 10 minutes.
When done, serve and enjoy with cooked salmon!

Nutrition:

Calories:95
Fat: 6g
Carbohydrates: 10g
Protein: 200g

Lunch Recipes

Chicken with Avocado Mix

Prep time: 6 minutes
Cooking time: 14 minutes
Servings: 2

Ingredients:

Chicken – 2 cups	Radish (sliced) – 2
Avocado (sliced) – ½	Parsley (chopped) for
Salt and pepper to	dressing
taste	

Directions:

Cut the chicken into slices and add it to the bowl.
Slice the radish and cut the avocado by placing on top of the chicken. When done, dress it with parsley and mix.
Add it to the round baking tray and place in the air fryer.
Let it cook for 14 minutes on 300 F.
When ready, add salt and pepper at the end to enjoy the salad.

Nutrition:

Calories:90	Carbohydrates: 45g
Fat: 16g	Protein: 110g

Bacon with Vegetables

Prep time: 6 minutes
Cooking time: 15 minutes
Servings: 3

Ingredients:

Bacon slices – 5	Carrots (grated) – 1
Oil – 1 ½ tsp.	cup
Lime juice – one lime	Peanuts (chopped) –
Soy sauce – 1/3 cup	¼ cup
Garlic (minced) – 2	Cilantro (chopped) –
cloves	½ cup
Red pepper flakes –	
2 tsp.	

Directions:

Grease oil in the round baking tray.
Add lime juice, soy sauce, garlic, red pepper flakes, carrots and peanuts.
Place the bacon slices over it.
Cook in the air fryer for 15 minutes on 300 F.
When done, garnish with parsley and enjoy!

Nutrition:

Calories:90	Carbohydrates: 10g
Fat: 4g	Protein: 257g

Eggs with Vegs

Prep time: 4 minutes
Cooking time: 6 minutes
Servings: 2

Ingredients:

Eggs (boiled) – 2	Yellow mustard – 1
Onion (chopped) – ½	tsp.
Celery (cut) – 6	Cheese (shredded) –
Dill pickles (diced) –	1 cup
2 cups	Salt and pepper to
Mayo – 1 cup	taste

Directions:

Chop the boiled eggs and add in a bowl.
Now add onions, celery, dill pickles, yellow mustard, and mayo. Mix it well together.
Pour the mixture in the round baking tray and cover it with shredded cheese.
Place it in the air fryer for 6 minutes on 300 F.
Add salt and pepper as desired. When ready, eat and enjoy!

Nutrition:

Calories:75	Carbohydrates: 20g
Fat: 9g	Protein: 100g

Avocado with Eggs

Prep time: 6 minutes
Cooking time: 10 minutes
Servings: 2

Ingredients:

Avocado (chopped) –	Lemon juice – 1 tbsp.
1	Salt and pepper to
Eggs boiled	taste
(chopped) – 2	Parsley to garnish
Tomato (chopped) –	
1	

Directions:

Get the round baking tray and place the chopped boiled eggs as a layer.
Add avocado, boiled eggs, tomato, and lemon juice.
Mix it well and add salt and pepper as desired. Cook in the air fryer for 10 minutes on 300 F.
When ready, garnish it with chopped parsley. Serve and enjoy the dish!

Nutrition:

Calories:90	Carbohydrates: 45g
Fat: 16g	Protein: 110g

Spaghetti with Mushroom Air Fryer Recipe

Prep time: 5 minutes
Cooking time: 15 minutes
Servings: 3

Ingredients:

Soy sauce – 5 tbsp.
Garlic (minced) – 2 cloves
Corn flour – 1 tbsp.
Red chili paste – 1 tbsp.
Beef steak (cut strips) – 1 lb.
Spaghetti – 1 pack
Oil – 2 tbsp.
Red pepper (sliced) – 1
Spring onion (sliced) – 1
Mushrooms (sliced) – 4 oz.
Coriander (chopped) – ½ oz.

Directions:

Get the round baking tray and add oil and beef steak.
Add soy sauce, garlic, corn flour, red chili paste, red pepper, spring onion, mushrooms and coriander. Mix well.
Place it in the air fryer for 15 minutes on 300 F.
Meanwhile, boil the spaghetti. When boiled, keep aside.
When the air fryer cooking is done, pour the mixture in the spaghetti and mix gently.
When ready, serve and enjoy!

Nutrition:

Calories:92
Fat: 11g
Carbohydrates: 45g
Protein: 108g

Catfish Fillets

Prep time: 5 minutes
Cooking time: 10 minutes
Servings: 3

Ingredients:

Catfish fillets – 2
Olive oil – 2 tbsp.
Shallot (chopped) – 1
Butter – 2 tbsp.
Olive oil – 1 tbsp.
Lemon juice – 1
Chives to garnish

Directions:

Mix olive oil, butter, lemon juice and shallots into a bowl. Mix well.
Now place the catfish on the baking tray and let it cook for 10 minutes in the air fryer on 300 F.
Pour the mixture in the fish and cover it again. Let it cook for 5 minutes.
When ready, sprinkle chives for garnishing.
Serve and enjoy the delicious lunch!

Nutrition:

Calories:75
Fat: 9g
Carbohydrates: 20g
Protein: 100g

Salmon Fillet Lunch Recipe

Prep time: 4 minutes
Cooking time: 20 minutes
Servings: 2

Ingredients:

Salmon fillets – 2
Parsley (chopped) – a bunch
Olive oil – 1 tsp.
For salad
Arugula – 2 cups
Onion (sliced) – 1
Lemon juice – 1
White vinegar – 1 tsp.
Dijon mustard – 1 tsp.
Salt and pepper to taste

Olive oil – 1 tbsp.
Salt and pepper to taste

Directions:

Heat the air fryer on 300F and place the salmon fish in a baking tray. Let it bake for 10 minutes with olive oil.
Add Dijon mustard and salt and pepper along with sprinkling parsley. Let it bake for total 20 minutes.
Meanwhile, prepare the salad by mixing arugula, onion, lemon juice, white vinegar, olive oil and salt and pepper together.
When the fish is ready, take it out and serve with the salad.

Nutrition:

Calories:90
Fat: 4g
Carbohydrates: 10g
Protein: 257g

Simple Asparagus Treat

Prep time: 6 minutes
Cooking time: 16 minutes
Servings: 2

Ingredients:

Asparagus – 2 lbs.
Butter – 1 tbsp.
Onion (chopped) – 1
Chicken broth – 6 cups
Sour cream (low-fat) – 2 tbsp.
Salt and pepper to taste

Directions:

Butter the round baking tray.
Add onion, chicken broth, sour cream and salt, and pepper with asparagus.
Place the tray in the air fryer.
Let it cook for 16 minutes on 300 F.
When ready, serve and enjoy!

Nutrition:

Calories:75
Fat: 9g
Carbohydrates: 20g
Protein: 100g

Salmon with Black Olives

Prep time: 4 minutes
Cooking time: 20 minutes
Servings: 3

Ingredients:

Salmon (1lb. Fillets)	Onion – 1 (chopped)
Olive oil – 2 tbsp.	Black olives (small
Tomatoes (2)	pieces) – ½ cup
Peas (1/2 cup)	Lemon Juice (2 tbsp.)
Basil (chopped) – a	Salt and pepper as
bunch	needed

Directions:

Sprinkle the salmon fillets with salt and pepper. Now apply some oil on the round baking tray and put the fillets.
Add the lemon juice over it by sprinkling basil. Keep this aside for a bit and in the hot pan, cook the onions, black olives, tomatoes, and peas.
Make sure they are fully cooked. Sprinkle salt and pepper at the end when cooked.
Now place the baking dish in the air fryer on 375 F and let it bake for 20 minutes.
When done, place the salmon fillet in place and pour the vegetable mixture and serve.

Nutrition:

Calories: 125	Carbohydrates: 10g
Fat: 7g	Protein: 40g

Eggs with Carrots and Peas

Prep time: 5 minutes
Cooking time: 20 minutes
Servings: 2

Ingredients:

Peas – 2 cups	Garlic cloves –
Olive Oil – 1/2 cup	minced
Onions – sliced	Cauliflower – 1
Carrots – 2 chopped	Soy sauce – 2 tbsp.
	Eggs – 2

Directions:

Whisk the eggs into a bowl and keep aside.
Grease oil in the round baking tray.
Add the peas, carrots, onions and cauliflower in the tray.
Mix minced garlic cloves with soy sauce.
Pour the egg and place the try in the air fryer.
Let it cook for 20 minutes on 300 F.
When ready, serve and enjoy the meal!

Nutrition:

Calories:90	Carbohydrates: 45g
Fat: 16g	Protein: 110g

Grounded Chicken with Mushrooms

Prep time: 5 minutes
Cooking time: 10 minutes
Servings: 3

Ingredients:

Grounded Chicken –	Cilantro (chopped) –
1 lb.	1 bunch
Mushrooms	Lemon juice – 1
(chopped) – 4 oz.	lemon
Onion (diced) – ½	Garlic sauce – 1 tsp.
Garlic cloves	Olive oil – 1 tbsp.
(minced) – 3	Lettuce – 1 bunch
Green onions	Avocado (sliced) – 1
(chopped) – 2	

Directions:

Grease the round baking tray with oil.
Add the minced garlic along with the chicken. Stir it well so the chicken cooks and gets soft to eat.
Add lemon juice and stir it well.
Add soy sauce, chili sauce, cilantro and green onions. Mix it well and let it cook in the air fryer on 300 F for 10 minutes.
When cooked, pour it into a bowl and dress it with onions and lettuce on the top with avocado slices.
Chop the mushrooms and sprinkle it as a last layer. Enjoy eating when ready!

Nutrition:

Calories:92	Carbohydrates: 45g
Fat: 11g	Protein: 108g

Chicken Broth with Vegetables

Prep time: 4 minutes
Cooking time: 15 minutes
Servings: 3

Ingredients:

Butter – 2 tbsp.	Cream (low-fat) – 1
Onion – ½ cup	can
Tomatoes (diced) – 2	Salt and pepper to
Chicken broth – 1	taste
can	Parsley (minced) – a
	bunch

Directions:

Add butter, onion, tomatoes, chicken broth, cream and salt, and pepper in a round baking bowl.
Place it in the air fryer.
Let it cook for 15 minutes on 300 F.
When done, pour it in a bowl with dressing it with chopped parsley.

Nutrition:

Calories:90	Carbohydrates: 45g
Fat: 16g	Protein: 110g

Chicken with Lettuce

Prep time: 5 minutes
Cooking time: 15 minutes
Servings: 3

Ingredients:

Chicken breast (sliced) – 12 oz.
Garlic (chopped) – 3 cloves
Avocado (chopped) – 1 cup
Red onion (diced) – 1
Lettuce (chopped) – 6 cups
Olive oil – 2 tbsp.
Balsamic vinegar – 2 tbsp.
Pepper to taste

Directions:

Add chicken in the round baking tray with garlic. Place it in the air fryer for 15 minute on 300 F.
When ready, cut the chicken into slices.
Add chicken along with the avocado, red onion, lettuce, olive oil, balsamic vinegar, and pepper in a bowl.
Mix it well and gently.
When ready, enjoy it with your friends and family.

Nutrition:

Calories:92
Fat: 11g
Carbohydrates: 45g
Protein: 108g

Beef Steak Air Fryer Recipe

Prep time: 4 minutes
Cooking time: 18 minutes
Servings: 3

Ingredients:

Balsamic Vinegar – 1/4 cup
Soy sauce – 1/2 cup
Worcestershire sauce – 2 tsp.
Onion powder – 1/2 tsp.
Smoke flavor liquid – 1/2 tsp
Garlic (chopped) – 2 tbsp.
Honey – 1/2 tbsp.
Olive oil – 1 tbsp.
Salt and pepper to taste
Cayenne pepper – 2 pinch
Beef Steak – 3

Directions:

Grease oil in the baking tray.
Mix Worcestershire sauce, salt and pepper, honey, cayenne pepper, garlic, soy sauce olive oil, onion powder and liquid smoke flavor by adding vinegar at the end. Stir well.
Now cover the beef with the sauce in the tray.
Place it in the air fryer for 18 minutes.
Let it cook on 350 F.
When ready, serve!

Nutrition:

Calories:75
Fat: 9g
Carbohydrates: 20g
Protein: 100g

Chicken Breast Air Fryer Recipe

Prep time: 6 minutes
Cooking time: 15 minutes
Servings: 2

Ingredients:

Olive oil – 2 tbsp.
Onion (chopped) – 2 tbsp.
Garlic (chopped) – 2 clove
Thyme (dried) – 1/2 tsp.
Salt and pepper to taste
Hot pepper sauce – 1/3 tsp.
Chicken breast – 3 pieces
Parsley – a bunch
Rosemary (dried) – 1 tsp.
Sage (powder) – 1 tsp.
Marjoram (dried) – 1/3 tsp.

Directions:

Grease oil in the baking tray.
Mix sage, thyme, salt and pepper, marjoram, rosemary, sage, onion and hot pepper sauce together. Stir well.
Now cover the chicken in the sauce and place the tray in the air fryer.
Let it cook for 15 minutes on 300 F.
When done, serve and enjoy the meal.

Nutrition:

Calories:29
Fat: 36g
Carbohydrates: 45g
Protein: 140g

Delicious Chicken Recipe for Lunch

Prep time: 6 minutes
Cooking time: 10 minutes
Servings: 3

Ingredients:

Boneless chicken – 1 lb.
Lettuce (chopped) – 1
Tomato (chopped) – 1
Cheese (low-fat) – ½ cup
Bacon slices – 3
Eggs boiled – 2
Ranch dressing (optional)
Pepper to taste
Parsley (chopped) – a bunch

Directions:

Add chicken in the round baking tray.
Add lettuce, tomato, cheese, eggs, pepper, and parsley. Mix well.
Now cut the bacon slices into pieces and spread it over the mixture.
Place the tray in the air fryer for 10 minutes on 300 F.
When ready, enjoy!

Nutrition:

Calories:90
Fat: 4g
Carbohydrates: 10g
Protein: 257g

Delicious Shell Spaghetti Recipe

Prep time: 4 minutes
Cooking time: 15 minutes
Servings: 3

Ingredients:

Oil – 1 tbsp.	Shell spaghetti – 2 pounds
Chicken breast (boneless) – 2 skinless	Salt to taste
Garlic (minced) – 2 cloves	Carrots (cut) – 2
Chile paste – 2 tbsp.	Onion (sliced) – 1
Soy sauce – ½ cup	Cabbage (chopped) – ½
Canola oil – 1 tbsp.	Ginger to taste
	Broccoli to taste (optional)

Directions:

Grease oil in the round baking tray.
Add chicken with garlic.
Mix Chile paste, soy sauce, salt, carrots, cabbage, ginger and broccoli.
Place the tray in the air fryer for 15 minutes on 300 F.
Meanwhile, boil the shell spaghetti.
When the mixture is ready, pour it in the cooked spaghetti and enjoy the meal!

Nutrition:

Calories:92	Carbohydrates: 45g
Fat: 11g	Protein: 108g

Delicious Kale with Cheese

Prep time: 6 minutes
Cooking time: 15 minutes
Servings: 3

Ingredients:

Green pepper – 1/8 cup	Kale – ½ cup
Red onion – 1/8 cup	Jalapeno – 5 slices
Tomatoes – 2 diced	Cheese – 1 slice
Spinach – 1 bunch	Salsa – 2 tbsp.
	Olive oil – 2 tbsp.

Directions:

Grease oil in the round baking tray.
Add spinach with green pepper, red onion, tomatoes, kale, jalapeno and salsa.
Cover the mixture with cheese.
Place the tray in the air fryer.
Cook for 15 minutes on 300 F.
When done, serve the healthy meal!

Nutrition:

Calories:78	Carbohydrates: 45g
Fat: 10g	Protein: 210g

Grounded Beef Air Fryer Recipe

Prep time: 6 minutes
Cooking time: 14 minutes
Servings: 3

Ingredients:

Oil – 2 tbsp.	Spinach – 1 bunch
Onion (chopped) – 1	Salt and pepper
Grounded beef – 1 lb.	Bell pepper – 2

Directions:

Grease oil in the baking tray. Add the onions and let it cook for 2 minutes in the air fryer on 300 F.
Now add grounded beef and cook it well for another 10 minutes. Stir with the onions so that it mixes with the taste.
Add salt and pepper according to taste when cooked.
Add spinach which should be cut into small pieces and stir the whole mixture well.
Cook for 15 minutes, open the lid in the middle and add the bell peppers which should be diced before. Mix lightly and cover it again for 2 minutes.
When cooked, it is ready to serve.

Nutrition:

Calories:45	Carbohydrates: 55g
Fat: 16g	Protein: 190g

Quick Shrimp Recipe

Prep time: 5 minutes
Cooking time: 10 minutes
Servings: 3

Ingredients:

Vegetable oil – 1 tbsp.	Onion (chopped) – 1
Curry paste – 1 tbsp.	Tomatoes (chopped) – 2
Shrimps – 1 lb.	Bell pepper (strips) – 1
Fish sauce – 1 tbsp.	Olive oil – 1/2 tbsp.
Lemon juice – 1 tbsp.	
Cilantro – 1 cup chopped	

Directions:

Add curry paste in the round baking tray.
Add shrimps and place it in the air fryer for 10 minutes on 300 F. Make sure the chicken is cooked well before you add any other ingredient.
Now add bell pepper, onion, fish sauce, tomatoes, and lemon juice. Stir well and make sure that the shrimps absorbs all the sauces.
Cook it for about 20 minutes and when done, sprinkle the cilantro to serve immediately.

Nutrition:

Calories:70	Carbohydrates: 45g
Fat: 16g	Protein: 104g

Spinach Mix Veggie Recipe

Prep time: 5 minutes
Cooking time: 10 minutes
Servings: 2

Ingredients:

Oil – 2 tbsp.	Spices (any of your
Spinach – 1 bunch	choice) – ½ tsp.
Mix vegetables – 1	Eggs – 2
pack	

Directions:

Grease the round baking tray with oil.
Add spinach, mix vegetables and spices.
Mix well.
Whisk eggs in a bowl and pour over the mixture.
Place the tray in the air fryer for 10 minutes on 300 F.
When done, serve and enjoy!

Nutrition:

Calories:75	Carbohydrates: 20g
Fat: 9g	Protein: 100g

Simple Spaghetti Recipe

Prep time: 6 minutes
Cooking time: 10 minutes
Servings: 2

Ingredients:

Oil – 1 tbsp.	Soy sauce – ½ tbsp.
Chili paste – 2 tbsp.	Cabbage
Garlic (chopped) – 2	(chopped) – 1
cloves	Spaghetti – 1 pack
Chicken breast	
(boneless) – 2	

Directions:

Grease the baking tray with oil.
Add chicken breast pieces, chili paste, garlic, soy sauce and cabbage.
Place the tray in the air fryer for 10 minutes.
Meanwhile, boil the spaghetti.
When the mixture is ready, mix it in the cooked spaghetti.
When done, serve and enjoy the meal!

Nutrition:

Calories:90	Carbohydrates: 10g
Fat: 4g	Protein: 257g

Spinach and Chicken Mix Recipe

Prep time: 6 minutes
Cooking time: 15 minutes
Servings: 3

Ingredients:

Oil – 1 tbsp.	Spinach – 1 bunch
White onions (sliced) – 2	Chicken (boneless) – 1 lb.
Garlic (minced) – 3 cloves	Salt to taste
	Cumin powder – 1 tsp.
Water – 2 cups	Black pepper to taste
Tomatoes – 2	

Directions:

Grease oil in the baking tray.
Add onion, garlic and chicken. Stir well.
Add water and let it cook in the air fryer for 10 minutes on 300 F.
Cook the spinach in the microwave for about 5 minutes. Add it in the baking tray with cumin powder, black pepper, and salt according to your taste.
Now add tomatoes and mix it well with the entire recipe.
When ready, serve immediately.

Nutrition:

Calories:92	Carbohydrates: 45g
Fat: 11g	Protein: 108g

Carrot and Onion Mix Spaghetti

Prep time: 4 minutes
Cooking time: 15 minutes
Servings: 3

Ingredients:

Spaghetti – 2 packs	Chili oil – ½ tbsp.
Soy sauce – 4 tbsp.	Red pepper – 1 pinch
Sesame oil – 4 tbsp.	Spring onions
Rice vinegar – 1 tbsp.	(sliced) – 1 bunch
Caster sugar – 1 tbsp.	Carrots (sliced) – 2

Directions:

Get the round baking tray.
Add soy sauce, sesame oil, rice vinegar, caster sugar, chili oil, red pepper, spring onions and carrots.
Place it in the air fryer for 15 minutes on 300 F.
Meanwhile, boil the spaghetti.
When done, mix both spaghetti and the cooked mixture.
Serve and enjoy!

Nutrition:

Calories:90	Carbohydrates: 45g
Fat: 16g	Protein: 110g

Chicken Mix Spaghetti

Prep time: 6 minutes
Cooking time: 15 minutes
Servings: 3

Ingredients:

Chicken breast (boneless) – 1 ½ pound
White sugar – ¾ cup
Soy sauce – ¾ cup
Mirin – ¾ cup
Ginger (grated) – 1 tbsp.
Carrots (chopped) – 3
Onions (sliced) – 2
Bamboo (shredded) – 1 can
Spaghetti – 1 pack

Directions:

Get the round baking tray.
Add chicken breast, white sugar, soy sauce, mirin, ginger, carrots, onions and bamboo.
Place the tray in the air fryer.
Cook for 15 minutes on 300 F.
Meanwhile, boil spaghetti.
When both done, mix them and enjoy the meal!

Nutrition:

Calories:89
Fat: 10g
Carbohydrates: 45g
Protein: 120g

Spaghetti with Sauces

Prep time: 5 minutes
Cooking time: 20 minutes
Servings: 2

Ingredients:

Sesame seeds – ½ cup
Spaghetti – 8 oz.
Chicken breast (cubes) – 1 lb.
Shrimps – 1 lb.
Balsamic vinegar – 2 tbsp.
White sugar – 1 tbsp.
Soy sauce – 2 ½ tbsp.
Garlic (minced) – 1 clove
Green Onions (chopped) – 5

Directions:

Add soy sauce and chicken breast in the round baking tray.
Cook it in the air fryer for 10 minutes on 300 F.
Add sesame seeds, shrimps, balsamic vinegar, white sugar, garlic and green onions. Cook for another 10 minutes.
Meanwhile, boil the spaghetti.
When the mixture is done, pour in the cooked spaghetti and enjoy!

Nutrition:

Calories:92
Fat: 11g
Carbohydrates: 45g
Protein: 108g

Lentils with Mushrooms

Prep time: 6 minutes
Cooking time: 20 minutes
Servings: 3

Ingredients:

Oil – 1 tbsp.
White onions (sliced) – 2
Garlic (minced) – 3 cloves
Lentils – ½ cup
Water – 2 cups
Mushrooms – 3 cups
Salt to taste
Cumin powder – 1 tsp.
Black pepper to taste

Directions:

Grease oil in the baking tray.
Add onion, garlic and then the lentils. Add water and let it cook for 10 minutes in the air fryer on 300 F.
Add mushrooms with cumin powder, black pepper, and salt according to your taste.
Cook for another 10 minutes
When ready, serve immediately and enjoy!

Nutrition:

Calories:75
Fat: 9g
Carbohydrates: 20g
Protein: 100g

Quick Eggplant Air Fryer Recipe

Prep time: 4 minutes
Cooking time: 16 minutes
Servings: 2

Ingredients:

Eggplants – 2 large
Salt to taste
Oil – 1/3 cup
Honey – 1 tbsp.
Paprika – 1 tsp.
Cumin powder – ½ tsp.
Garlic cloves (chopped) – 4
Lemon juice – 1
Soy sauce – 1 tbsp.
Parsley (chopped) – 1 bunch
Cheese – 2 ounces.

Directions:

Grease oil in the baking tray.
Mix salt, honey, paprika, cumin powder, garlic cloves, lemon juice, soy sauce and parsley in a bowl.
Place the eggplants in the baking tray and pour the mixture as well.
Spread cheese on the entire mixture.
Place tray in the air fryer for 16 minutes on 300 F.
When ready, serve and enjoy!

Nutrition:

Calories:90
Fat: 4g
Carbohydrates: 10g
Protein: 270g

Chicken and Avocado Recipe

Prep time: 6 minutes
Cooking time: 15 minutes
Servings: 3

Ingredients:

Red onion (chopped) – ½ cup	Garlic (minced) – 2 cloves
Cilantro (chopped) – 1 bunch	Tomatoes (diced) – 4
Jalapeno (minced) – 1	Avocados (cubed) – 4
Lime juice – 1 tbsp.	Boneless chicken (cubes) – 1 lb.

Directions:

Add chicken in the round baking tray along with lime juice.
Let it cook in the air fryer for 10 minutes on 300 F.
Add red onion, cilantro, jalapeno, garlic, tomatoes and avocados on top of the chicken.
Cook for another 15 minutes.
When ready, serve!

Nutrition:

Calories:92	Carbohydrates: 45g
Fat: 11g	Protein: 108g

Kale with Dressing

Prep time: 5 minutes
Cooking time: 10 minutes
Servings: 3

Ingredients:

Kale – 1	Chickpeas – 2 can
Cucumber (diced) – 1	Hemp Seeds – for toppings
Avocado (diced) – 1	
Tomatoes (diced) – 2	
For Dressing:	
Tahini – ½ cup	Garlic cloves (minced) – 1
Water – ¾ cup	Salt and pepper to taste
Lemon juice – 1	

Directions:

Get the round baking tray.
Mix kale, avocado, tomatoes, boiled chickpeas and hemp seeds.
Place it in the air fryer for 10 minutes on 300 F.
Meanwhile, prepare dressing: Mix tahini, water, garlic cloves, lemon juice and salt and pepper in a bowl. Blend well.
When the kale mix is ready, serve it with the delicious dressing.

Nutrition:

Calories:56	Carbohydrates: 45g
Fat: 10g	Protein: 167g

Sweet Potato Recipe

Prep time: 6 minutes
Cooking time: 10 minutes
Servings: 3

Ingredients:

Sausage – 1 lb.	Cilantro – 1 bunch
Sweet potatoes (diced) – 2	Hot sauce – 1 tbsp.
Eggs – 4	Cheese (shredded) – 2 cups
Avocado (diced) – 1	

Directions:

Get the round baking tray and add sweet potatoes as a layer at the bottom.
Whisk eggs in a bowl and keep aside.
Add sausage, avocado, cilantro and hot sauce in the baking tray.
Pour egg and cook in the air fryer for 10 minutes on 300 F.
When half cooked, sprinkle cheese and cook for 4 more minutes.
When ready, serve and enjoy!

Nutrition:

Calories:90	Carbohydrates: 45g
Fat: 16g	Protein: 110g

Asparagus Green Recipe

Prep time: 4 minutes
Cooking time: 20 minutes
Servings: 2

Ingredients:

Asparagus (chopped) – 24 spears	Green onion (sliced) – 4
Salsa – ½ cup	Avocado (mashed) – 1
Cilantro (chopped) – 1 tbsp.	Chicken breast – 1 lb.
Garlic (minced) – 2 cloves	

Directions:

Place the chicken breast in the round baking tray.
Add salsa, cilantro, green onion, garlic, avocado and asparagus.
Place the tray in the air fryer.
Let it cook for 20 minutes on 300 F.
When ready, serve and enjoy!

Nutrition:

Calories:90	Carbohydrates: 10g
Fat: 4g	Protein: 270g

Potatoes with Black Beans

Prep time: 6 minutes
Cooking time: 18 minutes
Servings: 3

Ingredients:

Potato (mashed) – 1
Black beans – 1 can
Lime juice – 1 tbsp.
Garlic (minced) – 2 cloves
Cheddar cheese (shredded) – 1/3 cup
Salt to taste

Directions:

Make a layer of mashed potato in the round baking dish.
Add black beans, lime juice, garlic and salt.
Sprinkle cheese to cover the mixture.
Place the try in the air fryer to cook for 18 minutes on 300 F.
When done, serve!

Nutrition:

Calories:75
Fat: 9g
Carbohydrates: 20g
Protein: 100g

Simple Chickpeas Recipe

Prep time: 6 minutes
Cooking time: 20 minutes
Servings: 2

Ingredients:

Oil – 2 tbsp.
Onions – 2
Garlic cloves – 2
Cumin powder – 1/2 tsp.
Coriander powder – 1 tsp.
Salt to add taste
Turmeric powder – 1 tsp.
Chickpeas – 2 cans
Cilantro – fresh, 1 cup

Directions:

Grease oil in the round baking tray.
Add chickpeas, onions, garlic, cumin powder, salt, coriander powder and turmeric powder.
Mix well and place the tray in the air fryer.
Let it cook for 20 minutes on 300 F.
When ready, garnish it with parsley and serve!

Nutrition:

Calories:90
Fat: 16g
Carbohydrates: 45g
Protein: 110g

Black Beans Corn Recipe

Prep time: 4 minutes
Cooking time: 14 minutes
Servings: 3

Ingredients:

Black beans – 2 cans
Mexican- style corn – 1 can
Tomatoes (chopped) – 2
Green onions (chopped) – 2 bunches
Cilantro leaves – for seasoning

Directions:

Get the round baking tray and add black beans.
Mix corn, tomatoes, green onions and cilantro leaves.
Place the try in the air fryer for 14 minutes on 300 F.
When ready, serve and enjoy the quick meal!

Nutrition:

Calories:92
Fat: 11g
Carbohydrates: 45g
Protein: 108g

Tasty Fish Sauce Chicken Recipe

Prep time: 6 minutes
Cooking time: 20 minutes
Servings: 3

Ingredients:

Vegetable oil – 1 tbsp.
Curry paste – 1 tbsp.
Boneless chicken – 1 lb.
Onion (chopped) – 1
Tomatoes (chopped) – 2
Lemon zest – 1 tbsp.
Bell pepper (strips) – 1
Olive oil – 1/2 tbsp.
Fish sauce – 1 tbsp.
Lemon juice – 1 tbsp.
Cilantro – a bunch

Directions:

Add the curry paste in the baking dish.
Add chicken. Place it in the air fryer for 10 minutes on 290 F.
Make sure that the chicken is cooked well before you add any other ingredient.
Now add bell pepper, onion, fish sauce, tomatoes, and lemon zest and lemon juice.
Stir it well and make sure that the chicken absorbs all the sauces.
Cook it for about 20 minutes.
When done, sprinkle the cilantro to serve immediately.

Nutrition:

Calories:78
Fat: 16g
Carbohydrates: 45g
Protein: 107g

Pita Bread Mix

Prep time: 6 minutes
Cooking time: 10 minutes
Servings: 3

Ingredients:

Grounded Chicken – 1 lb.	Cilantro (chopped) – 1 bunch
Mushrooms (chopped) – 4 oz.	Lemon juice – 1 lemon
Onion (diced) – ½	Garlic sauce – 1 tsp.
Garlic cloves (minced) – 3	Sesame oil – 1 tbsp.
Green onions (chopped) – 2	Lettuce – 1 bunch
	Avocado (sliced) – 1
	Pita bread – 3 (or more)

Directions:

Get the round baking dish and add chicken with mushrooms.
Mix onion, garlic, green onions, cilantro, lemon juice, garlic sauce, sesame oil and avocado.
Place the tray in the air fryer for 10 minutes on 300 F.
When the mixture is ready, add lettuce.
Take the pita bread and add mixture. Cover it by making a roll.
When done, serve and enjoy!

Nutrition:

Calories:90	Carbohydrates: 10g
Fat: 4g	Protein: 270g

Simple Shrimp Recipe

Prep time: 6 minutes
Cooking time: 18 minutes
Servings: 2

Ingredients:

Oil – 2 tbsp.	Salt and pepper to taste
Garlic cloves (minced) – 2	Shrimps (cleaned) – 1 lb.
Parsley (chopped) – a bunch	

Directions:

Grease the baking tray with oil.
Add shrimps with garlic cloves, salt and pepper and parsley.
Mix well until the ingredients are blended.
Place the tray in the air fryer for 18 minutes on 300 F.
When done, serve the simple and delicious shrimp recipe.

Nutrition:

Calories:90	Carbohydrates: 10g
Fat: 4g	Protein: 270g

Zucchini Mix Chicken Recipe

Prep time: 5 minutes
Cooking time: 18 minutes
Servings: 2

Ingredients:

Chicken breast (cubes) – 1 pound	Celery (sliced) – 2 stalks
Salt to taste	Oregano – ½ tsp.
Onion (chopped) – 1	Tomatoes (crushed) – 2
Garlic (chopped) – 2 cloves	Chickpeas – 1 can
Carrots (chopped) – 1	Zucchini (sliced) – 1
	Lemon juice – 1 tbsp.
	Butter – 1 tbsp.

Directions:

Grease butter in the round baking tray.
Add chicken cubes, onion, garlic, carrots, celery and oregano. Mix well.
Add tomatoes, zucchini and chickpeas with lemon juice.
Place the tray in the air fryer and cook for 18 minutes on 300 F.
When ready, serve and enjoy the meal!

Nutrition:

Calories:75	Carbohydrates: 20g
Fat: 9g	Protein: 100g

Boneless Chicken Mix Recipe

Prep time: 4 minutes
Cooking time: 15 minutes
Servings: 3

Ingredients:

Boneless chicken – 1 lb.	Bacon slices – 3
Lettuce (chopped) – 1	Eggs boiled – 2
Tomato (chopped) – 1	Ranch dressing (optional)
Cheese (low-fat) – ½ cup	Pepper to taste
	Parsley (chopped) – a bunch

Directions:

Add boneless chicken in the baking dish.
Place it in the air fryer for 10 minutes on 300 F.
Grab a bowl and add lettuce, tomato, cheese, eggs, pepper, and parsley. Mix well.
Add the mixture to the chicken along with bacon slices and let it cook for another 5 minutes.
Garnish parsley when cooked.
When ready, serve and enjoy the delicious meal!

Nutrition:

Calories:92	Carbohydrates: 45g
Fat: 11g	Protein: 108g

Red Beans with Lentils

Prep time: 6 minutes
Cooking time: 15 minutes
Servings: 3

Ingredients:

Oil – 1 tbsp.
Onions – sliced
Garlic cloves
Lentils – 1/2 cup
Red beans – 1/2 cup

Water – 2 cups
Spinach – 1 cup
Salt and pepper
Cumin powder – 1/2
tsp.

Directions:

Grease the round baking tray.
Add lentil and water. Cook in the air fryer for 10 minutes on 300 F.
When the water vanishes, add onion, red beans, spinach, salt and pepper and cumin powder.
Let it cook for 15 more minutes.
When ready, serve and enjoy!

Nutrition:

Calories:90
Fat: 4g

Carbohydrates: 10g
Protein: 270g

Salmon with Garlic Taste

Prep time: 6 minutes
Cooking time: 15 minutes
Servings: 3

Ingredients:

Maple syrup – 1/2 cup
Soy sauce – 2 tbsp.
Garlic powder – 1 tbsp.

Salt and pepper to taste
Salmon – 1 lb.
Oil – 1 tbsp.

Directions:

Grease the round baking tray with oil.
Add salmon with maple syrup and soy sauce. Blend well.
Add salt and pepper and garlic powder.
Place the tray in the air fryer for 15 minutes on 300 F.
When ready, serve and enjoy!

Nutrition:

Calories:90
Fat: 16g

Carbohydrates: 45g
Protein: 110g

Delicious Scallops Recipe

Prep time: 6 minutes
Cooking time: 10 minutes
Servings: 2

Ingredients:

Scallops – 1 lb.
Onions (chopped) – 1
Butter – 2 tbsp.
Mushrooms – ½ cup

Salt and pepper as needed
Lemon juice – 2 tbsp.

Directions:

Grease the baking tray with butter.
Add salt and pepper. Now add the mushrooms and onions and mix well so that all the mushrooms are covered with salt and pepper.
Now put the washed scallops in the mixture and place the tray in the air fryer for 10 minutes. Let it cook on 300 F.
Add the lemon juice and cover it when ready. Take it out after 5 minutes and enjoy!

Nutrition:

Calories:90
Fat: 11g

Carbohydrates: 85g
Protein: 108g

Easy Tilapia Recipe

Prep time: 5 minutes
Cooking time: 15 minutes
Servings: 3

Ingredients:

Tilapia (4- 5 fillet)
Lemon juice (4 tbsp.)
Butter – 2 tbsp.
Garlic cloves – 3

Parsley – a bunch
Salt and pepper as needed

Directions:

Wash the tilapia and keep it aside to dry.
While it dries, apply some butter on the round baking dish. Sprinkle salt and pepper on tilapia so that it can have the taste.
Now place the tilapia in the baking dish and sprinkle the garlic over it. Pour the lemon juice and place in the air fryer for 15 minutes on 375 F.
When done, take it out and dress it with minced parsley.
Serve and enjoy the meal!

Nutrition:

Calories:75
Fat: 9g

Carbohydrates: 20g
Protein: 100g

Halibut Fillets Recipe

Prep time: 4 minutes
Cooking time: 20 minutes
Servings: 2

Ingredients:

Halibut fillets – 6	Garlic powder – 1
Dill – 1 tbsp.	tbsp.
Onion powder – 1	Lemon pepper – 1
tbsp.	tbsp.
Parsley – 1 cup	Lemon juice – ½ cup
Paprika – 2 tbsp.	Butter – ½ tbsp.

Directions:

Grease the round baking tray with butter.
Wash the halibut fillets and let it dry.
Now you have to fill the fillets with the
mixture. Add onions, dill, paprika, salt, lemon
pepper, garlic powder with parsley.
Mix it well and then add the lemon juice.
Place it in the air fryer for 20 minutes on 300
F.
When ready, serve and enjoy!

Nutrition:

Calories:92	Carbohydrates: 45g
Fat: 11g	Protein: 108g

Garlic Shrimps Recipe

Prep time: 6 minutes
Cooking time: 10 minutes
Servings: 3

Ingredients:

Shrimps – 1 lb.	Salt and pepper to
Garlic cloves – 2	taste
Olive oil – 2 tbsp.	Parsley (chopped) –
Butter – 2 tbsp.	½ bunch
Red pepper – ½ tsp.	

Directions:

Make sure the shrimps are clean and
washed.
Grease the baking tray with oil. Add the
garlic, keep it chopped that would be better.
Now add butter and shrimps.
Place it in the air fryer for 10 minutes on 300
F.
When ready, add salt and pepper along with
red pepper. Mix well.
Garnish with parsley and serve!

Nutrition:

Calories:78	Carbohydrates: 45g
Fat: 16g	Protein: 110g

Cauliflower and Potatoes Mix

Prep time: 4 minutes
Cooking time: 10 minutes
Servings: 2

Ingredients:

Cauliflower (cut) – 1	Tomatoes (diced) – 2
Potatoes (peeled	Salt to taste
and chunks) – 3	Shredded cheese –
Oil – 1 tbsp.	½ cup
Cumin seeds – 1	Curry powder – 1 tsp.
tbsp.	

Directions:

Grease the round baking tray with oil.
Add layers by starting with potato chunks,
cauliflower, cumin seeds, salt, curry powder
and tomatoes on top.
Cover the mixture with shredded cheese.
Place the tray in the air fryer and cook for 10
minutes.
When ready, take it out and serve
immediately!

Nutrition:

Calories:90	Carbohydrates: 10g
Fat: 4g	Protein: 270g

Easy Chicken Recipe

Prep time: 5 minutes
Cooking time: 10 minutes
Servings: 3

Ingredients:

Chicken breast – 2	Oil 1 tbsp.
(cubes)	Oregano powder – 1
Lemon juice – 1 tbsp.	pinch
Salt and pepper to	Parsley (chopped) –
taste	a bunch

Directions:

Grease the round baking tray with oil.
Add chicken cubes and lemon juice. Blend
well.
Add salt and pepper, oregano and parsley.
Place it in the air fryer for 10 minutes on
350F.
When ready, serve and enjoy!

Nutrition:

Calories:75	Carbohydrates: 20g
Fat: 9g	Protein: 100g

Tasty Veggie Mix Chicken

Prep time: 5 minutes
Cooking time: 15 minutes
Servings: 3

Ingredients:

Butter – 2 tbsp.
Onion (chopped) – 1 cup
Celery (chopped) – 1 cup
Chicken broth (can) – 1
Vegetable broth (can) – 1
Chicken breast (chopped) – 1 pound
Carrots – 2 cups sliced
Basil – 1 tsp.
Oregano – 1 tsp.
Salt and pepper to taste

Directions:

Get the round baking tray and grease butter in it,
Now add celery with onions and stir well. Add chicken with vegetables and mix well.
Place the tray in the air fryer for 15 minutes on 300 F.
When cooked, add basil, carrots, and oregano with chicken breast pieces.
Cover the lid after mixing it well.
When done, add salt and pepper along with basil and serve!

Nutrition:

Calories:90
Fat: 16g
Carbohydrates: 45g
Protein: 110g

Beef Air Fryer Recipe

Prep time: 6 minutes
Cooking time: 15 minutes
Servings: 2

Ingredients:

Almond Butter – 2 tsp.
Broth of Beef – 2 ounce
Tomato soup – 2 cups
Water – 1 cup
Cabbage (shredded) – 2 cups
Onion (chopped) – 2
Carrots – 2
Green Bell pepper (diced) – 2 cup
Salt and pepper to taste

Directions:

Grab a round baking tray and mix beef broth with tomato soup. Now add water to it and mix well.
Place it in the air fryer for 5 minutes on 300 F.
Add onion, green bell pepper, cabbage, carrots and blend well. Let it cook for another 10 minutes.
When ready, add salt and pepper at the end.
Serve and enjoy!

Nutrition:

Calories:90
Fat: 4g
Carbohydrates: 10g
Protein: 270g

Side Dishes

Chicken Broth Mix Side Dish

Prep time: 4 minutes
Cooking time: 20 minutes
Servings: 3

Ingredients:

Olive oil – 1 tbsp.
Red onion (chopped) – 2
Garlic (minced) – 2 cloves
White rice – 2 cups
Chicken broth – 2 cups
Parsley (chopped0 – 1 cup
Salt and pepper to taste
Dried cherries – S cup
Hazelnuts for garnishing

Directions:

Add olive oil and garlic into the air fryer pot.
Mix red onion, chicken broth, rice, salt and pepper, dried cherries and parsley.
Cook for 20 minutes on 300 F.
When ready, garnish with hazelnuts to serve!

Nutrition:

Calories: 125
Fat: 7g
Carbohydrates: 10g
Protein: 40g

Sweet Potatoes Mix

Prep time: 4 minutes
Cooking time: 10 minutes
Servings: 3

Ingredients:

Sweet potatoes (mashed) – 2 lb.
Garlic cloves (minced) – 2
Salt and pepper to taste
Dried parsley – S tbsp.
Dried sage – S tbsp.
Dried rosemary – S tbsp.
Dried thyme – S tbsp.
Milk – S cup
Butter – 2 tbsp.
Grated parmesan – S cup

Directions:

Add butter and garlic into the air fryer pot.
Mix sweet potatoes, salt and pepper, parsley, sage, rosemary, thyme, milk and parmesan.
Cook for 10 minutes on 300 F.
When done, serve and enjoy!

Nutrition:

Calories:70
Fat: 6g
Carbohydrates: 10g
Protein: 10g

Avocado Jalapeno Side Dish

Prep time: 3 minutes
Cooking time: 15 minutes
Servings: 2

Ingredients:

Avocados (peeled) – 4
Lime juice – 2 tbsp.
Lemon juice – 2 tbsp.
Tomatoes (diced) – 2 cans
Red onion (diced) – ½ cup
Jalapeno pepper (minced) – 1 large
Garlic (minced) – 3 cloves
Salt and pepper to taste

Directions:

Mash avocados into the bowl.
Mix lime juice, lemon juice, tomatoes, red onions, jalapeno pepper, garlic with salt and pepper.
Pour the mixture into the air fryer and cook for 15 minutes on high pressure.
When done, serve and enjoy!

Nutrition:

Calories:90
Fat: 4g
Carbohydrates: 10g
Protein: 257g

Pink Rice Recipe

Prep time: 2 minutes
Cooking time: 15 minutes
Servings: 2

Ingredients:

Pink rice – 2 cups
Water – 2 S cups
Salt – S tbsp.

Directions:

Add pink rice and water into the air fryer pot.
Mix salt.
Cook for 15 minutes on 300 F.
When ready, serve!

Nutrition:

Calories: 115
Fat: 7g
Carbohydrates: 9g
Protein: 40g

Dried Cherries Mix Recipe

Prep time: 3 minutes
Cooking time: 15 minutes
Servings: 3

Ingredients:

Whole grain farro – 1 cup	Dried cherries (chopped) – S cup
Apple cider vinegar – S cup	Green onions (chopped) – 2
Lemon juice – 1 tbsp.	Mint leaves (chopped) – S cup
Olive oil – 1 tbsp.	Cherrie (cut in half) – 2 cups
Salt to taste	

Directions:

Add oil and whole grain farro into the air fryer pot.
Mix apple cider vinegar, lemon juice, salt, dried cherries, green onions and mint leaves.
Cook for 15 minutes on 300 F.
When ready, garnish cherries to serve!

Nutrition:

Calories: 125	Carbohydrates: 10g
Fat: 7g	Protein: 40g

Saffron Threads Special Recipe

Prep time: 2 minutes
Cooking time: 15 minutes
Servings: 2

Ingredients:

Saffron threads (crushed) – S tbsp.	Cinnamon powder – 1 tbsp.
Hot milk – 2 tbsp.	Honey – 1 tbsp.
Onion (chopped) – 1	Almonds (crushed) – S cup
Rice – 2 cups	Dried zante currants – S cup
Vegetable broth – 2 cups	
Salt and pepper to taste	

Directions:

Add hot milk and rice into the air fryer pot.
Mix onion, vegetable broth, salt and pepper, cinnamon powder, honey and zante currants.
Cook for 15 minutes on 300 F.
When ready, garnish saffron threads and almonds to serve!

Nutrition:

Calories: 105	Carbohydrates: 9g
Fat: 8g	Protein: 46g

Simple Muffin Mix

Prep time: 3 minutes
Cooking time: 15 minutes
Servings: 3

Ingredients:

Jiffy corn mix muffin – 2 (8.5 oz.)	Eggs – 2
Milk – 1 cup	Oil – 1 tbsp.

Directions:

Add muffin mix and milk into a bowl.
Whisk eggs and pour it in the mixture.
Grease baking tray with oil.
Pour the mixture into the baking tray.
Bake in the air fryer for 15 minutes on 300 F.
When ready, serve and enjoy!

Nutrition:

Calories: 165	Carbohydrates: 9g
Fat: 7g	Protein: 30g

White Rice with Herbs

Prep time: 2 minutes
Cooking time: 15 minutes
Servings: 2

Ingredients:

Olive oil – 2 tbsp.	Oregano (chopped) – 2 tbsp.
Onion (chopped) – 1	Rosemary (chopped) – 2 tbsp.
Garlic (chopped) – 2 cloves	Basil (chopped) – 2 tbsp.
Vegetable broth – 2 cups	Parsley (chopped) – S cup
Sun-dried tomatoes (chopped) – 2 cups	White rice – 2 cups
Salt to taste	
Bay leaf – 1	

Directions:

Add olive oil and onion into the air fryer pot.
Mix garlic, vegetable broth, sun-dried tomatoes, bay leaf, oregano, rosemary, basil and parsley.
Add rice.
Cook for 15 minutes on 300 F.
When ready, sprinkle salt and serve!

Nutrition:

Calories: 115	Carbohydrates: 9g
Fat: 7g	Protein: 40g

Quick Avocados Recipe

Prep time: 4 minutes
Cooking time: 10 minutes
Servings: 3

Ingredients:

Avocados (mashed) – 2
Small onion (chopped) – 1
Garlic (minced) – 1 clove
Tomato (diced) – 1
Lime juice – 1 tbsp.
Salt and pepper to taste
Cayenne powder – 1 tbsp.

Directions:

Add avocados and onion into a bowl.
Mix garlic, tomato, lime juice, cayenne powder with salt and pepper.
Pour the mixture into the round baking tray.
Cook for 10 minutes on 300 F.
When ready, serve!

Nutrition:

Calories:70
Fat: 6g
Carbohydrates: 10g
Protein: 10g

Chicken Broth with Grains

Prep time: 4 minutes
Cooking time: 10 minutes
Servings: 3

Ingredients:

Butter – 2 tbsp.
Chicken broth – 2 cups
Harvest grains blend – 1 (16 oz.)
Salt and pepper to taste

Directions:

Add butter and harvest grains blend into a bowl.
Mix salt and pepper with chicken broth.
Pour the mixture into the air fryer pot.
Cook for 10 minutes on 300 F.
When ready, serve and enjoy!

Nutrition:

Calories:96
Fat: 9g
Carbohydrates: 10g
Protein: 35g

Rice with Veg Broth

Prep time: 3 minutes
Cooking time: 10 minutes
Servings: 3

Ingredients:

Vegetable broth – 1 cup
Rice – 1 cup
Avocado (chopped) – 1
Cilantro (chopped) – S cup
Hot sauce – S cup
Salt and pepper to taste

Directions:

Add vegetable broth into the air fryer pot.
Mix rice, avocado, cilantro, hot sauce with salt and pepper.
Cook for 10 minutes on 300 F.
When ready, serve!

Nutrition:

Calories: 125
Fat: 7g
Carbohydrates: 10g
Protein: 40g

Sweet Potatoes with Cream

Prep time: 4 minutes
Cooking time: 15 minutes
Servings: 2

Ingredients:

Sweet potatoes (cubed) – 2 lbs.
Brown sugar – S cup
Butter – 2 tbsp.
Vanilla extract – S tbsp.
Cinnamon powder – 1 tsp.
Nutmeg powder – 1 tsp.
Egg – 1
Heavy cream – 2 tbsp.

Directions:

Add sweet potatoes and brown sugar into a bowl.
Mix butter, vanilla extract, cinnamon powder, nutmeg powder and heavy cream.
Whisk egg in a separate bowl and it to the mixture.
Pour the mixture into the round baking tray.
Cook in the air fryer for 15 minutes on 300 F.
When ready, serve and enjoy!

Nutrition:

Calories:70
Fat: 6g
Carbohydrates: 10g
Protein: 10g

Brown rice with Black Beans

Prep time: 2 minutes
Cooking time: 20 minutes
Servings: 3

Ingredients:

Brown rice – 1 cup	Tomatoes
Water – 1 cup	(chopped) – 1
Salt to taste	Avocado (diced) – 1
Black beans – 1 cup	Cilantro (chopped) –
	S cup

Directions:

Add brown rice and water into the air fryer pot.
Cook for 10 minutes on 300 F.
Mix salt, black beans, tomatoes, avocado and cilantro.
Cook for another 10 minutes.
When ready, enjoy!

Nutrition:

Calories: 159	Carbohydrates: 9g
Fat: 9g	Protein: 50g

Quinoa with Edamame

Prep time: 4 minutes
Cooking time: 20 minutes
Servings: 3

Ingredients:

Quinoa (rinsed) – 1 cup	Cucumber (chopped) – 1
Water – S cup	Edamame – 1 cup
Salt – S tsp.	Onions (chopped) – 2
Carrot (shredded) – S cup	Red cabbage (shredded) – 1 cup

Directions:

Add water and quinoa into the air fryer pot.
Cook for 10 minutes on 300 F.
Mix carrot, cucumber, edamame, onions and red cabbage.
Cook for another 10 minutes.
When ready, serve and enjoy!

Nutrition:

Calories: 115	Carbohydrates: 9g
Fat: 7g	Protein: 40g

Potatoes with Mayonnaise

Prep time: 3 minutes
Cooking time: 20 minutes
Servings: 2

Ingredients:

Potatoes (diced) – 2	Pickle juice – 1 tbsp.
Eggs – 3	Mustard – 1 tbsp.
Onion (chopped) – 1	Salt and pepper to
Mayonnaise – 1 tbsp.	taste
Parsley (chopped) – 1 cup	

Directions:

Add potatoes and eggs into the air fryer pot.
Mix onion, mayonnaise, parsley, pickle juice, mustard with salt and pepper.
Cook for 20 minutes on 300 F.
When ready, serve and enjoy!

Nutrition:

Calories: 125	Carbohydrates: 10g
Fat: 7g	Protein: 40g

Delicious Cauliflower Mix

Prep time: 4 minutes
Cooking time: 10 minutes
Servings: 3

Ingredients:

Cauliflower head – 1 small	Garlic (minced) – 2 cloves
Olive oil – 2 tbsp.	Chicken broth – 1
Salt and pepper to taste	cup
Parmesan (grated) – S cup	Thyme (chopped) – S cup
Onion (chopped) – 1	Butter – 1 tsp.
	Parsley (chopped) – 2 tbsp.

Directions:

Cut the cauliflower head into small pieces.
Add olive oil and cauliflower pieces into the air fryer pot.
Mix parmesan, onion, garlic, chicken broth, thyme, butter and parsley.
Cook for 10 minutes on 300 F.
When ready, serve and enjoy!

Nutrition:

Calories: 130	Carbohydrates: 3g
Fat: 3g	Protein: 40g

Navy Beans with Molasses

Prep time: 4 minutes
Cooking time: 10 minutes
Servings: 3

Ingredients:

Dried navy beans – 1 lb.	Molasses – S cup
Water – 2 cups	Ketchup – 1 tbsp.
Salt to taste	Brown sugar – 1 tbsp.
Bacon (slices) – 10 oz.	Dry mustard – 1 tbsp.
Onion (chopped) – 1	Pepper to taste

Directions:

Add navy beans and water into the air fryer pot.
Cook for 10 minutes on 300 F.
Mix bacon, onion, molasses, ketchup, brown sugar, dry mustard and pepper.
Cook for another 14 minutes.
When ready, serve and enjoy!

Nutrition:

Calories:70
Fat: 6g
Carbohydrates: 10g
Protein: 10g

Simple Sliced Potatoes

Prep time: 3 minutes
Cooking time: 10 minutes
Servings: 2

Ingredients:

Potatoes (sliced) – 1 lb.	Garlic cloves (minced) – 2
Olive oil – 1 tbsp.	Rosemary (dried) – 2 tbsp.

Directions:

Add potatoes and rosemary into a bowl.
Mix garlic.
Grease the baking tray with oil.
Pour the mixture into the baking tray.
Cook in the air fryer for 10 minutes on 300 F.
When ready, serve!

Nutrition:

Calories:96
Fat: 9g
Carbohydrates: 10g
Protein: 35g

Grains with Kale

Prep time: 4 minutes
Cooking time: 40 minutes
Servings: 3

Ingredients:

Grains blend – 16 oz.	Lemon juice – 1 tbsp.
Water – 2 cups	Olive oil – 2 tbsp.
Salt to taste	Feta (crumbled) – S cup
Kale leaves – 2 cups	
Red onion (chopped) – 1	

Directions:

Add grains blend and water into the air fryer pot.
Cook for 10 minutes on 300 F.
Mix kale leaves, salt, red onion, lemon juice and oil.
Cook for another 30 minutes.
When ready, sprinkle Feta and serve!

Nutrition:

Calories:70
Fat: 6g
Carbohydrates: 10g
Protein: 10g

Avocados with Cilantro

Prep time: 2 minutes
Cooking time: 20 minutes
Servings: 2

Ingredients:

Avocados (diced) – 2	Jalapeno peppers (chopped) – 2
Salt to taste	Cilantro (chopped) – ½ tbsp.
Tomato (diced) – 1	Lime juice – 2 tbsp.
Onion (diced) – 1	

Directions:

Add avocados and onion into the air fryer pot.
Mix salt, tomato, jalapeno peppers, cilantro and lime juice.
Cook for 20 minutes on 300 F.
When ready, serve and enjoy!

Nutrition:

Calories: 120
Fat: 2g
Carbohydrates: 10g
Protein: 50g

Mushrooms Mix Veg Broth

Prep time: 3 minutes
Cooking time: 10 minutes
Servings: 3

Ingredients:

Vegetable broth – 4 cups	Soy sauce – 4 tsp.
Mushrooms (sliced) – 4	Tofu (cubes) – 1/3 cup
Miso paste – ¼ cup	Green onions (sliced) – 2

Directions:

Add vegetable broth and mushrooms into the air fryer pot.
Mix miso paste, soy sauce, tofu and green onions.
Cook for 10 minutes on 300 F.
When ready, serve the delicious side dish!

Nutrition:

Calories: 115	Carbohydrates: 9g
Fat: 7g	Protein: 40g

Squash with Leeks

Prep time: 2 minutes
Cooking time: 20 minutes
Servings: 2

Ingredients:

Squash – 1 pound	Vegetable stock – 4 cups
Canola oil – 2 tbsp.	Salt and pepper to taste
Onion (chopped) – 1	
Leeks (cut) – 3 large	
Russet potatoes (chopped) – 3	

Directions:

Add squash and oil into the air fryer pot.
Mix onion, leeks, potatoes, vegetable stock with salt and pepper.
Cook for 20 minutes on 300 F.
When ready, serve!

Nutrition:

Calories:70	Carbohydrates: 10g
Fat: 6g	Protein: 10g

White Rice with Chicken Broth

Prep time: 4 minutes
Cooking time: 20 minutes
Servings: 3

Ingredients:

Butter – 1 tbsp.	Salt and pepper to taste
Onion (chopped) – 1	Peas – 1 cup
Celery stalk (chopped) – 1	Parsley (chopped) – S cup
Carrot (chopped) – 1	Sliced almonds – S cup
White rice – 2 cups	
Chicken broth – 2 cups	

Directions:

Add butter and onion into the air fryer pot.
Mix celery stalk, carrot, white rice, chicken broth, salt and pepper, peas and parsley.
Cook for 20 minutes on 300 F.
When ready, garnish almonds and serve!

Nutrition:

Calories: 125	Carbohydrates: 10g
Fat: 7g	Protein: 40g

Quick Asparagus Side Dish

Prep time: 4 minutes
Cooking time: 10 minutes
Servings: 3

Ingredients:

Asparagus – 2 lbs.	Sour cream (low-fat) – 2 tbsp.
Butter – 1 tbsp.	Salt and pepper to taste
Onion (chopped) – 1	
Chicken broth – 6 cups	

Directions:

Add asparagus and butter into the air fryer pot.
Mix onion, chicken broth with salt and pepper.
Cook for 10 minutes on 400 F.
When ready, serve with sour cream.

Nutrition:

Calories: 128	Carbohydrates: 2g
Fat: 3g	Protein: 49g

Pumpkin Quick Dish

Prep time: 3 minutes
Cooking time: 12 minutes
Servings: 2

Ingredients:

Pumpkin (peeled, sliced) – ¼
Ginger (cut) – 1
Soy sauce – 2 tbsp.
Tofu (cubed) – 3 oz.
Green onions (chopped) – 2
Red peppers (sliced) – 2
Sesame seeds – 2 tbsp.
Cilantro (chopped) – 2 tbsp.
Ginger pickles – 2 tbsp.

Directions:

Add pumpkin and ginger into the air fryer pot.
Cook for 2 minutes on 300 F.
Mix soy sauce, tofu, green onion, red peppers, sesame seeds and ginger pickles.
Cook for other 10 minutes.
When ready, garnish cilantro and serve!

Nutrition:

Calories: 115
Fat: 7g
Carbohydrates: 9g
Protein: 40g

Avocados with Orange Juice

Prep time: 4 minutes
Cooking time: 10 minutes
Servings: 3

Ingredients:

Avocados (mashed) – 2
Lime juice – ½ tbsp.
Orange juice – ½ tbsp.
Pineapple juice – ½ tbsp.
Ground cumin – 1 tsp.
Chopped Cilantro – ¼ tbsp.
Salt and pepper to taste

Directions:

Add avocados and lime juice into a bowl.
Mix orange juice, pineapple juice, ground cumin with salt and pepper.
Cook in the air fryer pot for 10 minutes on 300 F.
When ready, garnish cilantro to serve!

Nutrition:

Calories: 125
Fat: 7g
Carbohydrates: 10g
Protein: 40g

Sage with Chicken Broth

Prep time: 3 minutes
Cooking time: 15 minutes
Servings: 3

Ingredients:

Chicken broth – S cup
Butter – 1 tbsp.
Celery (chopped) – 1 cup
Onion (chopped) – 1
Bread loaf (cubed) – 1
Sage – 1 tbsp.
Salt to taste
Poultry seasoning – 1 tsp.

Directions:

Add chicken broth with butter into the air fryer pot.
Mix celery, onion, bread, sage, salt and poultry seasoning.
Cook for 15 minutes on 300 F.
When ready, serve!

Nutrition:

Calories: 102
Fat: 5g
Carbohydrates: 6g
Protein: 50g

Quinoa and Celery

Prep time: 4 minutes
Cooking time: 10 minutes
Servings: 2

Ingredients:

Butter – 1 tbsp.
Onion (chopped) – 1
Celery stalk (chopped) – 1
Quinoa (rinsed) – 1 cup
Chicken broth – 1 cup
Parsley (chopped) – 1 cup
Salt to taste

Directions:

Add butter and onion into the air fryer pot.
Mix celery stalk, quinoa, chicken broth, parsley and salt.
Cook for 10 minutes on 300 F.
When ready, serve and enjoy!

Nutrition:

Calories: 128
Fat: 3g
Carbohydrates: 2g
Protein: 50g

Tofu with Spinach

Prep time: 3 minutes
Cooking time: 15 minutes
Servings: 3

Ingredients:

Water – 2 ¼ cup
Tofu (cubes) – 2 oz.
Miso paste – 1 tbsp.

Spinach (chopped) –
½ cup
Green onion
(sliced) – 1

Directions:

Add water and tofu into the air fryer pot.
Mix miso paste, spinach and green onion.
Cook for 15 minutes on 300 F.
When ready, serve and enjoy!

Nutrition:

Calories:96
Fat: 9g

Carbohydrates: 10g
Protein: 35g

Green Onion Mix Avocados

Prep time: 2 minutes
Cooking time: 10 minutes
Servings: 3

Ingredients:

Avocados
(mashed) – 5
Lemon juice – 2 tbsp.
Green onion
(minced) – ½ cup

Cilantro (chopped) –
½ cup
Salt and pepper to
taste

Directions:

Add avocados and lemon juice into a bowl.
Mix green onion, cilantro with salt and
pepper.
Pour the mixture into the air fryer pot.
Cook for 10 minutes on 300 F.
When ready, serve and enjoy!

Nutrition:

Calories: 125
Fat: 7g

Carbohydrates: 10g
Protein: 40g

Onion Mix Tofu Side Dish

Prep time: 2 minutes
Cooking time: 20 minutes
Servings: 2

Ingredients:

Oil – 2 tbsp.
Onion (chopped) – 1
Garlic (chopped) – 2
cloves
Tofu – 2 cups
Soy sauce – 1 tbsp.

Carrots (grated) – 1
Salt and pepper to
taste
Spinach (chopped) –
2 cups

Directions:

Add oil and onion into the air fryer pot.
Cook for 10 minutes on 300 F.
Mix garlic, tofu, soy sauce, carrots, salt and
pepper with spinach.
Cook for another 10 minutes.
When ready, serve!

Nutrition:

Calories:70
Fat: 6g

Carbohydrates: 10g
Protein: 10g

Chili Tasty Rice Recipe

Prep time: 4 minutes
Cooking time: 10 minutes
Servings: 2

Ingredients:

Olive oil – 2 tbsp.
Onion (chopped) – 1
Green chilies
(chopped) – 1 tbsp.
Cumin powder – S
tbsp.

Chicken broth – 1
cup
Rice – 2 cups
Cilantro (chopped) –
S cup
Lime juice – 1 tbsp.
Hot sauce – S tbsp.

Directions:

Add olive oil and onion into the air fryer pot.
Mix green chilies, cumin powder, chicken
broth, rice, cilantro, lime juice and hot sauce.
Cook for 10 minutes on 300 F.
When ready, serve and enjoy!

Nutrition:

Calories: 115
Fat: 7g

Carbohydrates: 9g
Protein: 40g

Black Beans with Avocados

Prep time: 3 minutes
Cooking time: 10 minutes
Servings: 3

Ingredients:

Olive Oil – 2 tbsp.	Avocado – 1
Eggs – 4	Salsa – 1/2 cup
Black beans – 1 ounce	White rice – 2 cups
	Salt and pepper

Directions:

Whisk eggs into a bowl.
Add olive oil and black beans into the air fryer pot.
Mix avocado, salsa, white rice and salt.
Pour the egg mixture.
Cook in the air fryer for 10 minutes on 300 F.
When ready, serve!

Nutrition:

Calories: 105   Carbohydrates: 10g
Fat: 9g   Protein: 30g

Avocados and Salsa Recipe

Prep time: 4 minutes
Cooking time: 20 minutes
Servings: 3

Ingredients:

Avocados (chopped) – 2	Chili powder – ¼ tsp.
Salsa – 2 tbsp.	Salt and pepper to taste
Mayonnaise – 2 tbsp.	

Directions:

Add avocados and chili powder into the air fryer pot.
Mix salsa with salt and pepper.
Cook for 20 minutes on 300 F.
When ready, mix mayonnaise.
Serve and enjoy!

Nutrition:

Calories:70   Carbohydrates: 10g
Fat: 6g   Protein: 10g

Avocados with Tomatillos

Prep time: 2 minutes
Cooking time: 10 minutes
Servings: 2

Ingredients:

Avocados (peeled) – 3	Lime juice – 1 tbsp.
Tomatillos (chopped) – 3	Red pepper flakes – 1 tbsp.
Red onion (chopped) – 1	Hot pepper sauce – 2 drops
Tomatoes (chopped) – 2	Salt and pepper to taste

Directions:

Add avocados and tomatillos into a bowl.
Mix red onion, tomatoes, lime juice, red pepper flakes and hot pepper.
Pour the mixture into the air fryer pot.
Cook for 10 minutes on 300 F.
When ready, sprinkle salt and pepper to serve!

Nutrition:

Calories: 105   Carbohydrates: 10g
Fat: 9g   Protein: 30g

Chicken Granules Recipe

Prep time: 3 minutes
Cooking time: 20 minutes
Servings: 3

Ingredients:

Water – 2 cups	Salt and pepper
Gluten free chicken granules – 4 tsp.	Sage (dried) – 1/8 tsp.
Onion (minced) – 1 tbsp.	Thyme (dried) – 1/8 tsp.
Celery flakes – 1 tbsp.	White rice – 2 cups
Parsley (dried) – 1 tsp.	Butter – 2 tbsp.

Directions:

Add water and chicken granules into the air fryer pot.
Cook for 5 minutes on 300 F.
Mix onion, celery flakes, parsley, salt and pepper, sage, thyme, white rice and butter.
Cook for another 15 minutes.
When done, enjoy!

Nutrition:

Calories: 125   Carbohydrates: 10g
Fat: 7g   Protein: 40g

White Rice with Onions

Prep time: 4 minutes
Cooking time: 15 minutes
Servings: 3

Ingredients:

Oil – 2 tbsp.
Onion (chopped) – 2 tbsp.
White rice – 1 ½ cup
Chicken broth – 2 cups
Salsa – 1 cup

Directions:

Add oil and onion into the air fryer pot.
Mix white rice, chicken broth and salsa.
Cook for 15 minutes on 300 F.
When ready, serve and enjoy!

Nutrition:

Calories:96
Fat: 9g
Carbohydrates: 10g
Protein: 35g

Avocados with Bacon

Prep time: 4 minutes
Cooking time: 15 minutes
Servings: 3

Ingredients:

Avocados (mashed) – 4
Bacon (crumbled) – 4 slices
Tomato (chopped) – 1
Onion (chopped) – 1
Garlic (minced) – 1
Salt and pepper to taste
Hot pepper to taste

Directions:

Add avocados and bacon into a bowl.
Mix tomato, onion, garlic with salt and pepper.
Pour the mixture into the air fryer pot.
Cook for 15 minutes on 300 F.
When ready, serve and enjoy!

Nutrition:

Calories:70
Fat: 6g
Carbohydrates: 10g
Protein: 10g

Rice with Cheese Recipe

Prep time: 2 minutes
Cooking time: 25 minutes
Servings: 2

Ingredients:

Butter – 2 tbsp.
Onion (chopped) – 1
Arborio rice – 1 cup
Lemon juice – 1 tbsp.
Chicken broth – 1 cup
Peas – 2 cups
Parsley (chopped) – S cup
Parmesan cheese – S cup
Salt and pepper to taste

Directions:

Add onion and Arborio rice into the air fryer pot.
Cook for 10 minutes on 300 F.
Mix butter, lemon juice, chicken broth, peas, parsley, parmesan cheese with salt and pepper.
Cook for another 15 minutes.
When ready, serve!

Nutrition:

Calories:96
Fat: 9g
Carbohydrates: 10g
Protein: 35g

Ramen Noodles with Green Onions

Prep time: 4 minutes
Cooking time: 30 minutes
Servings: 3

Ingredients:

Water – 2 cups
Ramen Noodles – 1 pack
Water – 2 ½ cup
Soy sauce – 2 tbsp.
Mirin – 2 tbsp.
Rice vinegar – 1 tsp.
Mushrooms (sliced) – 5
Green onions (sliced) – 2
Ginger (minced) – 1 tsp.
Scallops – 8

Directions:

Add water and ramen noodles into the air fryer pot.
Cook for 10 minutes on 300 F.
Mix soy sauce, rice vinegar, mushrooms, green onions, ginger and scallops.
Cook for another 20 minutes.
When ready, serve and enjoy!

Nutrition:

Calories: 105
Fat: 9g
Carbohydrates: 10g
Protein: 30g

Avocados and Onions Mix

Prep time: 4 minutes
Cooking time: 15 minutes
Servings: 2

Ingredients:

Avocados (mashed) – 2	Garlic (minced) – 2 cloves
Tomatoes – 2	Lime juice – ½ tsp.
Onion (chopped) – 2	Salt and pepper to taste

Directions:

Add avocados and tomatoes into a bowl.
Mix onion, garlic, lime juice with salt and pepper.
Pour the mixture into the round baking tray.
Cook for 15 minutes on 300 F.
When done, serve and enjoy!

Nutrition:

Calories:70	Carbohydrates: 10g
Fat: 6g	Protein: 10g

Rice with Chicken Broth

Prep time: 3 minutes
Cooking time: 30 minutes
Servings: 3

Ingredients:

Onion (chopped) – ¼ cup	Chicken broth – 2 cups
Garlic (minced) – 2 cloves	Vegetable juice – 1 cup
Vegetable oil – tbsp.	Taco seasoning – 1 ½ tsp.
Instant rice – 3 cups	

Directions:

Add chicken broth with rice into the air fryer pot.
Add vegetable oil and cook for 10 minutes on 300 F.
Mix garlic, onion and vegetable juice.
Cook for another 20 minutes.
When done, garnish with taco and serve!

Nutrition:

Calories: 105	Carbohydrates: 10g
Fat: 9g	Protein: 30g

Potatoes with Eggs

Prep time: 2 minutes
Cooking time: 20 minutes
Servings: 3

Ingredients:

Potatoes (cubed) – 2	Tomatoes (chopped) – 2
Eggs (beaten) – 2	Salt and pepper to taste
Mayonnaise – 1 tbsp.	
Pickle juice – 1 tbsp.	
Onions (chopped) – 2	

Directions:

Add potatoes into the air fryer pot.
Mix eggs, mayonnaise, pickle juice, onions, tomatoes with salt and pepper.
Cook for 20 minutes on 300 F.
When done, serve and enjoy!

Nutrition:

Calories: 125	Carbohydrates: 10g
Fat: 7g	Protein: 40g

Avocados with Tomatoes

Prep time: 3 minutes
Cooking time: 15 minutes
Servings: 3

Ingredients:

Avocados (mashed) – 5	Cilantro (chopped) – ½ cup
Tomatoes (diced) – 3	Lime juice – 1 tbsp.
Serrano Chile (diced) – 1	Olive oil – 2 tbsp.
Garlic (chopped) – 3 cloves	Salt to taste

Directions:

Add avocados and garlic into a bowl.
Mix tomatoes, serrano Chile, cilantro, lime juice and salt.
Grease the baking tray with oil.
Pour the mixture into the baking tray.
Cook in the air fryer for 15 minutes on 300 F.
When ready, serve!

Nutrition:

Calories: 108	Carbohydrates: 10g
Fat: 3g	Protein: 40g

Asparagus with Hot Pepper Sauce

Prep time: 2 minutes
Cooking time: 15 minutes
Servings: 3

Ingredients:

Asparagus – 1 ½ pounds
Lime juice – 1 tbsp.
Fresh cilantro – 1 tbsp.
Green onions (sliced) – 2
Jalapeno pepper (minced) – ½
Garlic (minced) – 1 tbsp.
Tomato (diced) – 1
Worcestershire sauce – ½ tsp.
Hot pepper sauce – 1 dash
Salt and pepper to taste

Directions:

Add asparagus and lime juice into a bowl.
Mix green onions, jalapeno pepper, garlic, tomato, Worcestershire sauce, hot pepper sauce with salt and pepper.
Pour the mixture into the air fryer pot.
Cook for 15 minutes on 300 F.
When done, serve and enjoy!

Nutrition:

Calories: 119
Fat: 55g
Carbohydrates: 8g
Protein: 50g

Avocado with Lime Juice

Prep time: 2 minutes
Cooking time: 20 minutes
Servings: 3

Ingredients:

Serrano Chili – 2
Cilantro (chopped) – ½ cup
Onion (diced) – ¼ cup
Salt to taste
Avocados (chopped) – 2
Tomatoes – 1 cup
Lime juice – 1 tbsp.

Directions:

Add avocados and onion in a bowl.

Mix serrano chili, cilantro, salt, tomatoes and lime juice.
Pour the mixture in the baking tray.
Place in the air fryer to cook on high pressure for 20 minutes.
When ready, garnish cilantro and serve!

Nutrition:

Calories: 105
Fat: 9g
Carbohydrates: 10g
Protein: 30g

Delicious Mushroom Mix Side Dish

Prep time: 4 minutes
Cooking time: 20 minutes
Servings: 2

Ingredients:

Oil – ¼ cup
Flour (all-purpose)- ¼ cup
Bell pepper – 1
Onion (chopped)- 1
Chicken (chopped, breast) – 2 cups
Mushrooms- 4.5 ounce
Tomatoes – diced, 4.5 ounce
Sauce (any) – 2 tsp.
Garlic cloves – 3
Soy sauce – 1 tsp.
Sugar (white) – 1 tsp.
Salt and pepper to taste
Hot sauce – 3 drops

Directions:

Grease the baking tray with oil.
Add flour and chicken into a bowl.
Mix bell pepper, onion, mushrooms, tomatoes, sauce, garlic cloves, soy sauce, sugar, hot sauce with salt and pepper.
Pour the mixture into the baking tray.
Cook in the air fryer for 20 minutes on 300 F.
When ready, serve!

Nutrition:

Calories:70
Fat: 6g
Carbohydrates: 10g
Protein: 10g

Asparagus with Salsa

Prep time: 3 minutes
Cooking time: 10 minutes
Servings: 2

Ingredients:

Asparagus (chopped) – 24 spears
Salsa – ½ cup
Cilantro (chopped) – 1 tbsp.
Garlic (minced) – 2 cloves
Green onion (sliced) – 4
Avocado (mashed) – 1

Directions:

Add asparagus and salsa into a bowl.
Mix cilantro, garlic, green onion and avocado.
Pour the mixture in the round baking tray and place in the air fryer.
Cook for 10 minutes on 300 F.
When done, serve and enjoy!

Nutrition:

Calories:70
Fat: 6g
Carbohydrates: 10g
Protein: 10g

Broccoli with Chicken Broth Recipe

Prep time: 3 minutes
Cooking time: 20 minutes
Servings: 3

Ingredients:

Butter – ½ cup
Onion (chopped) – 1
Broccoli (frozen) – 1 pack
Chicken broth – 2 cans

Milk – 2 cups
Garlic powder – 1 tbsp.
Cornstarch – 2/3 cup
Water – 1 cup

Directions:

Add butter into the air fryer cooking pot.
Mix onion, broccoli, chicken broth, milk, garlic powder, cornstarch and water.
Cook in the air fryer for 20 minutes on 400 F.
When ready, serve and enjoy!

Nutrition:

Calories: 120
Fat: 5g
Carbohydrates: 10g
Protein: 34g

Edamame with Avocado

Prep time: 2 minutes
Cooking time: 15 minutes
Servings: 3

Ingredients:

Shelled Edamame – 6 oz.
Onion (chopped) – ½
Cilantro (chopped) – 1 bunch
Olive oil – 2 tbsp.

Avocado (cubed) – 1 large
Lemon juice – 1 tbsp.
Garlic sauce – 1 tbsp.
Salt and pepper to taste

Directions:

Grease baking tray with oil.
Add edamame and onion in a bowl.
Mix avocado, lemon juice, garlic sauce with salt and pepper.
Blend well.
Pour the mixture into the round baking tray and cook in the air fryer for 15 minutes on 300 F.
When ready, garnish cilantro and serve!

Nutrition:

Calories: 125
Fat: 7g
Carbohydrates: 10g
Protein: 40g

Main Dishes

Pork Loin Chops Quick Recipe

Prep time: 2 minutes
Cooking time: 25 minutes
Servings: 3

Ingredients:

Pork loin chops (boneless) – 4
White sugar – S tbsp.
Soy sauce – 1 tbsp.
Onion (sliced) – 1
Garlic cloves (minced) – 2
Shallot (diced) – 1 cup
Tomato paste – S cup
Salt and pepper to taste

Directions:

Add garlic and pork loin chops into the air fryer pot.
Cook for 10 minutes on 300 F.
Mix soy sauce, white sugar, onion, garlic, shallot, tomato paste with salt and pepper.
Cook for another 15 minutes.
When ready, serve and enjoy!

Nutrition:

Calories: 105
Fat: 9g
Carbohydrates: 10g
Protein: 30g

Chicken Steak with Tomato Paste

Prep time: 3 minutes
Cooking time: 15 minutes
Servings: 2

Ingredients:

Chicken steak – 1 lb.
Garlic cloves (minced) – 2
Mushrooms (chopped) – 1 cup
Celery stalks (chopped) – S cup
Carrots (chopped) – 1 cup
Potato (diced) – 1
Bay leaves – 2
Flour – 1 tbsp.
Salt and pepper to taste
Soy sauce – 1 tbsp.
Tomato paste – 1 tbsp.

Directions:

Add chicken and garlic into the air fryer pot.
Mix mushrooms, celery, carrots, potato, bay leaves, soy sauce, tomato paste, flour with salt and pepper.
Cook for 15 minutes on 400 F.
When ready, serve and enjoy the meal!

Nutrition:

Calories:95
Fat: 6g
Carbohydrates: 10g
Protein: 200g

Meat Breasts with Green Onions

Prep time: 4 minutes
Cooking time: 15 minutes
Servings: 3

Ingredients:

Red meat breasts – 1 lb.
Garlic cloves (minced) – 2
Onion (minced) – 1
Ginger (minced) – 1 tbsp.
Honey – 2 tbsp.
Brown sugar – 2 tbsp.
Rice vinegar – 2 tbsp.
Sesame oil – 2 tbsp.
Green onions (chopped) to garnish

Directions:

Add garlic and red meat breasts into the air fryer pot.
Mix onion, ginger, honey, brown sugar, and rice vinegar with sesame oil.
Cook for 15 minutes on 300 F.
When ready, garnish green onions and serve!

Nutrition:

Calories: 120
Fat: 6g
Carbohydrates: 10g
Protein: 50g

Grounded Beef with Kidney Beans

Prep time: 3 minutes
Cooking time: 10 minutes
Servings: 2

Ingredients:

Grounded beef – 1 lb.
Onion (chopped) – 1
Garlic cloves (minced) – 4
Tomatoes (crushed) – 2
Kidney beans – 2 cups
Chili powder – 1 tbsp.
Cumin powder – 1 tbsp.
Oregano powder – 1 tbsp.
Apple cider vinegar – 2 tbsp.
Salt and pepper to taste

Directions:

Add beef and onion into the air fryer pot.
Mix garlic, tomatoes, kidney beans, chili powder, cumin powder, oregano powder, apple cider with salt and pepper.
Cook for 10 minutes on 300 F.
When ready, serve and enjoy the meal!

Nutrition:

Calories: 112
Fat: 6g

Carbohydrates: 10g   Protein: 70g

Cod Fillet Recipe

Prep time: 2 minutes
Cooking time: 15 minutes
Servings: 3

Ingredients:

Miso paste – 3 tbsp.   Brown sugar – 1
Water – 2 tbsp.   tbsp.
Mirin – 2 tbsp.   Cod fillets – 7 oz.
Sake – 2 tbsp.

Directions:

Add miso paste and mirin into a bowl.
Mix sake, brown sugar and water.
Blend well.
Dip the cod fillets in the mixture and place
into the baking tray.
Cook the tray in the air fryer for 15 minutes
on 300 F.
When ready, serve!

Nutrition:

Calories:95   Carbohydrates: 10g
Fat: 6g   Protein: 200g

Spinach with Chicken

Prep time: 4 minutes
Cooking time: 20 minutes
Servings: 3

Ingredients:

Spinach – 1 cup   Cumin seeds – 2
Butter – 1 tbsp.   tbsp.
Onion (chopped) – 1   Cheese (low fat) – ½
Jalapeno (chopped   cup
or normal sized) – 1   Chicken (small
Sour cream (low   pieces or sliced) – 1
fat) – 1 tbsp.   lb.

Directions:

Add chicken and butter into the air fryer pot.
Mix spinach, onion, jalapeno, sour cream,
cumin seeds and cheese.
Cook for 20 minutes on 300 F.
When ready, serve and enjoy!

Nutrition:

Calories: 125   Carbohydrates: 10g
Fat: 7g   Protein: 40g

Beef with Cheese

Prep time: 3 minutes
Cooking time: 15 minutes
Servings: 2

Ingredients:

Grounded beef – 1   Salt and pepper
lb.   according to taste
Onion (chopped) – 1   Milk – 1 cup
Tomatoes   Olives (black) – ½
(chopped) – 2   cup
Red chili powder – 1   Cheese (low fat) – ½
tbsp.   cup

Directions:

Add grounded beef and onion into the air
fryer pot.
Mix tomatoes, red chili powder, milk, olives
and cheese with salt and pepper.
Cook for 15 minutes on 400 F.
When ready, serve!

Nutrition:

Calories: 105   Carbohydrates: 10g
Fat: 9g   Protein: 30g

Chicken and Beef Mix Recipe

Prep time: 2 minutes
Cooking time: 20 minutes
Servings: 3

Ingredients:

Butter – 1 tbsp.   Pepper and Salt as
Onion (chopped) – 1   taste
Garlic (cloves) – 2   Beef (grounded) – ½
Mushrooms – 2 cups   lb.
Cream (low fat) – 1   Carrots (chopped) –
cup   2
Chicken (shredded) –   Cheese (slices) (low
1 lb.   fat) – 4

Directions:

Add butter and onion into the air fryer pot.
Mix garlic, mushrooms, cream, chicken,
beef, carrots cheese with salt and pepper.
Cook for 20 minutes on 400 F.
When ready, serve and enjoy!

Nutrition:

Calories:95   Carbohydrates: 10g
Fat: 6g   Protein: 200g

Cheese and Ham Recipe

Prep time: 4 minutes
Cooking time: 20 minutes
Servings: 3

Ingredients:

Noodles (boiled) – 1 medium pack
Ham – 1 lb.
Cheese (shredded) – ½ cup
Cream (low fat) – 1 cup
Milk (Low-Fat) – 1 cup
Butter – 1 tbsp.

Directions:

Add butter and ham into the air fryer pot.
Cook for 10 minutes on 400 F.
Mix cheese, cream, milk and noodles.
Cook for another 10 minutes.
When ready, serve and enjoy!

Nutrition:

Calories:70
Fat: 6g
Carbohydrates: 10g
Protein: 10g

Broccoli and Cauliflower Mix

Prep time: 3 minutes
Cooking time: 15 minutes
Servings: 3

Ingredients:

Cauliflower head (chopped) – 1
Broccoli (chopped) – ½ cup
Cheese – 1 cup
Salt and pepper to taste
Coriander powder – 1 tsp.

Directions:

Add cauliflower with salt and pepper into a bowl.
Mix coriander powder, broccoli and cheese.
Pour the mixture into the baking tray.
Place the tray into the air fryer.
Cook for 15 minutes on 300 F.
When ready, serve and enjoy!

Nutrition:

Calories: 105
Fat: 9g
Carbohydrates: 10g
Protein: 30g

Beef Granules Mix Recipe

Prep time: 4 minutes
Cooking time: 15 minutes
Servings: 2

Ingredients:

Celery (chopped) – ½ stalk
Onion (chopped) – 1
Carrot (chopped) – ½
Ginger (grated) – 1 tsp.
Garlic (minced) – ½ tsp.
Chicken stock – 2 tbsp.
Bouillon beef granules – 3 tsp.
Mushrooms (chopped) – 1 cup
Chives (chopped) – 1 tbsp.

Directions:

Add celery and onion into the air fryer pot.
Mix carrot, ginger, garlic, chicken stock, beef granules, mushrooms, water and chives.
Cook for 15 minutes on 300 F.
When ready, serve and enjoy!

Nutrition:

Calories: 110
Fat: 7g
Carbohydrates: 6g
Protein: 60g

Chicken with Cream

Prep time: 2 minutes
Cooking time: 15 minutes
Servings: 3

Ingredients:

Green bell pepper (chopped) – 1
Sour Cream (low fat) – 1 tbsp.
Milk (skimmed or low fat) – 2 cups
Salsa – 1 tbsp.
Cheese (shredded) – 1 cup
Cilantro leaves (chopped) – ½ cup
Onions (cut properly in round shape) – 2
Chicken (slices) – 1 lb.

Directions:

Add onions and salsa into the air fryer pot.
Mix green bell pepper, sour cream, milk, cheese, cilantro and chicken.
Cook for 15 minutes on 300 F.
When ready, serve and enjoy the meal!

Nutrition:

Calories:96
Fat: 9g
Carbohydrates: 10g
Protein: 35g

Delicious Salsa Recipe

Prep time: 3 minutes
Cooking time: 15 minutes
Servings: 2

Ingredients:

Salsa – 2 tbsp.	Salt and pepper to taste
Tomato sauce as needed	Cheese Shredded (low fat) – 1 cup
Chipotle sauce – 1 tbsp.	Cilantro as needed
Chicken (chopped) – 1 lb.	

Directions:

Add salsa and chicken into the air fryer pot.
Mix tomato sauce, chipotle sauce, cheese, cilantro with salt and pepper.
Cook for 15 minutes on 300 F.
When ready, serve and enjoy!

Nutrition:

Calories: 105	Carbohydrates: 10g
Fat: 9g	Protein: 30g

Cauliflower with Ranch

Prep time: 3 minutes
Cooking time: 10 minutes
Servings: 3

Ingredients:

Cauliflower head (chopped) – 1	Onion powder – 1/2 tsp.
Sour cream – 1/2 cup	Garlic powder – 1/2 tsp.
Cheese (shredded) – ½ cup	Butter – 1 tbsp.
Ranch dressing – 1 tsp.	

Directions:

Add butter and cauliflower into the air fryer pot.
Mix sour cream, cheese, onion powder and garlic powder.
Cook for 10 minutes on 300 F.
When ready, garnish ranch to serve!

Nutrition:

Calories: 110	Carbohydrates: 6g
Fat: 7g	Protein: 60g

Mushrooms and Chicken Recipe

Prep time: 2 minutes
Cooking time: 20 minutes
Servings: 3

Ingredients:

Oil as needed	Milk – 2 cups
Onion (chopped) – 1	Salt and pepper to taste
Mushrooms (chopped) – 2 cups	Chicken (shredded) – 1 lb.
Garlic cloves (minced) – 2	Almonds for seasoning
Spinach – 2 cups	
Parsley (chopped) – 1 cup	

Directions:

Add oil and onion into the air fryer pot.
Mix mushrooms, garlic, spinach, parsley, milk, chicken with salt and pepper.
Cook for 20 minutes on 300 F.
When ready, serve with almond seasoning.

Nutrition:

Calories:70	Carbohydrates: 10g
Fat: 6g	Protein: 10g

Ramen Noodles with Mushrooms

Prep time: 4 minutes
Cooking time: 15 minutes
Servings: 3

Ingredients:

Ramen Noodles (boiled) – 1 pack	Green onions (sliced) – 2
Soy sauce – 2 tbsp.	Ginger (minced) – 1 tsp.
Rice vinegar – 1 tsp.	
Mushrooms (sliced) – 5	Butter – 1 tsp.
	Scallops (diced) – 8

Directions:

Add butter and scallops into the air fryer pot.
Mix soy sauce, rice vinegar, mushrooms, green onions and ginger.
Add ramen noodles.
Cook for 15 minutes on 300 F.
When ready, serve and enjoy!

Nutrition:

Calories:110	Carbohydrates: 10g
Fat: 6g	Protein: 200g

Chicken with Cajun

Prep time: 2 minutes
Cooking time: 15 minutes
Servings: 3

Ingredients:

Chicken (boneless) – 1 lb.
Oil – 2 tbsp.
Carrots (chopped) – 2
Onion (chopped) – 2
Cajun seasoning
Orange juice – 1 tbsp.
Peas – ½ cup
Chicken broth – 2 cups
Dill (chopped) – 2 tbsp.
Parsley (chopped) – ½ cup

Directions:

Add chicken and oil into the air fryer pot.
Mix carrots, onion, orange juice, peas, chicken broth, dill and parsley.
Cook for 15 minutes on 300 F.
When ready, garnish Cajun to serve!

Nutrition:

Calories:96
Fat: 6g
Carbohydrates: 10g
Protein: 200g

Chicken and Broccoli Mix

Prep time: 4 minutes
Cooking time: 10 minutes
Servings: 2

Ingredients:

Butter – 2 tbsp.
Mayonnaise – ½ cup
Mushroom soup – 2 cups
Salt and pepper according to taste
Onion (chopped) – 1
Chicken (mashed) – 1 lb.
Broccoli (chopped) – 1 cup

Directions:

Add butter and onion into the air fryer pot.
Mix mayonnaise, mushroom soup, chicken, broccoli with salt and pepper.
Cook for 10 minutes on 300 F.
When ready, serve!

Nutrition:

Calories: 125
Fat: 7g
Carbohydrates: 10g
Protein: 40g

White Rice with Chicken Bouillon

Prep time: 3 minutes
Cooking time: 15 minutes
Servings: 3

Ingredients:

Oil – 1 tbsp.
Red onion (chopped) – 1
Boneless chicken (chopped) – 4
Cilantro – 1 bunch
Garlic (chopped) – ½
Hominy – 1 can
White rice – 1 cup
Chicken bouillon – 1 cube
Salt and pepper to taste

Directions:

Add oil and chicken into the air fryer pot.
Mix red onion, cilantro, garlic, hominy, white rice, chicken bouillon with salt and pepper.
Cook for 15 minutes on 300 F.
When ready, serve and enjoy the rice!

Nutrition:

Calories: 110
Fat: 7g
Carbohydrates: 6g
Protein: 60g

Potatoes and Cauliflower Recipe

Prep time: 2 minutes
Cooking time: 15 minutes
Servings: 2

Ingredients:

Cauliflower (chopped) – 2 cups
Potatoes (mashed) – 2
Celery (chopped) – 1 cup
Carrots (chopped) – 1
Onions (chopped) – 1
Butter – 1/4 cup
Flour (all-purpose) – 1/3 cup
Salt and pepper to taste
Cheese (shredded) – 2 cups

Directions:

Add cauliflower and potatoes into the air fryer pot.
Mix celery, carrots, onion, butter, flour, cheese with salt and pepper.
Cook for 15 minutes on 300 F.
When ready, serve and enjoy the meal!

Nutrition:

Calories:95
Fat: 6g
Carbohydrates: 10g
Protein: 200g

Cauliflower Crumbs Recipe

Prep time: 4 minutes
Cooking time: 15 minutes
Servings: 2

Ingredients:

Cauliflower (chopped) – 3 cups	Bread crumbs – 1/2 cup
Butter – 1 tbsp.	Salt and pepper to taste
Milk – 1/2 cup	
Sour cream – 1 cup	

Directions:

Add butter and milk into the baking tray.
Mix sour cream, bread crumbs with salt and pepper.
Add cauliflower.
Place the baking tray into the air fryer and cook for 15 minutes on 300 F.
When ready, serve and enjoy!

Nutrition:

Calories:96	Carbohydrates: 10g
Fat: 9g	Protein: 35g

Carrots and Cauliflower Mix

Prep time: 3 minutes
Cooking time: 10 minutes
Servings: 3

Ingredients:

Cauliflower (pieces) – 2 cups	Garlic powder – 1 tsp.
Carrots (chopped) – 2	Salt and pepper to taste
Sour cream – ½ cup	Butter – 1 tbsp.
Apple Cider vinegar – 1/4 cup	

Directions:

Add butter and garlic powder into the round baking tray.
Mix cauliflower, carrots, apple cider vinegar with salt and pepper.
Place the baking tray into the air fryer.
Cook for 10 minutes on 300 F.
When ready, serve and enjoy!

Nutrition:

Calories:70	Carbohydrates: 10g
Fat: 6g	Protein: 10g

White rice with Black Beans

Prep time: 2 minutes
Cooking time: 15 minutes
Servings: 3

Ingredients:

Oil – 1 tsp.	Cumin powder – 1 tsp.
Onion (chopped) – 1	Cayenne powder – ¼ tsp.
Garlic (minced) – 2 cloves	Black beans (can) – 3 cups
White rice (boiled) – ¾ cup	
Vegetable broth – 1 cup	

Directions:

Add oil and onion into the air fryer pot.
Mix garlic, vegetable broth, cumin powder, cayenne powder, black beans and white rice.
Cook for 15 minutes on 300 F.
When ready, serve and enjoy!

Nutrition:

Calories:95	Carbohydrates: 10g
Fat: 6g	Protein: 200g

Pork with Onion

Prep time: 4 minutes
Cooking time: 15 minutes
Servings: 2

Ingredients:

Pork (grounded) – 1 lb.	Flour (all-purpose) – ¼ cup
Salt to taste	Sour cream – 2 cups
Eggs – 2	Chicken broth – 2 cups
Onion (chopped) – 1/3 cup	Fresh Dill – ¼ cup
Butter – 1 cup	

Directions:

Add pork and butter into the air fryer pot.
Mix eggs, onion, flour, sour cream, chicken broth and fresh dill with salt.
Cook for 15 minutes on 300 F.
When ready, serve and enjoy!

Nutrition:

Calories: 110	Carbohydrates: 6g
Fat: 7g	Protein: 60g

Beef and Bell Pepper Recipe

Prep time: 3 minutes
Cooking time: 20 minutes
Servings: 2

Ingredients:

Beef (grounded) – 2 lbs.	Sugar – 2 tsp.
Onion (chopped) – ½ cup	Vinegar – 3 tbsp.
Ginger powder– ½ tsp.	Soy sauce – 1 tbsp.
Salt and pepper to taste	Carrot – 1 large
	Green bell pepper – 1 large
	Water – ½ cup

Directions:

Add onion and ginger powder into the air fryer pot.
Mix sugar, vinegar, soy sauce, carrot, green bell pepper, water with salt and pepper.
Add beef and stir well.
Cook for 20 minutes on 300 F.
When ready, serve and enjoy the meal!

Nutrition:

Calories:95	Carbohydrates: 10g
Fat: 6g	Protein: 200g

Seashells Main Dish Recipe

Prep time: 4 minutes
Cooking time: 10 minutes
Servings: 3

Ingredients:

Seashells (boiled) – 1 pound	Garlic (minced) – 7 cloves
Spinach (chopped) – 1 pack	Red pepper flakes – 1 tsp.
Oil – 2 tbsp.	Salt for taste

Directions:

Add oil and spinach into the air fryer pot.
Mix garlic, red pepper flakes, salt and seashells.
Cook for 10 minutes on 300 F.
When ready, serve!

Nutrition:

Calories:70	Carbohydrates: 10g
Fat: 6g	Protein: 10g

Beef and Egg Recipe

Prep time: 2 minutes
Cooking time: 15 minutes
Servings: 3

Ingredients:

Butter – 1 tsp.	Nutmeg – ¼ tsp.
Onion (chopped) – 1	Ginger powder – ¼ tsp.
Beef (grounded) – 1 lb.	Beef Broth – 2 cups
Egg – 1	Sour cream – ½ cup
Salt and pepper to taste	

Directions:

Add butter and onion into the air fryer pot.
Mix beef, egg, nutmeg, ginger, beef broth, sour cream with salt and pepper.
Cook for 15 minutes on 300 F.
When ready, serve and enjoy!

Nutrition:

Calories: 110	Carbohydrates: 6g
Fat: 7g	Protein: 60g

Lettuce Mix Delight

Prep time: 2 minutes
Cooking time: 10 minutes
Servings: 2

Ingredients:

Lettuce (chopped) – 2 cups	Broccoli (chopped) – 2 cups
Cauliflower head (chopped) – 2 cups	Radish (chopped) – 1 cup
Cucumbers (diced) – 2	Beans (can) – 1
Onion (chopped) – 1	Tortilla chips to garnish
Carrots (chopped) – 2	

Directions:

Add lettuce and cauliflower into the air fryer pot.
Mix onion, carrots, broccoli, radish and beans.
Cook for 10 minutes on 300 F.
When ready, garnish tortilla chips.
Serve with cucumbers and enjoy!

Nutrition:

Calories: 125	Carbohydrates: 10g
Fat: 7g	Protein: 40g

Egg Noodles with Tuna

Prep time: 3 minutes
Cooking time: 15 minutes
Servings: 3

Ingredients:

Egg Noodles Pack (boiled) – 1 medium pack
Onion (chopped) – 1/4 cup
Peas – 1 cup
Tuna (can) – 2

Mushroom Soup – 1/2 cup
Mushrooms (sliced) – 1/2 cup
Potato Chips, Crushed to garnish

Directions:

Add onion and peas into the air fryer pot.
Mix tuna, mushroom soup, mushrooms and egg noodles.
Cook for 15 minutes on 300 F.
When ready, garnish potato chips and serve!

Nutrition:

Calories:95
Fat: 6g

Carbohydrates: 10g
Protein: 200g

Grounded Turkey with Jalapeno

Prep time: 4 minutes
Cooking time: 15 minutes
Servings: 2

Ingredients:

Ground Turkey – 1 Pound
Salt and pepper to taste
Parmesan Cheese, Grated – 1 tbsp.
Egg – 1
Olive Oil – 1 tbsp.

Jalapeno Pepper (chopped) – 1 Small
Spaghetti pack (boiled) – 1 (16 oz.)
Onion (chopped) – 1
Chipotle sauce – 2 tbsp.

Directions:

Add oil and turkey into the air fryer pot.
Mix cheese, egg, jalapeno pepper, onion, chipotle sauce, spaghetti with salt and pepper.
Cook for 15 minutes on 300 F.
When ready, serve and enjoy!

Nutrition:

Calories: 110
Fat: 7g

Carbohydrates: 6g
Protein: 60g

Cauliflower with Sour Cream

Prep time: 3 minutes
Cooking time: 15 minutes
Servings: 3

Ingredients:

Cauliflower head (chopped) – 1
Onion (sliced) – 1
Mayonnaise – 1/2 cup

Sour cream – 1/2 cup
Cheese (shredded) – 2 cups
Garlic powder – 1 tsp.

Directions:

Add mayonnaise and sour cream into a bowl.
Mix onion, cheese and garlic powder.
Pour the mixture into the round baking tray.
Place chopped cauliflowers over it.
Cook the dish in the air fryer for 15 minutes on 300 F.
When ready, enjoy!

Nutrition:

Calories:96
Fat: 9g

Carbohydrates: 10g
Protein: 35g

Spinach with Cheese

Prep time: 2 minutes
Cooking time: 15 minutes
Servings: 3

Ingredients:

Oil – 2 tbsp.
Butter – 1 tbsp.
Spinach (chopped) – 2 cups
Onion (chopped) – 1
Cheese (any, shredded) – 2 cups

Garlic (chopped, minced) – 1
Potato (mashed) – 1
Eggs – 2
Salt and pepper to taste
Milk – 1/2 cup

Directions:

Add oil and onion into the air fryer pot.
Mix butter, spinach, cheese, garlic, potato, eggs, milk with salt and pepper.
Cook for 15 minutes on 300 F.
When ready, serve!

Nutrition:

Calories:95
Fat: 6g

Carbohydrates: 10g
Protein: 200g

Italian Sausage Recipe

Prep time: 4 minutes
Cooking time: 30 minutes
Servings: 3

Ingredients:

Italian sausage – 1 lb.	Garlic Powder – 1/2 tsp.
Tomato Sauce Cans – 2 cups	Dried Basil – 1 tsp.
Diced Tomatoes Can – 1 cup	Dried Oregano – 1 tsp.
Bay Leaves – 2	Salt and pepper to taste
Italian Seasoning – 1 tbsp.	Spaghetti Pack (boiled) – 1 medium
	Oil – 2 tbsp.

Directions:

Add sausage and oil into the air fryer pot.
Cook for 10 minutes on 300 F.
Mix tomato sauce, bay leaves, Italian seasoning, garlic powder, basil, oregano salt and pepper.
Add spaghetti.
Cook for another 20 minutes.
When ready, serve and enjoy!

Nutrition:

Calories: 105	Carbohydrates: 10g
Fat: 9g	Protein: 30g

Cauliflower with Peas

Prep time: 4 minutes
Cooking time: 18 minutes
Servings: 2

Ingredients:

Peas – 2 cups	Garlic cloves (minced) – 2
Water – 1 cup	Cauliflower head (chopped) – 1
Onions (sliced) – 2	
Carrots (chopped) – 2	Soy sauce – 1 tbsp.
	Eggs – 2

Directions:

Add peas and water into the air fryer pot.
Cook for 4 minutes on 300 F.
Mix onion, carrots, garlic cloves, cauliflower, soy sauce and eggs.
Cook for another 15 minutes.
When ready, serve and enjoy!

Nutrition:

Calories:70	Carbohydrates: 10g
Fat: 6g	Protein: 10g

Pork Sausage Mix

Prep time: 3 minutes
Cooking time: 25 minutes
Servings: 3

Ingredients:

Ground pork sausage – 1 lb.	White Rice – 2 cups
Beaten eggs – 3	Soy Sauce – 1 tbsp.
Vegetable oil – 2 tbsp.	Peas – 2 cups
Cabbage (chopped) – 2 cups	Beans (can) – 1
Carrots (sliced) – 2	Onions (chopped) – 2
	Salt and pepper to taste

Directions:

Add oil and pork sausage into the air fryer pot.
Cook for 10 minutes on 300 F.
Mix oil, cabbage, carrots, white rice, soy sauce, peas, beans, onions with salt and pepper.
Cook for another 15 minutes.
When ready, serve and enjoy the meal!

Nutrition:

Calories: 125	Carbohydrates: 10g
Fat: 7g	Protein: 40g

Broccoli with Chicken Broth

Prep time: 4 minutes
Cooking time: 15 minutes
Servings: 2

Ingredients:

Butter – ½ cup	Chicken broth – 2 cups
Onion (chopped) – 1	Garlic powder – 1 tbsp.
Broccoli (frozen) – 3 cups	Rice – 3 cups

Directions:

Add butter and onion into the air fryer pot.
Mix broccoli, chicken broth, garlic powder and rice.
Cook for 15 minutes on 300 F.
When ready, serve!

Nutrition:

Calories: 105	Carbohydrates: 10g
Fat: 9g	Protein: 30g

Egg Noodles Recipe

Prep time: 3 minutes
Cooking time: 10 minutes
Servings: 3

Ingredients:

Egg Noodles (boiled) – 1 medium pack	Green bell pepper (chopped) – 1
Onion (chopped) – 1	Pepperoni – 2 cups
Garlic cloves (minced) – 2	Pizza sauce – 2 tbsp.
	Milk – 1 cup
	Mozzarella cheese (shredded) – 1 cup

Directions:

Add onion and garlic cloves into the air fryer pot.
Mix green bell pepper, pepperoni, pizza sauce, milk and cheese.
Add egg noodles.
Cook for 10 minutes on 300 F.
When ready, serve the delicious noodles!

Nutrition:

Calories:96	Carbohydrates: 10g
Fat: 9g	Protein: 35g

Spinach with Bell Pepper

Prep time: 4 minutes
Cooking time: 25 minutes
Servings: 3

Ingredients:

Milk – 1/2 cup	Bell Pepper (chopped) – 1
Spinach (chopped) – 1 cup	Eggs – 2
Cheese (Any, shredded) – 1 cup	Salt and pepper to taste
Onion (chopped) – 1	Mint (dried) – 1 tbsp.

Directions:

Add milk and spinach into the air fryer pot.
Cook for 10 minutes on 300 F.
Mix onion, bell pepper, eggs, salt and pepper with mint.
Cook for another 15 minutes.
When ready, serve and enjoy!

Nutrition:

Calories: 110	Carbohydrates: 6g
Fat: 7g	Protein: 60g

Cauliflower with Flour Mix

Prep time: 2 minutes
Cooking time: 15 minutes
Servings: 3

Ingredients:

Cauliflower head (chopped) – 2 cups	Cabbage (chopped) – 2 cups
Eggs – 2	Radish (chopped) – 1 cup
Salt to taste	
Coconut flour – 1/2 cup	

Directions:

Mix eggs and flour into a bowl.
Add the mixture into the round baking tray,
Mix salt, cauliflower, cabbage and radish.
Place the baking tray into the air fryer.
Cook for 15 minutes on 300 F.
When ready, serve!

Nutrition:

Calories:95	Carbohydrates: 10g
Fat: 6g	Protein: 200g

Spaghetti with Bacon Slices

Prep time: 4 minutes
Cooking time: 15 minutes
Servings: 2

Ingredients:

Spaghetti (boiled) – 1 medium pack	Eggs – 2
Oil – 2 tbsp.	Grated cheese – 2 cups
Bacon slices – 9	Salt and pepper to taste
Onion (chopped) – 1	
Garlic cloves (minced) – 2	Parsley (chopped) to garnish

Directions:

Add oil and bacon slices into the air fryer pot.
Mix onion, garlic, eggs, cheese, salt and pepper with spaghetti.
Cook for 15 minutes on 300 F.
When ready, garnish parsley to serve!

Nutrition:

Calories:70	Carbohydrates: 10g
Fat: 6g	Protein: 10g

Rigatoni Mix Recipe

Prep time: 3 minutes
Cooking time: 10 minutes
Servings: 3

Ingredients:

Garlic cloves (minced) – 2
Cheddar cheese – 2 cups
Dried oregano – 1 tbsp.
Olive oil – 1 tbsp.
Sausages – 1 lb.
Dried Chili flakes – 1 tbsp.
Tomatoes (chopped) – 2
Rigatoni (boiled) – 3 cups

Directions:

Add garlic and oil into the air fryer pot.
Mix sausages, cheese, oregano, chili flakes and tomatoes.
Add boiled rigatoni and cook for 10 minutes on 300 F.
When ready, serve and enjoy!

Nutrition:

Calories: 105
Fat: 9g
Carbohydrates: 10g
Protein: 30g

White Rice with Butter

Prep time: 2 minutes
Cooking time: 10 minutes
Servings: 2

Ingredients:

White rice – 3 cups
Butter – 1 tbsp.
Garlic cloves (minced) – 2
Onion (chopped) – 1
Lemon juice – 2 tbsp.
Chicken broth – 2 cups

Directions:

Add garlic with butter into the air fryer pot.
Mix onion, lemon juice, chicken broth and white rice.
Cook for 10 minutes on 300 F.
When ready, serve and enjoy!

Nutrition:

Calories:80
Fat: 6g
Carbohydrates: 10g
Protein: 200g

Grounded Beef with Green Onion

Prep time: 2 minutes
Cooking time: 25 minutes
Servings: 3

Ingredients:

Oil – 2 cups
Grounded beef – 2 cups
Green onion (chopped) – 2 cups
White rice – 2 cups
Butter – 2 tbsp.
Egg – 3

Directions:

Add oil and grounded beef into the air fryer pot.
Cook for 10 minutes on 300 F.
Mix green onion, white rice, butter and egg.
Cook for another 15 minutes.
When ready, serve and enjoy!

Nutrition:

Calories:90
Fat: 6g
Carbohydrates: 10g
Protein: 200g

White Rice with Peas

Prep time: 4 minutes
Cooking time: 15 minutes
Servings: 3

Ingredients:

Vegetable oil – 2 tbsp.
Eggs – 2
White Rice – 2 cups
Chicken (chopped) – 1 lb.
Celery (chopped) – ½ cup
Carrot (chopped) – 1
Peas – 2 cups
Green onion (chopped) – 2 cups
Soy sauce – 1 tbsp.

Directions:

Add vegetable oil with eggs into the air fryer pot.
Cook for 5 minutes on 300 F.
Mix chicken, white rice, celery, carrot, peas, green onion and soy sauce.
Cook for another 10 minutes.
When ready, serve the delicious rice!

Nutrition:

Calories: 125
Fat: 7g
Carbohydrates: 10g
Protein: 40g

White Rice with Eggs

Prep time: 3 minutes
Cooking time: 20 minutes
Servings: 3

Ingredients:

Eggs – 2
Vegetable oil – 1 tbsp.
Onion (chopped) – 1

White Rice – 2 cups
Soy Sauce – 2 tbsp.
Chicken (chopped) – 1 lb.

Directions:

Add onion and chicken into the air fryer pot.
Mix vegetable oil, eggs, white rice and soy sauce.
Cook for 20 minutes on 300 F.
When ready, serve!

Nutrition:

Calories:96
Fat: 9g

Carbohydrates: 10g
Protein: 35g

Chicken Breast with Chicken Stock

Prep time: 4 minutes
Cooking time: 20 minutes
Servings: 3

Ingredients:

Chicken breast – 1 lb.
Garlic cloves (minced) – 2
Onions (chopped) – 2
Chicken stock – 2 cups
Soy sauce – 1 tbsp.

Fish sauce – 1 tbsp.
Oil – 1 tbsp.
Rosemary – 1 pinch
Thyme – 1 pinch
Mushrooms (sliced) – 2 cups
Salt and pepper to taste

Directions:

Add oil and garlic cloves into the air fryer pot.
Mix onions, chicken stock, soy sauce, fish sauce, thyme, rosemary, mushrooms with salt and pepper.
Place the chicken steaks on the top.
Cook for 20 minutes on 300 F.
When ready, serve!

Nutrition:

Calories:90
Fat: 6g

Carbohydrates: 10g
Protein: 200g

Asparagus with Cheese

Prep time: 4 minutes
Cooking time: 10 minutes
Servings: 2

Ingredients:

Asparagus (chopped) – 2 cups
Eggs – 2
Parmesan cheese – 2 cups

Lemon – half
Olive oil – 2 tbsp.
Mint leaves to garnish

Directions:

Add asparagus and eggs into the air fryer pot.
Mix parmesan cheese, lemon and oil.
Cook for 10 minutes on 300 F.
When ready, garnish mint leaves to serve!

Nutrition:

Calories:70
Fat: 6g

Carbohydrates: 10g
Protein: 10g

Elbow Macaroni with Cheese

Prep time: 2 minutes
Cooking time: 30 minutes
Servings: 2

Ingredients:

Elbow macaroni – 1 small pack
Water – 2 cups
Butter – 2 tbsp.
Cheddar cheese – 2 cups

Salt and pepper to taste
Eggs – 2
Milk – 2 cups
Grounded mustard – 2 tbsp.

Directions:

Add water and macaroni into the air fryer pot.
Cook for 10 minutes.
Rinse the macaroni and add it back into the pot.
Mix butter, cheddar cheese, salt and pepper, eggs, milk and grounded mustard.
Cook for 20 minutes on 300 F.
When ready, serve and enjoy!

Nutrition:

Calories:70
Fat: 6g

Carbohydrates: 10g
Protein: 10g

Chicken Drumsticks with Honey

Prep time: 2 minutes
Cooking time: 10 minutes
Servings: 3

Ingredients:

Chicken drumsticks – 5
Peanut oil – 2 tbsp.
Red chili powder – 1 tbsp.
Garlic cloves (minced) – 2
Green onion (chopped) – 2
Ginger (sliced) – 1 tbsp.
Honey – 1 tbsp.
Flour – 1 cup

Directions:

Add red chili powder and green onion into a bowl.
Mix garlic, ginger, honey and flour.
Add peanut oil into air fryer pot.
Dip the chicken drumsticks into the mixture.
Place them in the air fryer.
Cook for 10 minutes on 300 F.
When ready, serve and enjoy!

Nutrition:

Calories:96
Fat: 9g
Carbohydrates: 10g
Protein: 35g

BBQ Meat Steaks

Prep time: 3 minutes
Cooking time: 20 minutes
Servings: 3

Ingredients:

Red meat steaks – 1 lb.
BBQ sauce – 2 cups
Salt and pepper to taste

Directions:

Add BBQ sauce with salt and pepper into a bowl.
Mix well.
Cover the red meat steaks into the mixture.
Place the steaks over the air fryer grill.
Let it cook for 20 minutes on 300 F.
When ready, serve and enjoy!

Nutrition:

Calories:125
Fat: 6g
Carbohydrates: 10g
Protein: 200g

Snacks and Appetizers

Eggplant Appetizer Recipe

Prep time: 2 minutes
Cooking time: 15 minutes
Servings: 2

Ingredients:

Eggplant (sliced) – 1	Flour – 1 cup
Salt to taste	Eggs – 2
Greek yogurt – 1 cup	Milk – 1 cup
Garlic cloves	Dried breadcrumbs –
(minced) – 2	2 cups
Lemon juice – S tbsp.	Oil – 2 tbsp.

Directions:

Add oil into the air fryer pot.
Mix eggplant, salt, Greek yogurt, garlic
cloves, lemon juice, flour, eggs, milk and
breadcrumbs.
Cook at 300 F for 15 minutes.
When ready, serve and enjoy!

Nutrition:

Calories:70	Carbohydrates: 10g
Fat: 6g	Protein: 10g

Olives and Feta Appetizer

Prep time: 2 minutes
Cooking time: 15 minutes
Servings: 2

Ingredients:

Olives – 2 cups	Twiggy sticks – 2
Feta – S cup	cups
White flour – 1 cup	Oil – 2 tbsp.
Bread crumbs – 1	
cup	

Directions:

Add oil into the air fryer pot.
Mix olives, feta, white flour and bread
crumbs.
Cook at 300 F for 15 minutes.
When ready, serve with twiggy sticks and
enjoy!

Nutrition:

Calories:96	Carbohydrates: 10g
Fat: 9g	Protein: 35g

Eschalot Recipe of Appetizer

Prep time: 4 minutes
Cooking time: 10 minutes
Servings: 3

Ingredients:

White wine – 1 cup	Gelatin leaves – 2
Red wine vinegar – S	Oysters – 12
tbsp..	Herbs (any) to
Eschalot (chopped) –	garnish
1 cup	

Directions:

Add white wine into the air fryer pot.
Mix wine vinegar, eschalot, gelatin leaves
and oysters.
Cook at 300 F for 10 minutes.
When ready, garnish herbs to enjoy!

Nutrition:

Calories: 125	Carbohydrates: 10g
Fat: 7g	Protein: 40g

Salmon Fillet Appetizer

Prep time: 2 minutes
Cooking time: 15 minutes
Servings: 3

Ingredients:

Salmon fillet (diced)–	Brandy – 2 tbsp.
1 lb.	Fennel bulb – 2 tbsp.
Dill – 2 tbsp.	Lemon wedges to
Salt to taste	serve
White sugar – 1 tbsp.	Rocket leaves – S
Peppercorn – 2 tbsp.	cup

Directions:

Add brandy and white sugar into the air fryer
pot.
Mix salmon fillet, dill, salt, peppercorn, fennel
bulb and rocket leaves.
Cook at 300 F for 15 minutes.
When ready, serve with lemon wedges and
enjoy!

Nutrition:

Calories:96	Carbohydrates: 10g
Fat: 9g	Protein: 35g

Oysters Appetizer

Prep time: 4 minutes
Cooking time: 15 minutes
Servings: 3

Ingredients:

Oysters – 12	Worcestershire
Salt to taste	sauce – 2 tbsp.
Pancetta (chopped) –	Chives (chopped) – 1
1 cup	tbsp.

Directions:

Add Worcestershire sauce into the air fryer pot.
Mix oysters, salt, pancetta and chives.
Cook at 300 F for 15 minutes.
When ready, serve and enjoy!

Nutrition:

Calories:70	Carbohydrates: 10g
Fat: 6g	Protein: 10g

Zucchini Mix Appetizer

Prep time: 3 minutes
Cooking time: minutes
Servings: 3

Ingredients:

Oil – 1 tbsp.	Mint leaves
Zucchini (sliced) – 2	(chopped) – 1 cup
cups	Milk – 1 cup
Cheese – 2 cups	

Directions:

Add oil into the air fryer pot.
Mix zucchini, cheese, mint and milk.
Cook at 300 F for 10 minutes.
When ready, serve and enjoy!

Nutrition:

Calories: 125	Carbohydrates: 10g
Fat: 7g	Protein: 40g

Chickpeas Appetizer Recipe

Prep time: 4 minutes
Cooking time: 10 minutes
Servings: 3

Ingredients:

Chickpeas – 1 small	Cumin powder – 2
can	tbsp.
Garlic cloves	Lemon juice – 1 tbsp.
(minced) – 2	Cheese (grated) – 1
Oil – 1 tbsp.	cup
Tahini paste – 2 tbsp.	

Directions:

Add oil into the air fryer pot.
Mix chickpeas, garlic, tahini paste, cumin powder, lemon juice and cheese.
Cook at 300 F for 10 minutes.
When ready, serve and enjoy!

Nutrition:

Calories:96	Carbohydrates: 10g
Fat: 9g	Protein: 35g

Fish Fillet Appetizer

Prep time: 2 minutes
Cooking time: 10 minutes
Servings: 2

Ingredients:

Fish fillets – 1 lb.	Lime leaves
Egg white – 1	(chopped) – S cup
Red curry paste – 2	Beans (boiled) – 2
tbsp.	cups
Fish sauce – 2 tbsp.	

Directions:

Add red curry paste and beans into the air fryer pot.
Mix fish fillets, egg whites, fish sauce and lime leaves.
Cook at 300 F for 10 minutes.
When ready, serve!

Nutrition:

Calories: 90	Carbohydrates: 20g
Fat: 8g	Protein: 25g

Ham Mix Appetizer

Prep time: 4 minutes
Cooking time: 15 minutes
Servings:

Ingredients:

Ham (chopped) – 1 lb.
Egg mayonnaise – 3 tbsp.
Parsley (chopped) – 1 cup
Eggs (boiled, chopped) – 2

Directions:

Add egg mayonnaise into the air fryer pot.
Mix ham, parsley and boiled eggs.
Cook at 300 F for 15 minutes.
When ready, serve and enjoy!

Nutrition:

Calories: 50
Fat: 8g
Carbohydrates: 40g
Protein: 45g

Corn Kernels Appetizer

Prep time: 4 minutes
Cooking time: 15 minutes
Servings: 2

Ingredients:

Oil – 2 tbsp.
Flour – 2 cups
Baking powder – 2 tbsp.
Pumpkin (chopped) – 2 cups
Corn kernels – 1 cup
Ham (chopped) – 1 lb.
Cheddar cheese – 1 cup
Shallots (chopped) – 2 cups
Milk – 1 cup
Greek yogurt – 2 tbsp.
Pumpkin kernels – 1 tbsp.

Directions:

Add oil into the air fryer pot.
Mix flour, baking powder, pumpkin, corn kernels, ham, cheddar cheese and shallots.
Add milk, Greek yogurt and pumpkin kernels.
Cook at 300 F for 15 minutes.
When ready, serve and enjoy!

Nutrition:

Calories:96
Fat: 9g
Carbohydrates: 10g
Protein: 35g

Rice Cracker Appetizer

Prep time: 2 minutes
Cooking time: 10 minutes
Servings: 3

Ingredients:

Rice crackers – 1 small pack
Apricots – 1 cup
Puffed corn – 2 cups
Pumpkin seeds – S cup

Directions:

Add apricots and corn into the air fryer pot.
Mix pumpkin seeds.
Cook at 300 F for 10 minutes.
When ready, apply the mixture on rice crackers to serve!

Nutrition:

Calories: 125
Fat: 7g
Carbohydrates: 10g
Protein: 40g

Chia Seeds Snack Recipe

Prep time: 4 minutes
Cooking time: 5 minutes
Servings: 3

Ingredients:

Cream cheese – 1 cup
Banana – 1
Coconut (shredded) – 1 cup
Chia seeds – S tbsp.

Directions:

Add cream cheese and coconut into the round baking tray.
Mix chia seeds with banana.
Place into the air fryer.
Cook at 300 F for 5 minutes.
When ready, serve!

Nutrition:

Calories: 20
Fat: 53g
Carbohydrates: 20g
Protein: 15g

Rice Cereal Appetizer

Prep time: 4 minutes
Cooking time: 10 minutes
Servings: 3

Ingredients:

Rice cereal – 2 cups
Icing sugar – 2 tbsp.
Cocoa powder – 4
tbsp.
Coconut (shredded) –
1 cup
Melted chocolate – 1
cup

Directions:

Add rice cereal into the air fryer pot.
Mix icing sugar, cocoa powder and coconut.
Cook at 300 F for 10 minutes.
When ready, cover the mixture with melted
chocolate to serve!

Nutrition:

Calories:70
Fat: 6g
Carbohydrates: 10g
Protein: 10g

Brown Rice Appetizer

Prep time: 3 minutes
Cooking time: 15 minutes
Servings: 3

Ingredients:

Brown rice (boiled) –
2 cups
Oil – 1 tbsp.
Tuna – 1 small can
Tomatoes
(chopped) – 2

Alfalfa sprouts – S cup
Directions:

Add oil into the air fryer pot.
Mix brown rice, tuna, tomatoes and alfalfa
sprouts.
Cook at 300 F for 15 minutes.
When ready, serve!

Nutrition:

Calories: 125
Fat: 7g
Carbohydrates: 10g
Protein: 40g

Nutella Mix Snack

Prep time: 2 minutes
Cooking time: 15 minutes
Servings: 2

Ingredients:

Pikelets – 1 small
packet
Nutella – 2 tbsp.
Vanilla frosting – 2
tbsp.
Pizza snack plates –
4

Directions:

Add pikelets into the air fryer pot.
Mix Nutella and vanilla frosting.
Cook at 300 F for 5 minutes.
When ready, apply the mixture on pizza
snack plates to serve!

Nutrition:

Calories: 90
Fat: 8g
Carbohydrates: 20g
Protein: 25g

Fruit Mix Appetizer

Prep time: 4 minutes
Cooking time: 15 minutes
Servings:

Ingredients:

Apples – 1 can
Peaches – 1 can
Filo pastry – 2 sheets
Oil – 1 tbsp.
Sugar – 1 tbsp.
Cinnamon powder –
2 tbsp.

Directions:

Add oil into the air fryer pot.
Mix apples, peaches, sugar and cinnamon
powder.
Place the pastry over the mixture.
Cook at 300 F for 15 minutes.
When ready, serve and enjoy!

Nutrition:

Calories:96
Fat: 9g
Carbohydrates: 10g
Protein: 35g

Rolled Oats Snack

Prep time: 2 minutes
Cooking time: 10 minutes
Servings: 3

Ingredients:

Butter – 1 tbsp.
Brown sugar – 2 tbsp.
Golden syrup – 2 tbsp.
Vanilla essence – 2 tbsp.

Rolled oats – 1 cup
Flour – S cup
Nuts – 1 cup
Dark chocolate (pieces) – 1 cup

Directions:

Add butter and brown sugar into the air fryer pot.
Mix golden syrup, vanilla essence, rolled oats, flour and nuts.
Add dark chocolate.
Cook at 300 F for 10 minutes.
When ready, serve and enjoy!

Nutrition:

Calories: 70
Fat: 8g
Carbohydrates: 30g
Protein: 25g

Butter Mix Appetizer

Prep time: 3 minutes
Cooking time: 10 minutes
Servings: 3

Ingredients:

Butter – 1 tbsp.
Flour – 2 cups
Salt to taste
Parmesan cheese – 1 cup

Oil – 2 tbsp.
Flour – 2 cups
Milk – 1 cup
Eggs – 2
Paprika – 1 tbsp.

Directions:

Add oil into the air fryer pot.
Mix butter, flour, parmesan cheese, flour, milk, eggs and paprika.
Pour the mixture into the round baking tray.
Place into the pot.
Cook at 300 F for 10 minutes.
When ready, serve and enjoy!

Nutrition:

Calories: 125
Fat: 7g
Carbohydrates: 10g
Protein: 40g

Delicious Quick Snack

Prep time: 4 minutes
Cooking time: 15 minutes
Servings: 3

Ingredients:

Pork (minced) – 1 lb.
Tomato sauce – 2 tbsp.
Barbeque sauce – 2 tbsp.

Worcestershire sauce – 2 tbsp.
Egg – 1
Oil – 2 tbsp.

Directions:

Add oil into the air fryer pot.
Mix pork, tomato sauce, barbeque sauce, Worcestershire sauce and egg.
Cook at 300 F for 15 minutes.
When ready, make small balls to serve!

Nutrition:

Calories: 60
Fat: 8g
Carbohydrates: 40g
Protein: 25g

Olives Mix Appetizer

Prep time: 4 minutes
Cooking time: 15 minutes
Servings:

Ingredients:

Black olives – 1 cup
Green olives – 1 cup
Lemon rind (sliced) – 2 tbsp.
Orange rind (sliced) – 2 tbsp.

Garlic cloves (minced) – 2
Onion (sliced) – 1
Oil – 1 tbsp.
Thyme (chopped) – S cup

Directions:

Add oil into the air fryer pot.
Mix black olives, green olives, lemon rind, orange rind, garlic cloves, onion and thyme.
Cook at 300 F for 15 minutes.
When ready, serve and enjoy!

Nutrition:

Calories:96
Fat: 9g
Carbohydrates: 10g
Protein: 35g

Delicious Muffin Snack

Prep time: 3 minutes
Cooking time: 15 minutes
Servings: 2

Ingredients:

Muffins – 4	Capers – 1 tbsp.
Tomato sauce – ½ cup	Ricotta – 2 cups
Red capsicum (sliced) – 1	Oregano leaves to garnish

Directions:

Add tomato sauce into the air fryer pot.
Mix red capsicum, capers and ricotta.
Cook at 300 F for 15 minutes.
When ready, apply the mixture on muffins.
Garnish with oregano leaves to serve!

Nutrition:

Calories: 90	Carbohydrates: 20g
Fat: 8g	Protein: 25g

Corn Tortillas Mix Snack

Prep time: 2 minutes
Cooking time: 10 minutes
Servings: 3

Ingredients:

Coriander (chopped) – S cup	Oil – 2 tbsp.
Lime juice – 1 tbsp.	Corn tortillas – 10
Tomatoes (diced) – 2	Lime wedges to serve
Onion (sliced) – 2	

Directions:

Add oil into the air fryer pot.
Mix coriander, lime juice, tomatoes, corn tortillas and onion.
Cook at 300 F for 10 minutes.
When ready, serve with lime wedges.

Nutrition:

Calories: 125	Carbohydrates: 10g
Fat: 7g	Protein: 40g

Ricotta Cheese Snack

Prep time: 3 minutes
Cooking time: 15 minutes
Servings: 3

Ingredients:

Yeast – 1 tbsp.	Baking powder – 1 tsp.
Sugar – 2 tbsp.	Oil – 1 tbsp.
Skim milk – 1 cup	Ricotta (shredded) – 1 cup
Warm water – 1 cup	
Flour – 2 cups	Honey to serve
Salt to taste	

Directions:

Add oil into the air fryer pot.
Mix yeast, sugar, skim milk, warm water, flour, salt, baking powder and ricotta.
Cook at 300 F for 15 minutes.
When ready, serve with honey and enjoy!

Nutrition:

Calories:70	Carbohydrates: 10g
Fat: 6g	Protein: 10g

Coconut Mix Snack

Prep time: 2 minutes
Cooking time: 15 minutes
Servings: 3

Ingredients:

Egg – 1	Sesame seeds – 2 tbsp.
Butter – 1 tbsp.	Peanut butter – 2 tbsp.
Flour – 2 cups	Honey – S cup
Rolled oats – 1 cup	Butter – 2 tbsp.
Coconut (shredded) – 1 cup	
Brown sugar – 1 cup	

Directions:

Add butter into the air fryer pot.
Mix egg, flour, rolled oats, coconut, brown sugar, sesame seeds and honey.
Cook at 300 F for 15 minutes.
When ready, spread peanut butter to serve!

Nutrition:

Calories:96	Carbohydrates: 10g
Fat: 9g	Protein: 35g

Lavash Bread Roll Appetizer

Prep time: 2 minutes
Cooking time: 15 minutes
Servings: 2

Ingredients:

Cheese dip – 1 cup	Carrot grated) – 2
Lavash bread – 3	cups
sheets	Broccoli sprouts – 1
	cup

Directions:

Add cheese dip into the air fryer pot.
Mix carrot and broccoli sprouts.
Cook at 300 F for 15 minutes.
When ready, add the mixture into the lavash bread sheet and roll.
Serve and enjoy!

Nutrition:

Calories: 90	Carbohydrates: 20g
Fat: 8g	Protein: 25g

Tuna and Cheese Snack

Prep time: 2 minutes
Cooking time: 15 minutes
Servings: 3

Ingredients:

Cucumber (sliced) – 1	Alfalfa sprouts – 1 tbsp.
Oil – 2 tbsp.	Tomato (chopped) – 1
Tuna – 1 small can	
Cheddar cheese – 2 cups	

Directions:

Add oil into the air fryer pot.
Mix tuna, cucumber, cheese and alfalfa sprouts.
Cook at 300 F for 15 minutes.
When ready, serve and enjoy the snack!

Nutrition:

Calories:70	Carbohydrates: 10g
Fat: 6g	Protein: 10g

Tuna Mix Lavash Roll Appetizer

Prep time: 3 minutes
Cooking time: 15 minutes
Servings: 3

Ingredients:

Oil – 1 tbsp.	Tuna – 1 can
Garlic cloves	Lavash bread
(minced) – 2	sheets – 2
Rosemary	Salt to taste
(chopped) – 2 tbsp.	

Directions:

Add oil into the air fryer pot.
Mix garlic, rosemary, tuna and salt.
Cook at 300 F for 15 minutes.
When ready, add the mixture into the lavash bread sheets and roll.
Serve and enjoy!

Nutrition:

Calories: 80	Carbohydrates: 20g
Fat: 8g	Protein: 25g

Nuts Mix Snack

Prep time: 4 minutes
Cooking time: 10 minutes
Servings: 2

Ingredients:

Honey – 1 tbsp.	Salt to taste
Oil – 2 tbsp.	Almond kernels – 1
Garlic clove	tbsp.
(minced) – 1 tbsp.	Cashew nuts – S cup
Chili powder – S	Brazil nuts – 1 cup
tbsp..	Macadamia nuts – S
Paprika – 1 tbsp.	cup

Directions:

Mix oil into the air fryer pot.
Add garlic clove, honey, chili powder, paprika, salt, almond kernels, cashew nuts, Brazil nuts and macadamia nuts.
Cook at 300 F for 10 minutes.
When ready, serve and enjoy!

Nutrition:

Calories: 125	Carbohydrates: 10g
Fat: 7g	Protein: 40g

Delicious Buttermilk Appetizer

Prep time: 4 minutes
Cooking time: 15 minutes
Servings: 2

Ingredients:

Flour – 2 cups	Cheddar cheese – 1
Mustard powder – 1	cup
tbsp.	Buttermilk – 1 cup
Sugar – 2 tbsp.	Egg – 1
Butter – 2 tbsp.	Flour for dusting

Directions:

Add buttermilk into the air fryer pot.
Mix flour, mustard powder, sugar, butter,
cheese and egg into the bowl.
Make small balls out of the mixture.
Place them into the pot.
Cook at 300 F for 15 minutes.
When ready, serve and enjoy!

Nutrition:

Calories: 90   Carbohydrates: 20g
Fat: 8g   Protein: 25g

Vita Weats Snack

Prep time: 3 minutes
Cooking time: 15 minutes
Servings:

Ingredients:

Ricotta – S cup	Tomatoes (sliced) – 2
Vita weats – 3	Snow pea sprouts
Cucumber (sliced) –	
1	

Directions:

Mix ricotta, cucumber, tomatoes and snow
peas into the bowl.
Add the mixture on the top of each vita
weats.
Place into the air fryer.
Cook at 300 F for 15 minutes.
When ready, serve and enjoy!

Nutrition:

Calories:96   Carbohydrates: 10g
Fat: 9g   Protein: 35g

Potatoes Mix Snack

Prep time: 2 minutes
Cooking time: 15 minutes
Servings: 3

Ingredients:

Potatoes (mashed) –	Grated cheese – 2
2	cups
Oil – 1 tbsp.	Tomato salsa – 2
	tbsp.

Directions:

Add oil into the air fryer pot.
Mix potatoes, grated cheese and tomato
salsa.
Cook at 300 F for 15 minutes.
When ready, serve!

Nutrition:

Calories: 90   Carbohydrates: 20g
Fat: 8g   Protein: 25g

Potatoes and Cheese Appetizer

Prep time: 2 minutes
Cooking time: 15 minutes
Servings: 3

Ingredients:

Potatoes (sliced) – 2	Pizza base – 6 small
small	Onion (sliced) – 1
Oil – 2 tbsp.	Parmesan cheese
Rosemary leaves – 2	(grated) – 2 cups
cups	Herbs to garnish

Directions:

Add oil into the air fryer pot.
Mix potatoes, rosemary leaves, onion and
parmesan cheese into the bow.
Paste the pizza base with the mixture.
Place into the air fryer.
Cook fat 300 F for 15 minutes.
When ready, garnish herbs to serve.

Nutrition:

Calories: 114   Carbohydrates: 10g
Fat: 9g   Protein: 50g

Chickpeas Snack

Prep time: 2 minutes
Cooking time: 10 minutes
Servings: 3

Ingredients:

Chickpeas – 1 small can	Cumin powder – 1 tbsp.
Oil – 1 tbsp.	Curry powder – 1 tbsp.
Salt to taste	
Sweet paprika – 1 tbsp.	

Directions:

Add oil into the air fryer pot.
Mix chickpeas, sweet paprika, salt, cumin powder and curry powder.
Cook at 400 F for 10 minutes.
When ready, serve and enjoy the crunchy chickpeas.

Nutrition:

Calories:95	Carbohydrates: 10g
Fat: 6g	Protein: 200g

Ham and Tomatoes Mix Appetizer

Prep time: 4 minutes
Cooking time: 10 minutes
Servings: 3

Ingredients:

Ham (chopped) – 2 tbsp.	Parsley (chopped) – S cup
Grated cheese – 2 cups	Milk – 1 cup
Flour – 2 cups	Oil – 1 tbsp.
Tomatoes (chopped) – 2	Egg – 1
	Salt to taste

Directions:

Add oil into the air fryer pot.
Mix ham, flour, tomatoes, milk, egg, salt and parsley.
Cook at 300 F for 10 minutes.
When ready, garnish cheese to serve!

Nutrition:

Calories:96	Carbohydrates: 10g
Fat: 9g	Protein: 35g

Sundried Tomatoes Snack

Prep time: 2 minutes
Cooking time: 10 minutes
Servings: 2

Ingredients:

Butter – 2 tbsp.	Paprika – 2 tbsp.
Sundried tomatoes – 2 cups	Oregano – 1 tbsp.
	Salt to taste

Directions:

Add butter into the air fryer pot.
Mix sundried tomatoes, paprika, oregano and salt.
Cook at 300 F for 10 minutes.
When ready, serve!

Nutrition:

Calories:70	Carbohydrates: 10g
Fat: 6g	Protein: 10g

Tortillas with Banana

Prep time: 4 minutes
Cooking time: 5 minutes
Servings: 2

Ingredients:

Tortillas – 2 mini	Banana (sliced) – 1
Fresh ricotta – 2 tbsp.	Honey – 1 tbsp.

Directions:

Add honey into the air fryer pot.
Mix fresh ricotta and banana.
Add tortillas.
Cook at 250 F for 5 minutes.
When ready, serve and enjoy the crunchy appetizer!

Nutrition:

Calories: 125	Carbohydrates: 10g
Fat: 7g	Protein: 40g

Kale Mix Snack

Prep time: 3 minutes
Cooking time: 10 minutes
Servings: 3

Ingredients:

Kale – 2 cups	Lemon zest – S tbsp.
Oil – 2 tbsp.	Almonds (chopped) –
Salt to taste	S cup

Directions:

Add oil into the air fryer pot.
Mix kale, salt, lemon zest and almonds.
Cook at 300 F for 10 minutes.
When ready, serve and enjoy!

Nutrition:

Calories:86	Carbohydrates: 10g
Fat: 6g	Protein: 200g

Beans Snack Recipe

Prep time: 3 minutes
Cooking time: 10 minutes
Servings: 3

Ingredients:

Beans – 1 small can	Pineapple juice – 2
Roll pastry – 6	tbsp.
	Oil – 2 tbsp.

Directions:

Add oil into the round baking tray.
Mix beans and pineapple juice with roll
pastry over it.
Place the baking tray into the air fryer.
Cook at 350 F for 10 minutes.
When ready, serve and enjoy!

Nutrition:

Calories:70	Carbohydrates: 10g
Fat: 6g	Protein: 10g

Cheesy Delicious Appetizer

Prep time: 2 minutes
Cooking time: 15 minutes
Servings: 3

Ingredients:

Rosemary	Vegetable stock – 2
(chopped) – 1 tbsp.	cups
Oil – 1 tbsp.	Parmesan cheese –
Onion (chopped) – 1	1 cup
Garlic cloves	Peas – 1 cup
(minced) – 2	Parsley (chopped) –
Rice – 2 cups	1 cup
White wine – S cup	Flour – 2 cups

Directions:

Add oil and rosemary into the air fryer pot.
Mix onion, garlic, rice, white wine, vegetable
stock, peas, parsley and flour.
Cook at 300 F for 15 minutes.
When ready, serve with cheese garnishing.

Nutrition:

Calories:95	Carbohydrates: 10g
Fat: 6g	Protein: 200g

Zucchini Snack

Prep time: 3 minutes
Cooking time: 10 minutes
Servings: 3

Ingredients:

Zucchini (chopped) –	Oil – 1 tbsp.
2 cups	Carrot (grated) – 1
Flour – 1 cup	Corn kernels – 1
Eggs – 2	tbsp.
Basil leaves	Red capsicum
(chopped) – 2 tbsp.	(sliced) – 1
Cheese (crumbled) –	
1 cup	

Directions:

Add flour and eggs into the bowl.
Mix zucchini, basil leaves, cheese, carrot,
corn kernels and red capsicum.
Add oil into the air fryer pot.
Pour the mixture into the pot.
Cook at 300 F for 10 minutes.
When ready, serve!

Nutrition:

Calories:95	Carbohydrates: 10g
Fat: 6g	Protein: 200g

Chicken Drumsticks Recipe

Prep time: 2 minutes
Cooking time: 10 minutes
Servings: 3

Ingredients:

Chicken drumsticks – 1 lb.
Buttermilk – 1 cup
Cornflakes crumbs – 1 cup
Chili powder – 1 tbsp.
Garlic (minced) – 1 tbsp.
Lemon juice – 1 tbsp.

Directions:

Add buttermilk into the air fryer pot.
Mix cornflakes, chili powder, garlic, lemon juice and chicken drumsticks.
Cook at 300 F for 10 minutes.
When ready, serve and enjoy!

Nutrition:

Calories: 125
Fat: 7g
Carbohydrates: 10g
Protein: 40g

Avocado Mix Appetizer

Prep time: 3 minutes
Cooking time: 10 minutes
Servings: 2

Ingredients:

Avocado (chopped) – 1 cup
Butter – 1 tbsp.
Egg – 1
Milk – 1 cup
Cheese (grated) – 1 cup
Flour – 2 cups
Chili powder – 1 tbsp.
Baking powder – 1 tsp.
Tomatoes (chopped) – 2

Directions:

Add butter and egg into the air fryer pot.
Mix avocado, milk, flour, chili powder, baking powder and tomatoes.
Cook at 300 F for 10 minutes.
When ready, garnish cheese to serve!

Nutrition:

Calories:96
Fat: 9g
Carbohydrates: 10g
Protein: 35g

Corncobs Recipe

Prep time: 2 minutes
Cooking time: 15 minutes
Servings: 2

Ingredients:

Corncobs – 6
Flour – 1 cup
Chives – S cup
Milk – 1 cup
Eggs – 3
Crab meat (minced) – 1 lb.
Oil – 2 tbsp.

Directions:

Add oil into the air fryer pot.
Mix flour, milk, eggs, corncobs, crabmeat and chives.
Cook at 350 F for 15 minutes.
When ready, serve!

Nutrition:

Calories:95
Fat: 6g
Carbohydrates: 10g
Protein: 200g

Dried Fruits Recipe

Prep time: 2 minutes
Cooking time: 10 minutes
Servings: 3

Ingredients:

Rolled oats – 1 cup
Dried apricots (chopped) – 1 cup
Dried apple (chopped) – 1 cup
Almonds (chopped) – 1 cup
Sunflower seed kernels – S cup
Cinnamon powder – 1 tbsp.
Bananas (mashed) – 2
Tahini sauce – 1 tbsp.
Egg – 1

Directions:

Add rolled oats into the air fryer pot.
Mix apricots, apple, almonds, sunflower seeds, cinnamon powder, and egg with tahini sauce.
Cook at 300 F for 10 minutes.
When ready, add bananas to enjoy the appetizer!

Nutrition:

Calories:96
Fat: 9g
Carbohydrates: 10g
Protein: 35g

Chicken Legs Recipe

Prep time: 3 minutes
Cooking time: 15 minutes
Servings: 2

Ingredients:

Soy sauce – 1 tbsp.	Ginger (chopped) – 1
Honey – 1 tbsp.	tbsp.
Garlic cloves	Chicken legs – 1 lb.
(minced) – 2	Green onion
	(chopped) to garnish

Directions:

Add honey and soy sauce into the air fryer pot.
Mix garlic, ginger, green onion and chicken legs.
Cook at 300 F for 15 minutes.
When ready, serve and enjoy!

Nutrition:

Calories:70	Carbohydrates: 10g
Fat: 6g	Protein: 10g

Celery Stalks Recipe

Prep time: 3 minutes
Cooking time: 15 minutes
Servings: 3

Ingredients:

Bread – 8 slices	Celery (thin slices) –
Vegemite – 1 cup	2 cups

Directions:

Add celery and vegemite into the air fryer pot.
Cook at 300 F for 15 minutes.
When ready, add the mixture between bread slices.
Serve and enjoy!

Nutrition:

Calories:98	Carbohydrates: 10g
Fat: 6g	Protein: 200g

Spring Onion Mix Snack

Try this simple recipe and you would eat it every dinner for sure!
Prep time: 3 minutes
Cooking time: 15 minutes
Servings: 2

Ingredients:

Cheddar cheese – 1	Spring onions
cup	(sliced) – 2
Sour cream – S cup	Eggs – 2
Flour – S cup	Butter – 2 tbsp.
Red capsicum	Chives to garnish
(diced) – 1	

Directions:

Add flour and eggs into the bowl.
Mix sour cream, red capsicum, spring onions and butter.
Pour the mixture into the round baking tray.
Cook at 300 F for 15 minutes.
When ready, garnish with chives and cheddar to serve!

Nutrition:

Calories:70	Carbohydrates: 10g
Fat: 6g	Protein: 10g

Cornmeal Mix Snack Recipe

Prep time: 2 minutes
Cooking time: 10 minutes
Servings: 2

Ingredients:

Oil – 2 tbsp.	Red chili (chopped) –
Cornmeal – 2 tbsp.	1
Flour – 1 cup	Buttermilk- S cup
Corn kernels – S cup	Egg – 1
Cheddar cheese – S	Butter to soften, if
cup	needed.

Directions:

Add oil into the air fryer pot.
Mix cornmeal, flour, corn kernels, red chili, buttermilk and egg.
Pour into the pot.
Cook at 300 F for 10 minutes.
When ready, garnish with cheese and serve!

Nutrition:

Calories: 125	Carbohydrates: 10g
Fat: 7g	Protein: 40g

Puff Pastry Appetizer

Prep time: 3 minutes
Cooking time: 15 minutes
Servings: 2

Ingredients:

Oil – 1 tbsp.
Onion (chopped) – 1
Salt to taste
Cumin seeds – S tbsp.
Turmeric powder – 1 tbsp.
Chili powder – S tsp.
Garlic clove (minced) – 1
Potatoes (mashed) – 2
Lemon juice – 1 tbsp.
Parsley (chopped) – S cup
Puff pastry – 3 sheets
Eggs – 2

Directions:

Add oil and onion into the air fryer pot.
Mix salt, cumin seeds, turmeric powder, chili powder, garlic, potatoes, lemon juice, eggs and parsley.
Cook at 300 for 15 minutes.
Place the puff pastries on top of the mixture and cook for another 5 minutes.
When ready, serve!

Nutrition:

Calories:70
Fat: 6g
Carbohydrates: 10g
Protein: 10g

Roasted Beef Snack Recipe

Prep time: 2 minutes
Cooking time: 15 minutes
Servings: 3

Ingredients:

Chickpeas – 1 small can
Tahini paste – 1 tbsp.
Garlic cloves (minced) – 1
Lemon juice – 1 tbsp.
Cumin powder – 1 tbsp.
Roasted beef (sliced) – 1 lb.
Tomatoes (chopped) – 2
Parsley (chopped) to garnish

Directions:

Add chickpeas and tahini into the air fryer pot.
Mix garlic cloves, lemon juice, cumin powder, roasted beef and tomatoes.
Cook at 300 F for 15 minutes
When ready, garnish with parsley and serve!

Nutrition:

Calories:96
Fat: 9g
Carbohydrates: 10g
Protein: 35g

Fish and Seafood

Tuna Fish Quick Recipe

Prep time: 5 minutes
Cooking time: 10 minutes
Servings: 2

Ingredients:

Onion (diced) – S large
Olive oil – 1 tbsp.
Tuna fish – 1 can
Tomatoes (diced) – 2
Chili powder – S tbsp.
Salt and pepper to taste

Directions:

Add onion and olive oil into the air fryer pot.
Add tomatoes, tuna fish, chili powder with salt and pepper. Mix well.
Let it cook for 10 minutes at 300 F.
When ready, serve with bread or any of your favorite side dish!

Nutrition:

Calories: 90
Fat: 10g
Carbohydrates: 21g
Protein:95g

Chipotle Mix Tilapia Recipe

Prep time: 4 minutes
Cooking time: 20 minutes
Servings: 4

Ingredients:

Olive oil – 2 tbsp.
Onion (diced) – 2
Garlic cloves (minced) – 3
Chili powder – 1 tbsp.
Chipotle powder – 1 tbsp.
Cumin powder – 1 tsp.
Salt to taste
Rinsed black beans – 1 small can
Tomatoes (diced) – 2
Tilapia fillets – 1 lb.
Lime juice – 2 tbsp.
Toppings: cream, cheese, avocado, cilantro (any)

Directions:

Add oil in the air fryer pot.
Mix onion, garlic cloves, lime juice and tilapia fillets.
Let it cook for 10 minutes at 300 F.
Now add chili powder, cumin powder, chipotle powder, salt and black beans. Mix well.
Add sweet potatoes and let it cook for 10 more minutes.
When done, serve and enjoy!

Nutrition:

Calories: 90
Fat: 8g
Carbohydrates: 20g
Protein: 25g

Peanut Butter with Mackerel Fillets

Prep time: 4 minutes
Cooking time: 14 minutes
Servings: 3

Ingredients:

Canola oil – S tbsp..
Peanut butter – 1 tbsp.
Soy sauce – 2 tbsp.
Cilantro (chopped) – S cup
Lime juice – 1 tbsp.
Mackerel fillets – 1 lb.
Red pepper flakes – 1 tbsp.
Cornstarch – 2 tbsp.
Green onions for garnishing

Directions:

Add canola oil in the air fryer pot.
Add mackerel fillets and cook at 300 F for 10 minutes.
Meanwhile, add peanut butter, cilantro, lime juice, soy sauce, red pepper flakes and cornstarch into a bowl. Stir well.
Add to the air fryer pot and cook for another 4 minutes.
When done, serve and enjoy with adding the garnishing of green onion!

Nutrition:

Calories:100
Fat: 6g
Carbohydrates: 10g
Protein: 20g

Shrimps Delight Recipe

Prep time: 4 minutes
Cooking time: 16 minutes
Servings: 3

Ingredients:

Oil – 2 tbsp.
Tomatoes (chopped) – 2
Onion – 1
Garlic cloves – 2 minced
Cumin powder – 1 tbsp.
Coriander powder – 1 tbsp.
Lemon rind – 2 strips
Shrimps – 1 lb.
Chopped parsley to garnish

Directions:

Add oil into the air fryer pot.
Mix red kidney beans. Lemon rind, coriander powder, cumin powder, garlic, onion, shrimps and tomatoes.
Cook at 300 F for 15 minutes.
When ready, serve!

Nutrition:

Calories:95
Fat: 6g
Carbohydrates: 10g
Protein: 200g

Kidney Beans with Tuna Fish

Prep time: 5 minutes
Cooking time: 15 minutes
Servings: 3

Ingredients:

Kidney beans – 2 cups
Tuna fish – 2 cans
Oil – 2 tbsp.
Curry paste – 2 tbsp.
Brown sugar – 1 tsp.
Fish sauce – 1 tbsp.
Coriander powder – 1 tbsp.
Rice to serve (boiled)

Directions:

Add oil into the air fryer pot.
Add curry paste, brown sugar, tuna fish, kidney beans, coriander powder and fish sauce.
Let it cook on high pressure for 15 minutes.
When done, serve with rice!

Nutrition:

Calories: 100g
Fat: 10g
Carbohydrates: 8g
Protein: 110g

Cod and Beans Recipe

Prep time: 5 minutes
Cooking time: 12 minutes
Servings: 2

Ingredients:

Black beans – 4 cup
Salsa – 2 cups
Oil – 2 tbsp.
Cod (chopped) – 1 lb.
Avocados (diced) – 2
Cheese to garnish

Directions:

Add oil and black beans in the air fryer pot.
Let it cook for 2 minutes at 300 F.
Mix salsa and avocados with cod.
Cook for another 10 minutes.
When done, garnish with shredded cheese and enjoy!

Nutrition:

Calories: 155
Fat: 7g
Carbohydrates: 10g
Protein: 40g

Delicious Tilapia Recipe

Prep time: 6 minutes
Cooking time: 10 minutes
Servings: 3

Ingredients:

Onions (chopped) – 2
Oil – 2 tbsp.
Carrots (sliced) – 2
Cumin powder – 1 tbsp.
Coriander powder – 1 tbsp.
Cayenne powder – 1 tbsp.
Cinnamon powder – ½ tbsp.
Tilapia (sliced) – 1 lb.
Tomato paste – 2 tbsp.
Lemon juice – 1 tbsp.
Cilantro to garnish

Directions:

Add oil into the air fryer pot.
Mix onions, carrots, coriander powder, cumin powder, cinnamon powder, and tomato paste with lemon juice.
Add tilapia slices.
Cook at 300 F for 15 minutes.
When ready, serve and enjoy!

Nutrition:

Calories:95
Fat: 6g
Carbohydrates: 10g
Protein: 200g

Halibut Mix Recipe

Prep time: 6 minutes
Cooking time: 10 minutes
Servings: 3

Ingredients:

Olive oil – 1 tbsp.
Onion (chopped) – 1
Garlic (minced) – 2 cloves
Brown sugar – ½ tsp.
Salt and pepper to taste
Black beans – 3 cups
Lime juice – 1 tbsp.
Halibut (sliced) – 1 lb.
Oregano powder – 1 tbsp.
Green bell pepper (chopped) – 1

Directions:

Add olive to the air fryer pot.
Mix onion and garlic.
Add black beans, salt and pepper, brown sugar, lime juice, bell pepper, halibut and oregano powder.
Cook at 300 F for 15 minutes.
When ready, serve!

Nutrition:

Calories: 90
Fat: 8g
Carbohydrates: 20g
Protein: 25g

Chickpeas with Crab

Prep time: 4 minutes
Cooking time: 14 minutes
Servings: 2

Ingredients:

Curry powder – 1 tbsp.
Black pepper – 1 tbsp.
Oil – 1 tbsp.
Salt to taste
Mustard seeds – 1 tbsp.
Garlic (minced) – 2 cloves
Red kidney beans – 3 cups
Chickpeas – 3 cups
Crabmeat – 1 lb.
Water – 1 cup

Directions:

Add oil to the air fryer pot. Add chickpeas and stir well.
Add curry powder, mustard seeds, chickpeas, kidney beans, garlic, water and black pepper.
Mix crab meat.
Cook at 300 F for 20 minutes.
When ready, serve and enjoy!
Nutrition:

Calories: 100g
Fat: 10g
Carbohydrates: 8g
Protein: 110g

Chickpeas and Shrimp Recipe

Prep time: 6 minutes
Cooking time: 14 minutes
Servings: 2

Ingredients:

Chickpeas – 2 cups
Shrimps – 1 lb.
Vegetable broth – 2 cups
Red lentils – 2 cups
Cumin powder – 1 tbsp.
Coriander powder – 1 tbsp.
Tomato paste – 2 tbsp.
Ginger (minced) – 1 tbsp.
Lime juice – 1 tbsp.
Chopped cilantro for garnishing

Directions:

Add ginger into the air fryer pot.
Mix shrimps, chickpeas, vegetable broth and lime juice.
Let it cook at 300 F for 4 minutes.
Now add cumin powder, coriander powder, red lentils and tomato paste.
Cook for another 10 minutes.
When ready, garnish with cilantro and serve!
Nutrition:

Calories: 90
Fat: 8g
Carbohydrates: 20g
Protein: 25g

Green Beans with Tilapia Fillets

Prep time: 5 minutes
Cooking time: 10 minutes
Servings: 3

Ingredients:

Green beans – 3 cups
Corn kernels – 2 cups
Pepper and salt to taste
Cumin powder – 1 tbsp.
Oil – 2 tbsp.
Spinach (chopped) – 3 cups
Tilapia fillets – 1 lb.
Cheese to garnish

Directions:

Add oil into the air fryer pot.
Mix cumin powder, salt and pepper, corn kernels, green beans and spinach with tilapia fillets.
Cook at 350 F for 15 minutes.
When ready, garnish cheese and enjoy!

Nutrition:

Calories:95
Fat: 6g
Carbohydrates: 10g
Protein: 200g

Sweet Potato with Cod Fillets

Prep time: 6 minutes
Cooking time: 10 minutes
Servings: 2

Ingredients:

Olive oil – 1 tbsp.
Onion (diced) – 1
Sweet potato – 1
Chili powder – 1 tbsp.
Cumin powder – 1 tbsp.
Salt to taste
Black beans – 3 cups
Black cod fillets – 1 lb.
Lime juice – 1 tbsp.
Tomatoes (diced) – 2

Directions:

Add oil into the air fryer pot.
Mix tomatoes, lime juice, black beans, salt, cumin powder, chili powder, sweet potatoes, black cod fillets and onion.
Cook at 300 F for 15 minutes.
When ready, serve and enjoy!

Nutrition:

Calories: 100g
Fat: 10g
Carbohydrates: 8g
Protein: 110g

Zucchini Mix Tuna Fish

Prep time: 6 minutes
Cooking time: 10 minutes
Servings: 3

Ingredients:

Oil – 2 tbsp.	Salsa – 2 tbsp.
Onion (chopped) – 1	Lime juice – 1 tbsp.
Black beans – 2 cups	Zucchini (sliced) – 1
Chili powder – 2 tbsp.	Chives – ½ cup
Tuna fish – 1 can	Chopped cilantro for
Cumin powder – 1 tbsp.	dressing

Directions:

Add oil to the air fryer pot.
Mix onion, chives, zucchini, lime juice, salsa, cumin powder, chili powder, tuna and black beans.
Cook at 350 F for 15 minutes.
When done, serve with cilantro dressing!

Nutrition:

Calories: 155	Carbohydrates: 10g
Fat: 7g	Protein: 40g

Mushrooms with Shrimps

Prep time: 4 minutes
Cooking time: 15 minutes
Servings: 2

Ingredients:

Olive oil – 1 tbsp.	Shrimps – 1 lb.
Chili powder – 2 tbsp.	Onions (chopped) – 1
Cardamom seeds – 2 tbsp.	Limes – 2
Mushrooms – 2 cups	Fish sauce – 2 tbsp.
	Tomatoes – 2

Directions:

Add oil and tomatoes into the air fryer pot.
Mix vegetable broth, limes, onions, mushrooms, cardamom seeds, and chili powder.
Add shrimps.
Cook at 300 F for 15 minutes.
When ready, serve and enjoy!

Nutrition:

Calories: 100g	Carbohydrates: 8g
Fat: 10g	Protein: 110g

Veg Taste Tuna Fish

Prep time: 6 minutes
Cooking time: 10 minutes
Servings: 3

Ingredients:

Corn – 2 cups	Bacon (sliced) – 4
Oil – 2 tbsp.	Vegetable broth – 2 cups
Onion (chopped) – 1	
Cornstarch – 1 tbsp.	Potato (sliced) – 1
Tuna fish – 1 can	Red pepper – ½ tsp.

Directions:

Add oil into the air fryer pot.
Mix tuna fish, onion, corn, cornstarch, bacon, potato, vegetable broth and red pepper.
Cook at 300 F for 10 minutes.
When ready, enjoy!

Nutrition:

Calories: 90	Carbohydrates: 20g
Fat: 8g	Protein: 25g

Avocado Mix Shrimps Recipe

Prep time: 5 minutes
Cooking time: 10 minutes
Servings: 3

Ingredients:

Cumin powder – 1 tsp.	Cilantro to garnish
Corn kernels – 2 cups	Avocado (diced) – 1
Shrimps – 1 lb.	Salt to taste
Tomatoes (sliced) – 2	Breadcrumbs – 1 tbsp.

Directions:

Add tomatoes into the air fryer pot.
Mix shrimps, breadcrumbs, avocado, corn kernels and cumin powder.
Add salt and cook for 10 minutes at 300 F.
When ready, garnish with cilantro and serve.

Nutrition:

Calories: 155	Carbohydrates: 10g
Fat: 7g	Protein: 40g

Cod Fillets with Squash

Prep time: 6 minutes
Cooking time: 10 minutes
Servings: 2

Ingredients:

Cod fillets – 1 lb.
Squash (chopped) –
2 cups
Salt to taste

Tomato sauce – 2
tbsp.
Beans – 2 cups
Cumin powder – 1
tbsp.

Directions:

Add cod fillets into the air fryer pot.
Mix squash, tomato sauce, beans and cumin powder.
Add salt.
Cook at 300 F for 10 minutes.
When ready, serve and enjoy!

Nutrition:

Calories:95
Fat: 6g

Carbohydrates: 10g
Protein: 200g

Tuna Fish with Squash Recipe

Prep time: 6 minutes
Cooking time: 10 minutes
Servings: 2

Ingredients:

Tuna fish –1 can
Squash (chopped) –
2 cups
Salt to taste

Tomato sauce – 2
tbsp.
Beans – 2 cups
Cumin powder – 1
tbsp.

Directions:

Add tuna into the air fryer pot.
Mix squash, tomato sauce, beans and cumin powder.
Add salt.
Cook at 300 F for 10 minutes.
When ready, serve and enjoy!

Nutrition:

Calories:95
Fat: 6g

Carbohydrates: 10g
Protein: 200g

Salmon with Ginger and Garlic

Prep time: 4 minutes
Cooking time: 15 minutes
Servings: 3

Ingredients:

Ginger (minced) – 2
tbsp.
Garlic cloves
(minced) – 4
Mustard seeds – 1
tbsp.
Vegetable oil – 1
tbsp.
Vegetable broth – 2
cups

Fenugreek – ½ tbsp.
Salmon (chopped) –
1 lb.
Coriander powder – 1
tbsp.
Cumin powder – 1
tbsp.
Baby spinach – 4
cups

Directions:

Add oil into the air fryer pot.
Mix salmon fillets, mustard seeds, garlic, fenugreek, cumin powder, coriander powder and vegetable broth.
Add chopped spinach.
Cook at 300 F for 15 minutes.
When ready, serve.

Nutrition:

Calories: 100g
Fat: 10g

Carbohydrates: 8g
Protein: 110g

Salmon with Onion and Potatoes

Prep time: 5 minutes
Cooking time: 10 minutes
Servings: 3

Ingredients:

Butter – 1 tbsp.
Cornstarch – 2 tbsp.
Red pepper flakes –
2 tbsp.
Salmon fillets – 1 lb.

Onion (chopped) – 1
Potatoes (cubes) – 2
Corn – 1 cup
Cooked bacon – 4
sliced chopped

Directions:

Add butter into the air fryer pot.
Mix salmon fillets, cornstarch, red pepper flakes, onion, potatoes, corn and bacon.
Cook at 300 F for 10 minutes.
When ready, serve and enjoy!

Nutrition:

Calories: 100g
Fat: 19g

Carbohydrates: 8g
Protein: 110g

Salmon with Veg Broth

Prep time: 6 minutes
Cooking time: 14 minutes
Servings: 3

Ingredients:

Olive oil – 2 tbsp.
Onion (chopped) – 1
Vegetable broth – 2 cups
Salmon fillets – 1 lb.
Potatoes (diced) – 3

Thyme – 1 tsp.
Apple cider vinegar – 2 tbsp.
Carrots (sliced) – 2
Parsley to garnish

Directions:

Add oil into the air fryer pot.
Mix vegetable broth, thyme, apple cider vinegar, salmon fillets, carrots, potatoes and onion.
Cook at 300 F for 14 minutes.
When done, garnish with chopped parsley and serve.

Nutrition:

Calories: 100g
Fat: 10g

Carbohydrates: 8g
Protein: 110g

Black Beans with Mackerel

Prep time: 6 minutes
Cooking time: 10 minutes
Servings: 2

Ingredients:

Black beans – 4 cups
Onions (chopped) – 3
Olive oil – 2 tbsp.
Salt to taste
Mackerel fillets – 1 lb.
Oregano – 1 tbsp.

Chili powder – 1 tbsp.
Green chilies – ½ cup
Cilantro leaves to garnish

Directions:

Add oil into the air fryer pot.
Mix onions, mackerel fillets, salt, oregano, green chilies, and chili powder with black beans.
Cook at 300 F for 10 minutes.
When done, serve and enjoy the meal.

Nutrition:

Calories: 155
Fat: 7g

Carbohydrates: 10g
Protein: 40g

Chicken Stock Fish Recipe

Prep time: 4 minutes
Cooking time: 10 minutes
Servings: 3

Ingredients:

Chicken stock – 2 cups
Ginger – 1 tbsp.
Sesame oil – 2 tbsp.

Fish (any) – 1 lb.
Salt to taste
Green onions (chopped) – 3

Directions:

Add sesame oil into the air fryer pot.
Mix chicken stock, fish, ginger, salt and green onions
Cook at 300 F for 10 minutes.
When ready, serve!

Nutrition:

Calories:95
Fat: 6g

Carbohydrates: 10g
Protein: 200g

Celery and Salmon Fillets

Prep time: 5 minutes
Cooking time: 15 minutes
Servings: 2

Ingredients:

Salmon fillets – 1 lb.
Celery – 3 stalks chopped
Garlic cloves – 2
Onion (chopped) – 2

Salt and pepper to taste
Green onion (chopped) – 2 cups

Directions:

Add salmon fillets into the air fryer pot.
Mix celery, garlic, salt and pepper, onion and green onion.
Cook at 300 F for 15 minutes.
When ready, serve and enjoy!

Nutrition:

Calories: 155
Fat: 7g

Carbohydrates: 10g
Protein: 40g

Cod with Mushrooms

Prep time: 6 minutes
Cooking time: 10 minutes
Servings: 3

Ingredients:

Butter – 2 tbsp.	Garlic cloves – 2
Onion (chopped) – 1	Thyme (chopped) – 2
Salt to taste	cups
Cod fillets – 1 lb.	Flour – 2 tbsp.
Mushrooms	Parmesan cheese
(chopped) – 3 cups	(shredded) – 2 cups

Directions:

Add butter and onion into the air fryer pot.
Mix mushrooms, cod, garlic cloves, thyme,
chicken stock and flour.
Add salt.
Cook at 300 F for 10 minutes.
When ready, sprinkle shredded cheese on it
and enjoy!

Nutrition:

Calories: 90	Carbohydrates: 20g
Fat: 8g	Protein: 25g

Carrots and Tuna Fish Recipe

Prep time: 6 minutes
Cooking time: 10 minutes
Servings: 3

Ingredients:

Olive oil – 2 tbsp.	Salt to taste
Onion (chopped) – 1	Tuna fish – 1 lb.
Carrots (chopped) – 1	Vegetable broth – 4 cups
Garlic (minced) – 2 cloves	Pumpkin seeds – 2 tbsp.
Curry powder – 2 tsp.	Parsley to garnish

Directions:

Add oil into the air fryer pot.
Add vegetable broth, tuna fish, pumpkin
seeds, salt, curry powder, garlic, carrots and
onion.
Cook at 300 F for 10 minutes.
When done, serve!

Nutrition:

Calories: 100g	Carbohydrates: 8g
Fat: 10g	Protein: 110g

Salmon with Mushrooms and Bell Pepper

Prep time: 5 minutes
Cooking time: 10 minutes
Servings: 2

Ingredients:

Oil – ¼ cup	Tomatoes – diced – 2
Flour (all-purpose)- ¼ cup	Garlic cloves – 3
Bell pepper – 1	Soy sauce – 1 tsp.
Onion (chopped)- 1	Sugar (white) – 1 tsp.
Salmon fillets (sliced) – 1 lb.	Salt and pepper to taste
Mushrooms- 4.5 ounce	Hot sauce – 3 drops

Directions:

Add oil into the air fryer pot.
Mix bell pepper, chicken, mushrooms,
tomatoes, onion, soy sauce, garlic, sugar
and hot sauce.
Add salt and pepper with flour.
Cook at 300 F for 15 minutes.
When done, serve and enjoy!

Nutrition:

Calories: 109g	Carbohydrates: 8g
Fat: 10g	Protein: 110g

Cod and Chicken Broth

Prep time: 6 minutes
Cooking time: 5 minutes
Servings: 3

Ingredients:

Butter – ½ cup	Garlic powder – 1 tbsp.
Onion (chopped) – 1	Cod fillets (sliced) – 1 lb.
Broccoli (frozen) – 1 pack	Cornstarch – 2/3 cup
Chicken broth – 2 cans	Water – 1 cup

Directions:

Add butter and onion into the air fryer pot.
Mix cod, onion, cornstarch, water, garlic
powder, broccoli and chicken broth.
Cook at 300 F 15 minutes.
When ready, serve and enjoy!

Nutrition:

Calories: 155	Carbohydrates: 10g
Fat: 7g	Protein: 40g

Spinach with Tuna Fish

Prep time: 4 minutes
Cooking time: 10 minutes
Servings: 2

Ingredients:

Butter – 2 tbsp.
Onion – 1 chopped
Garlic – 2 cloves
Cumin powder – 1 tbsp.
Paprika – 1 tbsp.
Tuna fish – 1 can

Tomatoes (chopped) – 2
Vegetable broth – 2 cups
Spinach – 1 small bunch chopped
Cilantro for garnishing

Directions:

Add butter into the air fryer pot.
Mix tuna fish, onion, garlic, and cumin powder, paprika and vegetable broth.
Add tomatoes and spinach.
Cook at 300 F for 10 minutes.
When ready, enjoy!

Nutrition:

Calories:95
Fat: 6g

Carbohydrates: 10g
Protein: 200g

Cauliflower with Mackerel

Prep time: 6 minutes
Cooking time: 10 minutes
Servings: 3

Ingredients:

Cauliflower (cut) – 1
Potatoes (peeled and chunks) – 3
Oil – 1 tbsp.
Cumin seeds – 1 tbsp.

Mackerel fish – 1 lb.
Tomatoes (diced) – 2
Salt to taste
Curry powder – 1 tsp.

Directions:

Add oil into the air fryer pot.
Mix curry powder, mackerel, tomatoes and cumin seeds.
Add cauliflower and potatoes with salt.
Cook at 300 F for 10 minutes.
When ready, serve and enjoy!

Nutrition:

Calories: 155
Fat: 7g

Carbohydrates: 10g
Protein: 40g

Sweet Potato with Tilapia

Prep time: 5 minutes
Cooking time: 10 minutes
Servings: 2

Ingredients:

Sweet potatoes (cubes) – 2 lbs.
Garlic cloves – 2
Salt to taste
Tilapia fillets – 1 lb.

Sage – 1 tbsp.
Rosemary – 1 tbsp.
Butter – 2 tbsp.
Grated cheese – 2 cups

Directions:

Add garlic cloves into the air fryer pot,
Mix sage, butter and rosemary.
Add sweet potatoes with salt.
Cook at 300 F for 10 minutes.
When ready, enjoy the tasty meal!

Nutrition:

Calories: 90
Fat: 8g

Carbohydrates: 20g
Protein: 25g

Kale with Tuna

Prep time: 4 minutes
Cooking time: 10 minutes
Servings: 3

Ingredients:

Kale (chopped) – 12 cups
Lemon juice – 2 tbsp.
Oil – 1 tbsp.
Tuna fish – 1 can

Garlic (minced) – 1 tbsp.
Soy sauce – 1 tsp.
Salt and pepper to taste

Directions:

Add oil into the air fryer pot.
Mix tuna fish, garlic, soy sauce, lemon juice, kale and salt and pepper.
Cook at 300 F for 10 minutes.
When ready, enjoy!

Nutrition:

Calories: 90
Fat: 8g

Carbohydrates: 20g
Protein: 25g

Spinach with Salmon and Seashells

Prep time: 5 minutes
Cooking time: 10 minutes
Servings: 3

Ingredients:

Seashells – 1 pound
Spinach (chopped) –
1 pack
Oil – 2 tbsp.
Garlic (minced) – 7
cloves

Salmon (chopped) –
1 lb.
Red pepper flakes –
1 tsp.
Salt for taste

Directions:

Add oil into the air fryer pot.
Mix tuna fish, garlic, red pepper flakes,
spinach and seashells with salt.
Cook at 300 F for 15 minutes.
When the pot beeps, serve and enjoy!

Nutrition:

Calories: 100g
Fat: 10g

Carbohydrates: 8g
Protein: 110g

Paprika Mix Salmon

Prep time: 6 minutes
Cooking time: 8 minutes
Servings: 3

Ingredients:

Onion (chopped) – 1
Garlic (chopped) – 2
cloves
Carrots (chopped) –
1
Celery (sliced) – 2
stalks
Ginger root
(minced) – 1 tbsp.
Paprika – ½ tsp.

Cumin powder – ½
tsp.
Oregano – ½ tsp.
Tomatoes
(crushed) – 2
Salmon fillets – 1 lb.
Zucchini (sliced) – 1
Lemon juice – 1 tbsp.
Salt to taste

Directions:

Add lemon juice into the air fryer pot.
Add onion, garlic, celery, ginger root,
oregano, cumin powder, paprika and carrots.
Add tomatoes and zucchini along with salt.
Cook at 300 F for 15 minutes.
When ready, serve and enjoy!

Nutrition:

Calories:95
Fat: 6g

Carbohydrates: 10g
Protein: 200g

Zucchini with Salmon Fillets

Prep time: 4 minutes
Cooking time: 10 minutes
Servings: 2

Ingredients:

Canola oil – 2 tbsp.
Onion (chopped) – 1
Zucchini (chopped) –
1
Salmon fillets – 1 lb.
Black beans – 3 cups

Tomatoes (diced) – 2
Salt and pepper to
taste
Corn – ½ cup
Parsley to garnish

Directions:

Add oil into the air fryer pot.
Mix salmon fillets, onion, black beans,
tomatoes, corn, zucchini and salt and
pepper.
Cook at 300 F for 10 minutes.
When done, garnish with parsley and serve.

Nutrition:

Calories:95
Fat: 6g

Carbohydrates: 10g
Protein: 200g

Black Beans with Ham and Salmon

Prep time: 4 minutes
Cooking time: 9 minutes
Servings: 3

Ingredients:

Ham hock – 2 lb.
Salmon (chopped) –
1 lb.
Onion (chopped) – 1
Garlic cloves
(minced) – 2

Black beans – 2 cups
Bay leaves – 2
Oregano powder – 2
tbsp.

Directions:

Add onion and bay leaves into the air fryer
pot.
Mix ham hock, garlic, black beans and
oregano powder.
Cook at 300 F for 9 minutes.
When done, serve and enjoy the meal!

Nutrition:

Calories:95
Fat: 6g

Carbohydrates: 10g
Protein: 200g

Tuna Fish with white Beans

Prep time: 6 minutes
Cooking time: 10 minutes
Servings: 3

Ingredients:

Olive oil – 1 tbsp.	White beans – 3 cups
Garlic (minced) – 2 tbsp.	Salt and pepper to taste
Spinach – 2 cups	Tuna fish – 1 can
Tomatoes – 2	Cheese to garnish

Directions:

Add oil into the air fryer pot.
Mix garlic and spinach.
Add tomatoes, white beans and salt and pepper.
Cook at 300 F for 10 minutes.
When ready, garnish with cheese and serve!

Nutrition:

Calories: 100g	Carbohydrates: 8g
Fat: 10g	Protein: 11

Kale and Salmon Fillets

Prep time: 5 minutes
Cooking time: 8 minutes
Servings: 3

Ingredients:

Olive oil – 2 tbsp.	Salt and pepper
Tomatoes (chopped) – 2	Kale (chopped) – 2 cups
Potatoes (chopped) – 2	Salmon fillets – 1 lb.

Directions:

Add oil into the air fryer pot.
Mix salmon fillets, potatoes, tomatoes, salt and pepper with kale.
Cook at 300 F for 10 minutes.
When done, serve and enjoy!

Nutrition:

Calories:95	Carbohydrates: 10g
Fat: 6g	Protein: 200g

Cod with Celery Stalk

Prep time: 6 minutes
Cooking time: 10 minutes
Servings: 2

Ingredients:

Carrots (sliced) – 2	Garlic (minced) – 2 tbsp.
Vegetable broth – 2 cups	Thyme (dried) – 2 tbsp.
Cod (cubed) – 1 lb.	Celery stalks – 4
Salt to taste	Cornstarch – 1 tbsp.
Cauliflower florets – 4 cups	

Directions:

Add vegetable broth into the air fryer pot.
Add celery stalks, cornstarch, cod, thyme, garlic, cauliflower, salt and carrots.
Cook at 300 F for 15 minutes.
When ready, serve and enjoy!

Nutrition:

Calories: 90	Carbohydrates: 20g
Fat: 8g	Protein: 25g

Squash with Salmon Fish

Prep time: 6 minutes
Cooking time: 10 minutes
Servings: 3

Ingredients:

Squash – 1 lb.	Nutmeg powder – 2 tbsp.
Butter – 2 tbsp.	Half and half – ½ cup
Onion (chopped) – 1	Salmon fish (cubes) – 1 lb.
Garlic cloves – 2 minced	
Chicken broth – 3 cups	

Directions:

Add butter into the air fryer pot.
Mix squash, chicken broth, salmon, garlic, onion, nutmeg powder, chicken breast and half and half.
Cook at 300 F for 10 minutes.
When done, serve and enjoy!

Nutrition:

Calories: 100g	Carbohydrates: 8g
Fat: 10g	Protein: 110g

Beef and Salmon

Prep time: 4 minutes
Cooking time: 10 minutes
Servings: 3

Ingredients:

Grounded beef – 1 lb.	Tomatoes (cubes) – 2
Onion (diced) – 1	Celery stalks (chopped) – 2
Garlic cloves (minced) – 2	Salt and pepper to taste
Beans (any) – 2 cups	Cumin powder – 2 tbsp.
Salmon fillets – 1 lb.	
Potato (cubes) –1	

Directions:

Add onion and potato into the air fryer pot.
Mix grounded beef, salmon fillets, garlic, beans, tomatoes, celery stalks and cumin powder.
Cook at 300 F for 10 minutes.
When done, serve and enjoy!

Nutrition:

Calories:95	Carbohydrates: 10g
Fat: 6g	Protein: 200g

Mackerel with Sweet Potatoes

Prep time: 6 minutes
Cooking time: 10 minutes
Servings: 2

Ingredients:

Butter – 2 tbsp.	Salt and pepper to taste
Onion – 1	
Sweet potatoes – 2	Cornstarch – 1 tbsp.
Corn – 2 cups	Red pepper flakes – ½ tsp.
Mackerel fish – 1 lb.	
Chicken broth – 2 cups	

Directions:

Add butter and onion into the air fryer pot.
Add chicken broth to it and stir well.
Mix sweet potato, corn, salt and pepper, mackerel fillets, cornstarch and red pepper flakes.
Cook on 300 F for 20 minutes.
When ready, serve!

Nutrition:

Calories: 90	Carbohydrates: 20g
Fat: 8g	Protein: 25g

Noodles and Tuna Fish

Prep time: 4 minutes
Cooking time: 15 minutes
Servings: 3

Ingredients:

Tuna fish – 1 lb.	Salt to taste
Noodles – 1 small pack	Chicken stock – 4 cups
Bok choy – 1 lb.	Hot water – 2 cups

Directions:

Add chicken stock into the air fryer pot.
Mix tuna fish, Bok choy, noodles, salt and hot water in the pot.
Cook at 300 F for 10 minutes.
When ready, serve and enjoy!

Nutrition:

Calories: 155	Carbohydrates: 10g
Fat: 7g	Protein: 40g

Shrimps with Spices

Prep time: 4 minutes
Cooking time: 10 minutes
Servings: 2

Ingredients:

Onion (sliced) – 1	Cinnamon powder – ½ tsp.
Garlic (minced) – 2 cloves	Salt and pepper to taste
Carrots (diced) – 2	
Shrimps – 1 lb.	Parsley (dried) – 1 tsp.
Sweet potatoes (diced) – 2	Tomatoes (diced) – 1 can
Cumin powder – ½ tsp.	Oil – 2 tbsp.
Turmeric powder – ½ tsp.	

Directions:

Add oil into the air fryer pot.
Mix onion, shrimps, garlic, cumin powder, turmeric powder and tomatoes.
Now add carrots and sweet potatoes. Mix well.
Add salt and pepper.
Cook at 300 F for 10 minutes.
When done, serve with garnishing of parsley on it.

Nutrition:

Calories: 100g	Carbohydrates: 8g
Fat: 10g	Protein: 110g

Tilapia with Broccoli

Prep time: 6 minutes
Cooking time: 5 minutes
Servings: 2

Ingredients:

Vegetable broth – 2 cups
Broccoli – 3 cups
Tilapia (cubed) – 1 lb.
Cumin powder – 1 tbsp.
Cayenne powder – 1 tbsp.
Green onion – 3
Salt to taste

Directions:

Add vegetable broth into the air fryer pot.
Mix broccoli, cumin powder, tilapia cubes, green onion and cayenne powder with salt.
Cook at 300 F for 15 minutes.
When ready, serve and enjoy!

Nutrition:

Calories: 100g
Fat: 10g
Carbohydrates: 8g
Protein: 110g

Cabbage with Salmon Fish

Prep time: 6 minutes
Cooking time: 15 minutes
Servings: 3

Ingredients:

Sesame oil – ½ tsp.
Canola oil – 1 tbsp.
Chile paste – 2 tbsp.
Garlic (chopped) – 2 cloves
Salmon fish (cubes) – 4
Soy sauce – ½ cup
Onion (sliced) – 1
Cabbage (chopped) – ½
Carrots (chopped) – 2
Noodles (cooked) – 8 ounces

Directions:

Add sesame oil and canola oil into the air fryer pot.
Mix garlic and salmon cubes.
Now add onion, soy sauce, Chile paste, cabbage and carrots.
Cook at 300 F for 15 minutes.
When ready, serve with noodles.

Nutrition:

Calories: 90
Fat: 8g
Carbohydrates: 20g
Protein: 25g

Cauliflower Mix Black Cod

Prep time: 6 minutes
Cooking time: 10 minutes
Servings: 3

Ingredients:

Cauliflower (chopped) – 1
Vinegar – 1/2 tbsp.
For Sauce
Milk – 1/2 cup
Cheese – ½ cup
Salt to taste
Black cod (chopped) – 1 lb.

Basil – ½ cup

Directions:

Add vinegar and salt in the air fryer pot.
Mix cauliflower and black cod chopped.
Cook at 300 F for 15 minutes.
Meanwhile, prepare sauce: mix milk, cheese and basil.
When ready, serve by pouring the sauce over it to enjoy!

Nutrition:

Calories: 100g
Fat: 10g
Carbohydrates: 8g
Protein: 110g

Salmon Fillet with Eggplant

Prep time: 4 minutes
Cooking time: 14 minutes
Servings: 3

Ingredients:

Potatoes (sliced) – 2
Eggplant (sliced) – 2
Zucchini (sliced) – 2
Onion (chopped) – 1
Salmon fillets – 1 lb.
Red Pepper – 1 tbsp.
Garlic cloves – 2
Tomato – 2
Oil – 1 tbsp.
Salt and pepper to taste
Water – hot, ½ cup

Directions:

Add oil into the air fryer pot.
Mix salmon fillets, onion, red pepper, tomato, garlic pepper, salt and pepper with water.
Add potatoes, eggplant and zucchini.
Cook at 300 F for 10 minutes.
When ready, serve and enjoy!

Nutrition:

Calories: 155
Fat: 7g
Carbohydrates: 10g
Protein: 40g

Tuna Fish with Tomato Paste

Prep time: 5 minutes
Cooking time: 10 minutes
Servings: 2

Ingredients:

Potatoes – 4
Tomatoes – 4
Water – ½ cup
Tomato paste – 1 can
Tuna fish – 1 can
Salt and pepper to taste
Basil – 1/2 chopped
Oil – 1 tbsp.

Directions:

Add oil into the air fryer pot.
Mix water, tomato paste, tuna fish, basil and salt and pepper. Stir well.
Add potatoes and tomatoes.
Cook at 300 F for 15 minutes.
When ready, enjoy!

Nutrition:

Calories:95
Fat: 6g
Carbohydrates: 10g
Protein: 200g

Tilapia with Carrots and Zucchini

Prep time: 5 minutes
Cooking time: 10 minutes
Servings: 2

Ingredients:

Zucchini (sliced) – 1
Carrots (sliced) – 2
Onion (sliced) – 1
Tilapia fillets – 1 lb.
Salt to taste
Dill – 1 tbsp.

Directions:

Add salt, dill and onion into the air fryer pot.
Mix zucchini, tilapia fillets and carrots.
Cook at 300 F for 15 minutes.
When ready, serve and enjoy!

Nutrition:

Calories:95
Fat: 6g
Carbohydrates: 10g
Protein: 200g

Poultry

Chicken Tenders Recipe

Prep time: 3 minutes
Cooking time: 10 minutes
Servings: 2

Ingredients:

Chicken tenders – 1 lb.
Garlic cloves (minced) – 2
Paprika – 2 tbsp.
Oregano powder – 2 tbsp.
Salt and pepper to taste
Oil – 2 tbsp.
Onion (chopped) – 1
Peas (frozen) – 2 cups
Flour (all-purpose) – 1 cup
Chicken stock – 1 cup
Egg – 1

Directions:

Add oil into the air fryer pot.
Mix chicken tenders, garlic, paprika, oregano, onion, peas, flour and chicken stock.
Add egg with salt and pepper.
Cook at 300 F for 10 minutes.
When ready, serve and enjoy!

Nutrition:

Calories:96
Fat: 9g
Carbohydrates: 10g
Protein: 35g

Chicken with Eggs

Prep time: 3 minutes
Cooking time: 20 minutes
Servings: 3

Ingredients:

Cornstarch – 1 tbsp.
Egg whites – 2
Chicken (sliced) – 1 lb.
Soy sauce – 1 tbsp.
Sesame oil – 1 tbsp.
Wine vinegar –1 tbsp.
Ginger (grated) – 1 tbsp.
Garlic cloves (minced) – 2 tbsp.
Salt and pepper to taste

Directions:

Mix cornstarch and egg whites into the bowl.
Add the mixture into the air fryer pot.
Mix chicken, soy sauce, sesame oil, wine vinegar, ginger, garlic with salt and pepper.
Cook at 300 F for 20 minutes.
When ready, serve!

Nutrition:

Calories:70
Fat: 16g
Carbohydrates: 20g
Protein: 20g

Chicken Thighs with Stock

Prep time: 2 minutes
Cooking time: 20 minutes
Servings: 2

Ingredients:

Chicken thighs – 1 lb.
Salt and pepper to taste
Oil – 3 tbsp.
Butter – 1 tbsp.
Flour – 2 tbsp.
Chicken stock – 1 cup
Lemon juice – 2 tbsp.
Bread for serving

Directions:

Add oil into the air fryer pot.
Mix chicken thighs, butter, flour, chicken stock, lemon juice with salt and pepper.
Cook at 300 F for 20 minutes.
When ready, serve with bread to enjoy!

Nutrition:

Chicken Breast with Marsala

Prep time: 3 minutes
Cooking time: 20 minutes
Servings: 2

Ingredients:

Chicken breast (sliced) – 1 lb.
Marsala wine – 1 cup
Cumin powder – 1 tbsp.
Salt and pepper to taste
Butter – 2 tbsp.
Parsley leaves (chopped) – 1 cup

Directions:

Add chicken breast and butter into the air fryer.
Mix Marsala wine, cumin powder, butter with salt and pepper.
Cook at 300 F for 20 minutes.
When ready, garnish parsley to serve!

Nutrition:

Calories: 190
Fat: 8g
Carbohydrates: 20g
Protein: 23g

Chicken with Beans

Prep time: 2 minutes
Cooking time: 30 minutes
Servings: 3

Ingredients:

Oil – 2 tbsp.
Tomatoes (diced) – 2
Onion (diced) – 1
Garlic cloves (minced) – 2
Chili powder – 2 tbsp.
Paprika – 2 tbsp.
Cumin powder – 1 tsp.

Chicken (pieces) – 1 lb.
Beans – 2 cups
Corn kernels – 2 cups
Cilantro leaves for garnishing

Directions:

Add oil into the air fryer pot.
Mix tomatoes, onion, garlic cloves, chili powder, paprika, cumin powder, corn kernels and chicken.
Cook at 300 F for 20 minutes.
Add beans and cook for another 10 minutes.
When ready, garnish cilantro and serve!

Nutrition:

Calories:96
Fat: 9g

Carbohydrates: 10g
Protein: 35g

White Beans with Chicken

Prep time: 3 minutes
Cooking time: 25 minutes
Servings: 2

Ingredients:

White beans – 2 cans
Jalapeno pepper (minced) – 1
Poblano peppers (chopped) – 2
Onion (chopped) – 1
Oil – 3 tbsp.
Garlic cloves (minced) – 2
Salt and pepper to taste

Coriander powder – 1 tbsp.
Chicken broth – 2 cups
Chicken (sliced) – 1 lb.
Chili powder – 1 tbsp.
Cilantro leaves for garnishing
Tortilla chips – for topping

Directions:

Add oil into the air fryer pot.
Mix garlic, coriander powder, chili powder, onion, Poblano peppers, jalapeno peppers, chicken broth and chicken.
Cook at 300 F for 15 minutes.
Add white beans.
Cook for another 10 minutes.
When ready, garnish cilantro and tortilla chips to serve!

Nutrition:

Calories: 90
Fat: 8g

Carbohydrates: 20g
Protein: 25g

Roasted Chicken with Mayo

Prep time: 3 minutes
Cooking time: 10 minutes
Servings:

Ingredients:

Roasted chicken – 1 lb.
Raisins – 1 cup
Oil – 2 tbsp.
Almonds (sliced) – 1 cup
Scallions (chopped) – 2
Mayonnaise – 1 cup

Greek yogurt – S cup
Curry powder – 2 tbsp.
Sugar – S tsp.
Salt and pepper to taste
Cilantro leaves for garnishing

Directions:

Add oil into the air fryer pot.
Mix roasted chicken, raisins, almonds, scallions, curry powder, sugar with salt and pepper.
Cook at 300 F for 10 minutes.
Mix mayonnaise and green yogurt into the bowl.
When the chicken is ready, garnish cilantro leaves.
Serve with mayo mixture to enjoy!

Nutrition:

Calories:70
Fat: 6g

Carbohydrates: 10g
Protein: 10g

Butter and Chicken Mix

Prep time: 2 minutes
Cooking time: 15 minutes
Servings: 3

Ingredients:

Chicken breasts – 1 lb.
Salt and pepper to taste
Butter – 2 tbsp.
Lemon juice- 2 tbsp.

Chicken stock – 2 cups
Capers (minced) – S cup
Parsley (chopped) – 1 cup

Directions:

Add butter into the air fryer pot.
Mix lemon juice, chicken stock, capers, parsley, chicken with salt and pepper.
Cook at 300 F for 15 minutes.
When ready, serve and enjoy!

Nutrition:

Calories:95
Fat: 6g

Carbohydrates: 10g
Protein: 200g

Ham and Chicken Recipe

Prep time: 3 minutes
Cooking time: 15 minutes
Servings: 3

Ingredients:

Butter – 2 tbsp.
Ham (cubed) – S lb.
Cheese (grated) – 1 cup
Chicken breast (pieces) – 1 lb.
Flour (all-purpose) – 1 cup
Milk – 2 cups
Chicken broth – 2 cups
Cayenne – 1 tsp.
Salt and pepper to taste

Directions:

Add butter into the air fryer pot.
Mix flour, milk, cayenne powder with salt and pepper into the bowl.
Dip ham and chicken into the mixture.
Place into the pot. Cook at 300 F for 15 minutes.
Add chicken broth and cook for another 4 minutes.
When ready, serve and enjoy!

Nutrition:

Calories:95
Fat: 6g
Carbohydrates: 10g
Protein: 200g

Chicken Pieces with Shallots

Prep time: 2 minutes
Cooking time: 20 minutes
Servings: 3

Ingredients:

Chicken breast (pieces) – 1 lb.
Lemongrass stalks – 2
Ginger (minced) – 2 tbsp.
Carrot (pieces) – 1
Celery stalks (pieces) – 2
Bay leaf – 1
Shallot (pieces) – 1
Chile powder – 1 tbsp.
Baby spinach – 2 cups
Salt and pepper to taste

Directions:

Add chicken breast into the air fryer pot.
Mix lemongrass, ginger, carrot, celery stalks, bay leaf and shallots.
Add Chile powder, baby spinach with salt and pepper.
Cook at 300 F for 20 minutes.
When ready, serve!

Nutrition:

Calories:96
Fat: 9g
Carbohydrates: 10g
Protein: 35g

Carrots and Chicken Recipe

Prep time: 2 minutes
Cooking time: 10 minutes
Servings: 2

Ingredients:

Carrots (sliced) – 2
Celery (sliced) – 4 stalks
Onion (sliced) – 1
Thyme – 1 cup
Bay leaf – 1
Salt and pepper to taste
Chicken thighs – 1 lb.
Egg noodles – 4 cups
Lemon juice – 2 tbsp.
Chicken broth – S cup

Directions:

Add chicken broth into the air fryer pot.
Mix carrots, celery, onion, thyme, bay leaf, lemon juice and chicken thighs.
Cook at 400 F for 10 minutes.
Add egg noodles and cook for another 10 minutes.
When ready, serve and enjoy!

Nutrition:

Calories: 90
Fat: 8g
Carbohydrates: 20g
Protein: 25g

Chicken Chipotle Mix Beans

Prep time: 2 minutes
Cooking time: 20 minutes
Servings: 3

Ingredients:

Chicken breast (pieces) – 1 lb.
Chili powder – 1 tsp.
Salt and pepper to taste
Tomatoes (diced) – 2
Chicken broth – 2 cups
Cumin powder – 1 tbsp.
Black beans – 1 cup
Red bell pepper (chopped) – 1
Chipotle sauce – 2 tbsp.
Lime juice – 1 tbsp.
Cilantro leaves for garnishing

Directions:

Add lime juice into the air fryer pot.
Mix chicken breast, chili powder, tomatoes, chicken broth, cumin powder, red bell pepper and chipotle sauce.
Add black beans with salt and pepper.
Cook at 300 F for 20 minutes.
When ready, serve and enjoy!

Nutrition:

Calories:95
Fat: 6g
Carbohydrates: 10g
Protein: 200g

Chicken with Garlic

Prep time: 2 minutes
Cooking time: 15 minutes
Servings: 2

Ingredients:

Roasted chicken (sliced) – 1 lb.
Salt and pepper to taste
Lemon juice – 1 tbsp.
Butter – 2 tbsp.
Onion (chopped) – 1
Carrots (chopped) – 2
Garlic cloves (minced) – 2

Directions:

Add roasted chicken into the air fryer pot.
Mix lemon juice, butter, onion, carrots, garlic with salt and pepper.
Cook at 300 F for 15 minutes.
When ready, serve and enjoy!

Nutrition:

Calories: 90
Fat: 8g
Carbohydrates: 20g
Protein: 25g

Duck Recipe with Air Fryer

Prep time: 3 minutes
Cooking time: 20 minutes
Servings: 2

Ingredients:

Thyme – 1 cup
Garlic cloves (minced) – 2
Frozen duck (slices) – 1 lb.
Shallots (minced) – 2
Balsamic vinegar – 2 tbsp.
Corn kernels – 2 cups

Directions:

Add garlic into the air fryer pot.
Mix thyme, duck, shallots, corn kernels and balsamic vinegar.
Cook at 400 F for 20 minutes.
When ready, serve and enjoy!

Nutrition:

Calories:70
Fat: 6g
Carbohydrates: 10g
Protein: 10g

Chicken with Mushrooms

Prep time: 2 minutes
Cooking time: 20 minutes
Servings: 3

Ingredients:

Oil – 2 tbsp.
Soy sauce – 2 tbsp.
Chicken thighs (sliced) – 1 lb.
Garlic cloves (minced) – 2
Jalapeno peppers (chopped) – 2
Mushrooms (chopped) – 2 cups
Cabbage (chopped) – 2 cups
Chicken stock – S cup
Salt and pepper to taste
Noodles – 3 cups
Cilantro and peanuts for garnishing

Directions:

Add oil into the air fryer pot.
Mix soy sauce, chicken thighs, garlic, jalapeno peppers, mushrooms and cabbage.
Add chicken stock, noodles with salt and pepper.
Cook at 300 F for 20 minutes.
When ready, serve with cilantro and peanuts dressing.

Nutrition:

Calories:70
Fat: 6g
Carbohydrates: 10g
Protein: 10g

Simple Chicken Wings Recipe

Prep time: 2 minutes
Cooking time: 20 minutes
Servings: 3

Ingredients:

Chicken wings – 1 lb.
Butter – 2 tbsp.
Garlic cloves (minced) – 2
Hot sauce – 1 tbsp.
Salt and pepper to taste

Directions:

Add butter into the air fryer pot.
Mix chicken wings, garlic, hot sauce with salt and pepper.
Cook at 300 F for 20 minutes.
When ready, serve!

Nutrition:

Calories: 90
Fat: 8g
Carbohydrates: 20g
Protein: 25g

Chicken with Basil

Prep time: 3 minutes
Cooking time: 20 minutes
Servings: 3

Ingredients:

Chicken breasts – 1 lb.	Breadcrumbs – 2 cups
Salt and pepper to taste	Tomato sauce – 2 cups
Flour (all-purpose) – 2 tbsp.	Basil leaves (chopped) to garnish
Oil – 2 tbsp.	

Directions:

Add oil into the air fryer pot.
Mix chicken breasts, flour, breadcrumbs, tomato sauce with salt and pepper.
Cook at 300 F for 20 minutes.
When ready, garnish basil to serve!

Nutrition:

Calories:95	Carbohydrates: 10g
Fat: 6g	Protein: 200g

Creamy Fettucine Recipe

Prep time: 3 minutes
Cooking time: 20 minutes
Servings: 3

Ingredients:

Fettucine (boiled) – 12 oz.	Heavy cream – 2 cups
Oil – 2 tbsp.	Nutmeg powder – 2 tbsp.
Chicken (cubed) – 1 lb.	Butter – 2 tbsp.
Salt and pepper to taste	

Directions:

Add oil into the air fryer pot.
Mix chicken, heavy cream, nutmeg, butter, fettucine with salt and pepper.
Cook at 300 F for 20 minutes.
When ready, serve and enjoy!

Nutrition:

Calories:96	Carbohydrates: 10g
Fat: 9g	Protein: 35g

Chicken with Apricots

Prep time: 2 minutes
Cooking time: 20 minutes
Servings: 3

Ingredients:

Apricot preserves – 2 tbsp.	Thyme – 2 tbsp.
Grilled chicken (sliced) – 1 lb.	Oregano – 2 tbsp.
Cheese (grated) – 2 cups	Salt and pepper to taste
	Onion (sliced) – 1

Directions:

Add onion and oregano into the air fryer pot.
Mix apricot preserves, chicken, cheese, thyme with salt and pepper.
Cook at 300 F for 20 minutes.
When ready, serve and enjoy!

Nutrition:

Calories:96	Carbohydrates: 10g
Fat: 9g	Protein: 35g

Chicken with Potatoes

Prep time: 3 minutes
Cooking time: 15 minutes
Servings: 2

Ingredients:

Red potatoes (cubed) – 2	Chicken (cubed) – 1 lb.
Cumin seeds – 1 tbsp.	Red pepper flakes – 2 tbsp.
Oil – 2 tbsp.	Salt and pepper to taste
Garlic cloves (minced) – 2	Cilantro leaves (chopped) to garnish

Directions:

Add oil into the air fryer pot.
Mix red potatoes, cumin seeds, garlic, chicken, red pepper flakes with salt and pepper.
Cook at 300 F for 15 minutes.
When ready, garnish cilantro to serve!

Nutrition:

Calories:96	Carbohydrates: 10g
Fat: 9g	Protein: 35g

Roasted Chicken with Broccoli

Prep time: 2 minutes
Cooking time: 20 minutes
Servings: 3

Ingredients:

Roasted chicken – 1 lb.
Oil – 2 tbsp.
Salt and pepper to taste
Lemon juice – 2 tbsp.
Butter – 1 tbsp.
Broccoli – 2 cups
Mushrooms – 2 cups

Directions:

Add oil into the air fryer pot.
Mix roasted chicken, lemon juice, butter, broccoli, mushrooms with salt and pepper.
Cook at 300 F for 20 minutes.
When ready, serve!

Nutrition:

Calories: 90
Fat: 8g
Carbohydrates: 20g
Protein: 25g

Chicken Tenders with Mayo

Prep time: 3 minutes
Cooking time: 10 minutes
Servings: 3

Ingredients:

Chicken tenders – 1 lb.
Cheese (grated) – 1 cup
Mayonnaise – 1 cup
Sauce
Honey – 2 tbsp.
Tomato paste – 1 cup
Apple cider vinegar – 1 tbsp.
Salt and pepper to taste

Salt and pepper to taste
Water – 2 tbsp.

Directions:

Add chicken tenders into the air fryer pot.
Mix cheese, mayonnaise, apple cider vinegar with salt and pepper.
Cook at 300 F for 10 minutes.
Meanwhile, mix honey, tomato paste, water with salt and pepper.
When ready, serve chicken with the sauce to enjoy!

Nutrition:

Calories:95
Fat: 6g
Carbohydrates: 10g
Protein: 200g

Creamy Stock Recipe

Prep time: 2 minutes
Cooking time: 15 minutes
Servings: 2

Ingredients:

Green bell pepper (chopped) – 1
Chicken (shredded) – 1 lb.
Cabbage – 1 cup
Cream of chicken stock – S cup
Buttermilk – 1 cup
Salt and pepper to taste

Directions:

Add buttermilk into the air fryer pot.
Mix green bell pepper, chicken, cabbage, cream of stock with salt and pepper.
Cook at 300 F for 15 minutes.
When ready, serve and enjoy!

Nutrition:

Calories: 90
Fat: 8g
Carbohydrates: 20g
Protein: 25g

Chicken with Brown Sugar

Prep time: 2 minutes
Cooking time: 20 minutes
Servings: 3

Ingredients:

Brown sugar – 2 tbsp.
Oyster sauce – 1 tbsp.
Sesame oil – 1 tbsp.
Soy sauce – 1 tbsp.
Ginger (chopped) – 2 tbsp.
Garlic cloves (minced) – 2
Chicken (cubed) – 1 lb.
White rice (boiled) – 2 cups
Scallions (chopped) – 1 cup
Water – 3 cups
Cilantro leaves (chopped) to garnish

Directions:

Add oil and scallions into the air fryer pot.
Mix brown sugar, oyster sauce, soy sauce, ginger, garlic, chicken and water.
Cook at 300 F for 20 minutes.
Add rice and cook for another 10 minutes.
When ready, garnish cilantro to serve!

Nutrition:

Calories:96
Fat: 9g
Carbohydrates: 10g
Protein: 35g

Chicken Thighs with Chili

Prep time: 3 minutes
Cooking time: 10 minutes
Servings: 3

Ingredients:

Chili powder – 2 tbsp.   Chicken thighs – 1 lb.
Cayenne pepper – 2   Tomatoes (sliced) – 2
tbsp.   Oil – 2 tbsp.
Salt and pepper to
taste

Directions:

Add oil into the air fryer pot.
Mix cayenne powder, chili powder, tomatoes,
chicken thighs with salt and pepper.
Cook at 300 for 10 minutes.
When ready, serve and enjoy!

Nutrition:

Calories:70   Carbohydrates: 10g
Fat: 6g   Protein: 10g

Rum Mixed Chicken Recipe

Prep time: 2 minutes
Cooking time: 10 minutes
Servings: 3

Ingredients:

Dark rum – 2 tbsp.   Chile peppers – 2
Soy sauce – 2 tbsp.   tbsp.
Brown sugar – 1   All spice – 2 tbsp.
tbsp.   Chicken wings – 1 lb.
Garlic cloves
(minced) – 2

Directions:

Add chicken wings into the air fryer pot.
Mix dark rum, soy sauce, brown sugar, garlic
cloves, Chile peppers and all spice.
Cook at 400 F for 10 minutes.
When ready, serve and enjoy!

Nutrition:

Calories:96   Carbohydrates: 10g
Fat: 9g   Protein: 35g

Tomato Sauce Chicken Recipe

Prep time: 3 minutes
Cooking time: 15 minutes
Servings: 2

Ingredients:

Garlic powder – 1   Rice (boiled) – 2
tbsp.   cups
Dried cumin – 1 tbsp.   Tomato sauce – 2
Salt and pepper to   cups
taste – 1 tbsp.   Red bell pepper
Chicken boneless   (sliced) – 1
(sliced) – 1 lb.   Onion (sliced) – 1
Garlic cloves
(minced) – 2

Directions:

Add garlic and cumin into the air fryer pot.
Mix chicken, tomato sauce, red bell pepper,
onion with salt and pepper.
Cook at 300 F for 15 minutes.
Add rice and cook for another 4 minutes.
When ready, serve and enjoy!

Nutrition:

Calories:95   Carbohydrates: 10g
Fat: 6g   Protein: 200g

Simple Chicken Pieces Recipe

Prep time: 2 minutes
Cooking time: 10 minutes
Servings: 3

Ingredients:

Chicken breasts   Egg – 1
(pieces) – 1 lb.   Breadcrumbs – 1 cup
Flour (all-purpose) –   Parsley leaves
1 cup   (chopped) to garnish

Directions:

Mix egg and flour into the bowl.
Dip chicken into the mixture.
Dip the same chicken into breadcrumbs.
Place it into the air fryer.
Cook at 400 F for 10 minutes.
When ready, garnish parsley to serve!

Nutrition:

Calories: 90   Carbohydrates: 20g
Fat: 8g   Protein: 25g

Jalapeno and Avocado Chicken

Prep time: 3 minutes
Cooking time: 15 minutes
Servings: 2

Ingredients:

Oil – 2 tbsp.
Onion (chopped) – 1
Jalapenos
(chopped) – 1 cup
Chicken (sliced) – 1
lb.

Red kidney beans –
2 cups
Avocados
(chopped) – 2
Cilantro leaves
(chopped) to garnish

Directions:

Add oil into the air fryer pot.
Mix onion, jalapenos, chicken, red kidney
beans and avocados.
Cook at 300 F for 15 minutes.
When ready, garnish cilantro to serve!

Nutrition:

Calories:96
Fat: 9g

Carbohydrates: 10g
Protein: 35g

Jalapeno and Avocado Chicken

Prep time: 3 minutes
Cooking time: 15 minutes
Servings: 2

Ingredients:

Oil – 2 tbsp.
Onion (chopped) – 1
Jalapenos
(chopped) – 1 cup
Chicken (sliced) – 1
lb.

Red kidney beans –
2 cups
Avocados
(chopped) – 2
Cilantro leaves
(chopped) to garnish

Directions:

Add oil into the air fryer pot.
Mix onion, jalapenos, chicken, red kidney
beans and avocados.
Cook at 300 F for 15 minutes.
When ready, garnish cilantro to serve!

Nutrition:

Calories:96
Fat: 9g

Carbohydrates: 10g
Protein: 35g

Chicken with Spices

Prep time: 2 minutes
Cooking time: 15 minutes
Servings: 2

Ingredients:

Oil – 2 tbsp.
Garlic cloves
(minced) – 2
Lemon juice – 2 tbsp.
Oregano – 2 tbsp.

Salt and pepper to
taste
Chicken breast – 1
lb.
Cheese (grated) to
garnish

Directions:

Add oil into the air fryer pot.
Mix garlic cloves, lemon juice, oregano,
chicken breast with salt and pepper.
Cook at 400 F for 15 minutes.
When ready, garnish cheese to serve!

Nutrition:

Calories:95
Fat: 6g

Carbohydrates: 10g
Protein: 200g

Chicken with Turmeric

Prep time: 3 minutes
Cooking time: 20 minutes
Servings: 3

Ingredients:

Butter – 2 tbsp.
Onion (chopped) – 1
Carrots (chopped) –
1
Flour (all-purpose) –
2 cups
Salt and pepper to
taste

Chicken broth – 2
cups
Turmeric powder – 1
tbsp.
Eggs – 1
Chicken (sliced) – 1
lb.

Directions:

Add butter into the air fryer pot.
Mix onion, carrots, flour, chicken broth,
turmeric powder, eggs, chicken with salt and
pepper.
Cook at 300 F for 20 minutes.
When ready, serve and enjoy!

Nutrition:

Calories: 90
Fat: 8g

Carbohydrates: 20g
Protein: 25g

Chicken Rigatoni Pasta

Prep time: 3 minutes
Cooking time: 10 minutes
Servings: 3

Ingredients:

Rigatoni pasta (boiled) – 1 lb.	Red pepper flakes – 1 tbsp.
Oil – 1 tbsp.	Parsley (chopped) – 1 tbsp.
Salt and pepper to taste	Basil leaves (chopped) to garnish
Onion (chopped) – 1	
Marinara sauce – 1 tbsp.	

Directions:

Add oil into the air fryer pot.
Mix onion, marinara sauce, red pepper flakes, parsley, rigatoni pasta with salt and pepper.
Cook at 300 F for 10 minutes.
When ready, garnish basil leaves to serve!

Nutrition:

Calories: 90	Carbohydrates: 20g
Fat: 8g	Protein: 25g

Chicken Wings with Hot Sauce

Prep time: 2 minutes
Cooking time: 10 minutes
Servings: 2

Ingredients:

Flour (all-purpose) – 2 cups

Cayenne powder – 2 tbsp.	Butter – 1 tbsp.
Oil – 2 tbsp.	Salt to taste
Chicken wings – 1 lb.	Lemon juice – 1 tbsp.
	Hot sauce – 1 tbsp.

Directions:

Add oil into the air fryer pot.
Mix cayenne powder, flour, salt, butter and lemon juice into the bowl.
Dip the chicken wings and place into the pot.
Cook at 400 F for 10 minutes.
Add hot sauce.
When ready, serve and enjoy!

Nutrition:

Calories:96	Carbohydrates: 10g
Fat: 9g	Protein: 35g

Chicken with Hot Sauce

Prep time: 3 minutes
Cooking time: 10 minutes
Servings: 3

Ingredients:

Chicken breasts (pieces) – 1 lb.	Red bell pepper (sliced) – 1
Chili powder – 1 tbsp.	Green onions (chopped) – 1 cup
Tomato sauce – 2 cups	Sour cream – 2 cups
Hot sauce – 2 tbsp.	Black olives (halves) – 1 cup
Jalapeno sauce – 2 tbsp.	Taco seasoning

Directions:

Add chicken breasts into the air fryer pot.
Mix chili powder, tomato sauce, hot sauce, jalapeno sauce, red bell pepper and green onions.
Add sour cream and black olives.
Cook at 300 F for 10 minutes.
When ready, garnish with taco seasoning to serve!

Nutrition:

Calories: 90	Carbohydrates: 20g
Fat: 8g	Protein: 25g

Chicken with Scallions

Prep time: 2 minutes
Cooking time: 15 minutes
Servings: 2

Ingredients:

Chicken (diced) – 1 lb.	Lemon juice – 1 tbsp.
Scallions (chopped) – 2 cups	Salt and pepper to taste
Dill – 1 tbsp.	Parsley (chopped) to garnish

Directions:

Add chicken into the air fryer pot.
Mix scallions, dill, lemon juice, parsley with salt and pepper.
Cook at 300 F for 15 minutes.
When ready, serve and enjoy!

Nutrition:

Calories:170	Carbohydrates: 10g
Fat: 6g	Protein: 10g

Chicken Breast with Cheese

Prep time: 2 minutes
Cooking time: 15 minutes
Servings: 3

Ingredients:

Chicken breasts
(pieces) – 1 lb.
Salt and pepper to
taste
Eggs – 3
Breadcrumbs – 1 cup

Parmesan cheese –
1 cup
Basil (dried) – 2 tbsp.
Lemon zest – 1 tbsp.
Soy sauce – 2 tbsp.
Basil leaves
(chopped) – 1 cup

Directions:

Whisk eggs into the bowl.
Dip the chicken into the eggs and cover with
breadcrumbs.
Place the chicken into the air fryer pot.
Add lemon zest, soy sauce, parmesan
cheese with salt and pepper.
Cook at 300 F for 15 minutes.
When ready, serve!

Nutrition:

Calories:70
Fat: 6g

Carbohydrates: 10g
Protein: 10g

Chicken with Cheese and Sauce

Prep time: 2 minutes
Cooking time: 20 minutes
Servings: 3

Ingredients:

Oil – 3 tbsp.
Worcestershire
sauce – 2 tbsp.
Garlic cloves
(minced) – 2
Chile powder – 2
tbsp.
Lemon juice – 2 tbsp.
Onion (chopped) – 1

Chicken (pieces) – 1
lb.
Cheddar cheese
(grated) – 1 cup
Bacon slices – 4
Tomatoes
(chopped) – 2
Salt and pepper to
taste

Directions:

Add oil into the air fryer pot.
Mix Worcestershire sauce, garlic cloves,
Chile powder, lemon juice and onion.
Add chicken, bacon slices and tomatoes.
Cook at 300 F for 16 minutes.
Add cheese with salt and pepper.
Cook for another 5 minutes.
When ready, serve and enjoy!

Nutrition:

Calories: 90
Fat: 8g

Carbohydrates: 20g
Protein: 25g

Cheese and Broccoli Chicken Recipe

Prep time: 3 minutes
Cooking time: 15 minutes
Servings: 2

Ingredients:

Butter – 2 tbsp.
Chicken breasts – 1
lb.
Broccoli – 3 cups
White rice (boiled) –
2 cups

Chicken stock – 1
cup
Sour cream – 1 cup
Lemon juice – 1 tbsp.
Cheddar cheese
(grated) – 1 cup

Directions:

Add butter into the air fryer pot.
Mix chicken breasts, broccoli, chicken stock,
sour cream and lemon juice.
Cook at 300 F for 15 minutes.
Add rice and cook for another 4 minutes.
When ready, sprinkle cheese to serve!

Nutrition:

Calories:96
Fat: 9g

Carbohydrates: 10g
Protein: 35g

Garlic Chicken Thighs Recipe

Prep time: 3 minutes
Cooking time: 19 minutes
Servings: 3

Ingredients:

Chicken thighs – 1 lb.
Soy sauce – 2 tbsp.
Salt and pepper to
taste
Bay leaves – 2

Garlic cloves
(minced) – 2
Corn kernels – 2
cups
Rice (boiled) – 2
cups

Directions:

Add soy sauce into the air fryer pot.
Mix chicken thighs, bay leaves, garlic cloves,
corn kernels with salt and pepper.
Cook at 300 F for 15 minutes.
Add rice and cook for another 4 minutes.
When ready, serve and enjoy!

Nutrition:

Calories:96
Fat: 9g

Carbohydrates: 10g
Protein: 35g

Mushroom and Pepper Chicken Recipe

Prep time: 3 minutes
Cooking time: 20 minutes
Servings: 3

Ingredients:

Chicken (pieces) – 1 lb.
Cheddar cheese – 2 cups
Green bell pepper (chopped) – 1
Red bell pepper (chopped) – 1
Salt and pepper to taste
Cayenne pepper – 2 tbsp.
Onion (diced) – 1
Mushrooms (chopped) – 1 S cup

Directions:

Add onion into the air fryer pot.
Mix chicken, green bell pepper, red bell pepper, cayenne pepper, mushrooms with salt and pepper.
Cook at 300 F for 20 minutes.
When ready, garnish cheese to serve!

Nutrition:

Calories:70
Fat: 6g
Carbohydrates: 10g
Protein: 10g

Chicken with Lemon Juice

Prep time: 2 minutes
Cooking time: 15 minutes
Servings: 2

Ingredients:

Thyme – 1 tbsp.
Salt and pepper to taste
Oil – 2 tbsp.
Yellow onion (chopped) – 1
Olives (halves) – 1 cup
Chicken (shredded) – 1 lb.
White wine – 1 cup
Lemon juice – 1 tbsp.
Garlic cloves (minced) – 2

Directions:

Add oil into the air fryer pot.
Mix onion, thyme, olives, chicken. White wine, lemon juice and garlic.
Cook at 300 F for 15 minutes.
When ready, serve and enjoy!

Nutrition:

Calories:95
Fat: 6g
Carbohydrates: 10g
Protein: 200g

Chicken and Bow Pasta Recipe

Prep time: 2 minutes
Cooking time: 15 minutes
Servings: 2

Ingredients:

Bow tie pasta (boiled) – 1 lb.
Chicken breast (sliced) – 1 lb.
Italian seasoning – 2 tbsp.
Salt and pepper to taste
Onion (sliced) – 1
Garlic cloves (minced) – 2
Red pepper flakes – 2 tbsp.
Ricotta cheese – 2 cups
Basil leaves (chopped) – 1 cup

Directions:

Add onion with salt and pepper into the air fryer pot.
Mix paste, chicken, onion, garlic cloves, red pepper flakes and ricotta cheese.
Cook at 300 F for 15 minutes.
When ready, pour Italian seasoning.
Serve with garnishing basil.

Nutrition:

Calories:96
Fat: 9g
Carbohydrates: 10g
Protein: 35g

Chicken with Breadcrumbs

Prep time: 2 minutes
Cooking time: 10 minutes
Servings: 3

Ingredients:

Butter – 2 tbsp.
Parsley (chopped) – 2 cups
Salt and pepper to taste
Chicken breast (sliced) – 1 lb.
Eggs – 3
Flour (all-purpose) – 2 cups
Oil – 3 tbsp.
Breadcrumbs – 2 cups

Directions:

Add oil into the air fryer pot.
Mix parsley, chicken breast, egg, flour, butter and breadcrumbs.
Cook at 300 F for 10 minutes.
When ready, serve and enjoy!

Nutrition:

Calories: 90
Fat: 8g
Carbohydrates: 20g
Protein: 25g

Chicken with Buttermilk

Prep time: 3 minutes
Cooking time: 15 minutes
Servings: 2

Ingredients:

Lemon zest – 2 tbsp.
Brown sugar – 1 tbsp.
Buttermilk – 1 cup
Chicken drumsticks – 1 lb.
Salt and pepper to taste
Thyme – 2 tbsp.
Mayonnaise – 1 cup
Oil – 2 tbsp.
Cayenne powder – 2 tbsp.

Directions:

Add oil into the air fryer pot.
Mix lemon zest, brown sugar, buttermilk, chicken drumsticks, thyme, cayenne powder with salt and pepper.
Cook at 300 F for 15 minutes.
When ready, serve with mayonnaise and enjoy!

Nutrition:

Calories:70
Fat: 6g
Carbohydrates: 10g
Protein: 10g

Chili Garlic Turkey Recipe

Prep time: 3 minutes
Cooking time: 15 minutes
Servings: 2

Ingredients:

Onion (sliced) – 1
Tomatoes (sliced) – 2
Garlic cloves (minced) – 2
Chili garlic sauce – 2 tbsp.
Sugar – 1 tbsp.
Turkey (minced) – 1 lb.
Ginger (grated) – 2 tbsp.
Oil – 3 tbsp.
Scallions (chopped) – 2 cups

Directions:

Add oil into the air fryer pot.
Mix onion, tomatoes, garlic, chili garlic sauce, sugar, turkey, ginger and scallions.
Cook at 300 F for 15 minutes.
When ready, serve!

Nutrition:

Calories:70
Fat: 6g
Carbohydrates: 10g
Protein: 10g

Vegetable and Chicken Fettucine Recipe

Prep time: 2 minutes
Cooking time: 20 minutes
Servings: 3

Ingredients:

Chicken breast (sliced) – 1 lb.
Garlic cloves (minced) – 2
Heavy cream – 1 cup
Salt and pepper to taste
Fettucine (boiled) – 1 lb.
Parmesan cheese (grated) – 1 cup
Oil – 2 tbsp.
Cabbage (chopped) – 2 cups
Carrots (sliced) – 1 cup

Directions:

Add garlic cloves and chicken into the air fryer pot.
Mix heavy cream, fettucine, parmesan cheese, oil, cabbage, carrot with salt and pepper.
Cook at 300 F for 20 minutes.
When ready, serve and enjoy!

Nutrition:

Calories:96
Fat: 9g
Carbohydrates: 10g
Protein: 35g

Chicken with Black beans

Prep time: 2 minutes
Cooking time: 15 minutes
Servings: 2

Ingredients:

Chicken breasts (pieces) – 1 lb.
Salt and pepper to taste
Butter – 2 tbsp.
Parsley leaves (chopped) – 1 cup
Black beans – 2 cups
Tomatoes (chopped) – 1

Directions:

Add butter into the air fryer pot.
Mix black beans, tomatoes, parsley, chicken with salt and pepper.
Cook at 300 F for 15 minutes.
When ready, serve and enjoy!

Nutrition:

Calories:96
Fat: 9g
Carbohydrates: 10g
Protein: 35g

Chicken with Lemon Zest

Prep time: 3 minutes
Cooking time: 15 minutes
Servings: 2

Ingredients:

Breadcrumbs – 2 cups
Lemon zest – 2 tbsp.
Thyme – 1 tbsp.
Salt and pepper to taste
Flour (all-purpose) – 2 cups
Chicken breast (sliced) – 1 lb.
Oil – 2 tbsp.

Directions:

Add flour and lemon zest into the bowl.
Mix thyme, breadcrumbs with salt and pepper.
Cover the chicken with oil and dip into the mixture.
Add chicken into the air fryer pot.
Cook at 300 F for 15 minutes.
When ready, serve and enjoy!

Nutrition:

Calories: 90
Fat: 8g
Carbohydrates: 20g
Protein: 25g

Chicken and White Rice

Prep time: 3 minutes
Cooking time: 15 minutes
Servings: 3

Ingredients:

Garlic cloves (minced) – 2
Chicken (sliced) – 1 lb.
Tomatoes (chopped) – 2
Potatoes (chopped) – 2
White rice (boiled) – 2 cups
Cilantro leaves (chopped) – 1 cup
Chili powder – 1 tbsp.
Cayenne powder – 1 tbsp.
Water – 3 cups

Directions:

Add garlic cloves and chicken into the air fryer pot.
Cook at 300 F for 15 minutes.
Mix tomatoes, potatoes, white rice, cilantro, chili powder and cayenne powder with water.
Cook for another 15 minutes.
When ready, serve and enjoy the meal!

Nutrition:

Calories:70
Fat: 6g
Carbohydrates: 10g
Protein: 10g

Chicken with Delicious Sauce

Prep time: 3 minutes
Cooking time: 15 minutes
Servings: 3

Ingredients:

Chicken (boneless, pieces) – 1 lb.
Sugar – S cup
Bay leaves – 2
Sauce
Ketchup – 1 tbsp.
Soy sauce – 2 tbsp.
White vinegar – 2 tbsp.
Garlic cloves (minced) – 2
Salt and pepper to taste
Ginger (minced) – 2 tbsp.
Brown sugar – 1 tbsp.

Directions:

Add chicken into the air fryer pot.
Mix sugar, bay leaves, garlic cloves with salt and pepper.
Cook at 300 F for 15 minutes.
Meanwhile, mix ketchup, soy sauce, white vinegar, ginger and brown sugar.
When the chicken is ready, serve with the sauce to enjoy!

Nutrition:

Calories: 90
Fat: 8g
Carbohydrates: 20g
Protein: 25g

Meat Recipes

Beef with Beans Recipe

Prep time: 5 minutes
Cooking time: 20 minutes
Servings: 4

Ingredients:

Beans – 2 cups
Beef stock – 2 cups
Grounded beef – 4 cups
Yellow mustard – 2 cups
Onion (minced) – 1

Chili powder – S tbsp.
Cumin powder – 1 tbsp.
White vinegar – 1 tbsp.
Salt and pepper to taste

Directions:

Add beans into the air fryer pot.
Mix beef stock, yellow mustard, onion, chili powder and salt and pepper.
Add grounded beef and cumin powder. Mix well.
Cook at 300 F for 20 minutes.
When ready, serve and enjoy!

Nutrition:

Calories: 90
Fat: 10g

Carbohydrates: 21g
Protein:95g

Beef Steak with Mustard

Prep time: 4 minutes
Cooking time: 15 minutes
Servings: 3

Ingredients:

Soy sauce – ½ cup
Wine vinegar – ¼ cup
Sugar (brown) – ¼ cup
Green onions (sliced) – ¼ cup

Garlic (chopped) – 1 tbsp.
Mustard powder – 1 tbsp.
Beef Steak – 2 pounds
Sesame seeds – 2 tbsp.

Directions:

Add garlic into the air fryer pot.
Mix soy sauce, wine vinegar, sugar, and mustard powder and sesame seeds into the bowl.
Add the mixture into the pot with beef steaks.
Sprinkle green onions.
Cook at 300 F for 15 minutes.
When ready, serve!

Nutrition:

Calories: 100
Fat: 20g

Carbohydrates: 8g
Protein:60g

Beef and Pork Mix Recipe

Prep time: 4 minutes
Cooking time: 30 minutes
Servings: 2

Ingredients:

Onion (chopped) – 1
Beef (grounded) – 2/3 pound
Pork (grounded) – 1/3 pound
Salt and pepper to taste

Nutmeg – ¼ tsp.
Ginger powder – ¼ tsp.
Beef Broth – 2 cups
Sour cream – ½ cup

Directions:

Add beef broth into the air fryer pot.
Mix ginger, nutmeg, salt and pepper and onion.
Add beef and pork.
Cook at 400 F for 30 minutes.
When ready, serve with sour cream.

Nutrition:

Calories:100
Fat: 6g

Carbohydrates: 10g
Protein: 20g

Grounded Beef with Pork and Veal

Prep time: 5 minutes
Cooking time: 15 minutes
Servings: 2

Ingredients:

Grounded Beef – 1 pound
Veal (grounded) – ½ pound
Pork (grounded) – ½ pound

Salt and pepper to taste
Onion (chopped) – 1/3 cup
Sour cream – 2 cups
Fresh Dill – ¼ cup

Directions:

Add onion into the air fryer pot.
Mix fresh dill, flour, butter, cream, onion, pork, veal and grounded beef.
Cook at 300 F for 15 minutes.
When ready, serve with sour cream and enjoy!

Nutrition:

Calories: 90
Fat: 10g

Carbohydrates: 21g
Protein:95g

Ground Beef with Spinach Leaves

Prep time: 6 minutes
Cooking time: 35 minutes
Servings: 2

Ingredients:

Ground beef – 1 lb.
Onion (chopped) – 1
Garlic (minced) – 2 cloves
Tomato sauce – 2 cups
Worcestershire sauce – 1 tbsp.
Beef broth – 2 cups
Tomatoes – 2 diced
Spinach leaves – S bunch chopped
Salt and pepper to taste
Cheese to dress

Directions:

Add beef broth into the air fryer pot.
Mix onion, garlic, tomato sauce, Worcestershire sauce and tomatoes.
Add beef and let it cook for 15 minutes.
Mix spinach leaves with salt and pepper.
Cook at 300 F for 20 more minutes.
When ready, serve with sprinkling cheese over it!

Nutrition:

Calories: 155
Fat: 7g
Carbohydrates: 10g
Protein: 40g

Beef Worcestershire Recipe

Prep time: 4 minutes
Cooking time: 20 minutes
Servings: 2

Ingredients:

Balsamic Vinegar – ½ cup
Soy sauce – ¼ cup
Garlic (chopped) – 3 tbsp.
Honey – 2 tbsp.
Salt and pepper to taste
Worcestershire sauce – 1 tsp.
Onion powder – 1 tsp.
Smoke flavor liquid – 1 tsp.
Cayenne pepper – 1 pinch
Beef Steaks – 2 (½ pound)

Directions:

Add garlic and soy sauce into the air fryer pot.
Mix balsamic vinegar, soy sauce, honey, salt and pepper, Worcestershire sauce, onion powder and cayenne powder. Stir well.
Add the beef steak.
Pour the mixture over it.
Cook at 350 F for 20 minutes.
When ready, take it out and serve!

Nutrition:

Calories: 100
Fat: 20g
Carbohydrates: 8g
Protein:60g

Beef Steak Quick Air fryer Recipe

Prep time: 6 minutes
Cooking time: 30 minutes
Servings: 3

Ingredients:

Oil – ½ cup
Worcestershire sauce – ¼ cup
Soy sauce – 6 tbsp.
Garlic (chopped) – ¼ cup
Onion (chopped) – 1
Salt and pepper to taste
Rosemary (dried) – 1 tbsp.
Steak seasoning – 2 tbsp.
Steak sauce – 2 tbsp.
Delmonico beef steaks – 4 (10 ounce)

Directions:

Add oil in the air fryer pot.
Place the beef steaks. Cook at 300 F for 15 minutes.
Mix onion, garlic and rosemary.
Add Worcestershire sauce, soy sauce, steak seasoning, steak sauce with salt and pepper. Stir well.
Cook for another 15 minutes.
When done, serve and enjoy!

Nutrition:

Calories: 90
Fat: 8g
Carbohydrates: 20g
Protein: 25g

Maple Syrup Mix Beef Recipe

Prep time: 5 minutes
Cooking time: 15 minutes
Servings: 2

Ingredients:

Soy sauce – ½ cup
Maple syrup – ¼ cup
Garlic (chopped) – 6 cloves
Ginger (grated) – 1 tbsp.
Mustard powder – 1 tsp.
Sesame oil – 1 tsp.
Hot pepper sauce – ¼ tsp.
Beer – ½ cup
Beef steak – 4 (10 ounce)

Directions:

Add sesame oil into the air fryer pot.
Mix soy sauce, garlic, ginger, mustard powder, hot pepper sauce, maple syrup and beer into the bowl.
Add beef steak into the pot.
Pour the mixture over it.
Cook at 400 F for 15 minutes.
Serve when ready!

Nutrition:

Calories: 155
Fat: 7g
Carbohydrates: 10g
Protein: 40g

Quick Beef Recipe

Prep time: 4 minutes
Cooking time: 20 minutes
Servings: 2

Ingredients:

Canola Oil – 1 Tbsp.
Ground Beef – 1/4 Cup
Sliced Green Onion, Separated Green and White Parts – 1

Short Grain Rice, Cooked – 3 Cups
Sesame Oil – 1 tsp.
Butter – 1 tsp.
Egg – 1

Directions:

Add canola oil into the air fryer pot.
Mix green onion, sesame oil, butter and egg.
Add grounded beef and rice.
Cook at 300 F for 20 minutes.
When ready, serve!

Nutrition:

Calories: 100g
Fat: 10g

Carbohydrates: 8g
Protein: 110g

Beef Mix Carrot Recipe

Prep time: 5 minutes
Cooking time: 25 minutes
Servings: 3

Ingredients:

Beef (grounded) – 2 pounds
Onion (chopped) – ½ cup
Ginger powder– ½ tsp.
Salt and pepper to taste

Sugar – 2 tsp.
Vinegar – 3 tbsp.
Soy sauce – 1 tbsp.
Ginger powder – ½ tsp.
Carrot – 1 large
Green bell pepper – 1 large

Directions:

Add beef into the air fryer pot.
Mix soy sauce, vinegar, ginger powder, salt and pepper and ginger powder.
Cook at 300 F for 15 minutes.
Add green bell pepper and carrots. Cook for another 10 minutes.
When ready, serve and enjoy!

Nutrition:

Calories: 155
Fat: 7g

Carbohydrates: 10g
Protein: 40g

White Rice with Chopped Meat Recipe

Prep time: 4 minutes
Cooking time: 15 minutes
Servings: 3

Ingredients:

Eggs – 1-2
Vegetable oil – 1 Tbsp.
Finely Chopped Onion – 1
Cold Cooked White Rice – 2 Cups

Soy Sauce – 2 Tbsp.
Black Pepper, Ground – 1 Tsp.
Red Meat Chopped and Cooked – 1 Cup

Directions:

Whisk eggs into the bowl and set aside.
Add vegetable oil into the air fryer pot.
Mix onion, white rice, soy sauce and pepper.
Cook at 300 F for 15 minutes.
Mix the eggs with red meat. Cook for another 20 minutes.
When ready, serve and enjoy!

Nutrition:

Calories: 90
Fat: 8g

Carbohydrates: 20g
Protein: 25g

Grounded Pork with Carrots and Rice

Prep time: 4 minutes
Cooking time: 20 minutes
Servings: 2

Ingredients:

Ground Pork Sausage – 1 lb.
Beaten Eggs – 5
Vegetable Oil – 3 tbsp.
Cored and Shredded Cabbage – 1/2
Finely Chopped Carrots – 3
Cold, Cooked White Rice – 6 Cups

Soy Sauce – 1/4 Cup Or To Taste
Thawed, Green Pea – 1 Frozen Package Of 6 Ounce
Drained, Can Bean Sprouts – 1 Package of 14.5 Ounce
Finely Chopped Onions – 3
Salt and pepper to taste

Directions:

Add vegetable oil into the air fryer pot.
Mix pork sausage along with cabbage, carrots, white rice, soy sauce, green pea, bean sprouts, onions with salt and pepper.
Cook at 300 F for 20 minutes.
When ready, serve and enjoy!

Nutrition:

Calories:100
Fat: 6g

Carbohydrates: 10g
Protein: 20g

Beef with Cheese Mix

Prep time: 6 minutes
Cooking time: 20 minutes
Servings: 2

Ingredients:

Garlic Cloves – 3	Olive Oil – 2 tbsp.
Cheddar Cheese – 1 cup	Dried Chili Flakes – 1 Pinch
Grounded beef – 2 lb.	Chopped Tomatoes – 2
Dried Oregano – 2 tsp.	

Directions:

Add beef into the air fryer pot.
Mix garlic cloves, dried oregano, chili flakes and chopped tomatoes with grounded beef.
Cook at 300 F for 20 minutes.
When ready, garnish cheese to serve!

Nutrition:

Calories: 100	Carbohydrates: 8g
Fat: 20g	Protein:60g

Beef with Herbs Recipe

Prep time: 5 minutes
Cooking time: 20 minutes
Servings: 3

Ingredients:

Olive oil – 3 tbsp.	Marjoram (dried) – ¼ tsp.
Onion (chopped) – 1 tbsp.	Salt and pepper to taste
Garlic (chopped) – 1 clove	Hot pepper sauce – 1/8 tsp.
Thyme (dried) – 1 tsp.	Beef Steak – 4 pieces
Rosemary (dried) – ½ tsp.	Parsley – 1 ½ tbsp.
Sage (powder) – ¼ tsp.	

Directions:

Add oil into the air fryer pot.
Mix onion, garlic, thyme, rosemary, sage, marjoram. Hot pepper sauce, parsley with beef steak.
Add salt and pepper.
Cook at 300 F for 20 minutes.
When ready, serve and enjoy!

Nutrition:

Calories: 100g	Carbohydrates: 8g
Fat: 10g	Protein: 110g

Grounded Beef with Bacon Slices

Prep time: 5 minutes
Cooking time: 10 minutes
Servings: 2

Ingredients:

Spaghetti (boiled) – 1 Pound	Parmesan Cheese (grated) – 1/2 Cup
Olive Oil – 1 tbsp.	Salt and pepper to taste
Diced Bacon Slices – 8	Fresh Parsley (chopped) – 2 tbsp.
Onion (chopped) – 1	Grounded beef – 2 lb.
Garlic clove (minced) – 1	

Directions:

Add oil into the air fryer pot.
Mix bacon slices, onion, garlic, parmesan cheese, parsley, beef with salt and pepper.
Cook at 300 F for 10 minutes.
Add spaghetti and cook for another 10 minutes.
When ready, serve and enjoy!

Nutrition:

Calories: 155	Carbohydrates: 10g
Fat: 7g	Protein: 40g

Beef with Potato Air fryer Recipe

Prep time: 6 minutes
Cooking time: 20 minutes
Servings: 2

Ingredients:

Beef Steak pieces – 4 large	Beef soup cans – 2
Potatoes (cubed) – 10	Garlic salt – 2 tsp.
Carrots (baby) – 8 ounce	Celery salt – 1 tsp.
Celery (chopped) – 1 cup	Black pepper to taste
	Mixed vegetables (frozen) – 1 small bag

Directions:

Add potatoes into the air fryer pot.
Mix carrots, celery, beef soup cans, garlic salt, celery salt, black pepper and mixed vegetables.
Add beef steaks.
Cook at 300 F for 20 minutes.
When ready, serve and enjoy!

Nutrition:

Calories: 90	Carbohydrates: 21g
Fat: 10g	Protein:95g

Beef Breast Pieces with Celery

Prep time: 4 minutes
Cooking time: 30 minutes
Servings: 2

Ingredients:

Butter – 2 tbsp.
Onion (chopped) – 1 cup
Celery (chopped) – 1 cup
Beef broth (can) – 1
Beef breast piece (chunks) – 2 lb.
Vegetable broth (can) – 1
Carrots – 2 cup sliced
Basil – 1 tsp.
Oregano – 1 tsp.
Salt and pepper according to taste

Directions:

Add butter into the air fryer pot.
Mix onion, celery, beef broth, beef breast pieces, carrots, vegetable broth and basil.
Add oregano with salt and pepper.
Cook at 300 F for 30 minutes.
When ready, serve and enjoy!

Nutrition:

Calories:100
Fat: 6g
Carbohydrates: 10g
Protein: 20g

Beef Steak with Tomato Soup

Prep time: 4 minutes
Cooking time: 20 minutes
Servings: 2

Ingredients:

Beef steaks – 4
Butter – 1 tsp.
Broth of Beef – 14 ounce
Tomato soup – 10.74 ounce
Water – 1 ½ cup
Cabbage (shredded) – 3 cups
Onion (chopped) – 1
Green Bell pepper (diced) – ½ cup
Salt and pepper to taste

Directions:

Add beef steaks into the air fryer pot.
Mix butter, broth, tomato soup, water, cabbage, onion, green bell pepper with salt and pepper.
Cook at 300 F for 20 minutes.
When ready, serve and enjoy!

Nutrition:

Calories: 90
Fat: 8g
Carbohydrates: 20g
Protein: 25g

Simple Beef Recipe

Prep time: 4 minutes
Cooking time: 20 minutes
Servings: 3

Ingredients:

Beef breast – 2
Lemon juice- 1 tbsp.
Salt and pepper to taste
Oil – 1 tbsp.
Oregano – 1 pinch
Parsley (chopped) – 1 cup

Directions:

Add lemon juice with oregano into the air fryer pot.
Mix oil, parsley and beef breast.
Cook at 300 F for 20 minutes.
When ready, serve and enjoy!

Nutrition:

Calories: 100g
Fat: 10g
Carbohydrates: 8g
Protein: 110g

Beef with Mushrooms Air Fryer Recipe

Prep time: 6 minutes
Cooking time: 20 minutes
Servings: 2

Ingredients:

Oil – ¼ cup
Bell pepper – 1
Onion (chopped)- 1
Beef (chopped, breast) – 2 cups
Mushrooms- 4.5 ounce
Tomatoes – diced, 4.5 ounce
Garlic cloves – 3
Soy sauce – 1 tsp.
Salt and pepper to taste
Hot sauce – 3 drops

Directions:

Add oil into the air fryer pot.
Mix bell pepper, onion, beef, mushrooms, tomatoes, garlic, soy sauce, hot sauce with salt and pepper.
Cook at 300 F for 20 minutes.
When ready, serve and enjoy!

Nutrition:

Calories: 155
Fat: 7g
Carbohydrates: 10g
Protein: 40g

Jalapeno Mix Beef

Prep time: 5 minutes
Cooking time: 30 minutes
Servings: 3

Ingredients:

Salt to taste
Lemon Juice – 1
Jalapeno – 1
Oregano – 1/2 tsp.
Cumin powder – 1/2 tsp.

Cayenne pepper – 1/2 tsp.
Oil – 2 tbsp.
Beef (sliced) – 1 lb.
Cabbage – 2 cups

Directions:

Add lemon juice into the air fryer pot.
Mix salt, jalapeno, oregano, cumin powder, cayenne pepper, oil, beef and cabbage.
Cook at 300 F for 30 minutes.
When ready, serve!

Nutrition:

Calories: 100
Fat: 20g

Carbohydrates: 8g
Protein:60g

Beef with Paprika Recipe

Prep time: 4 minutes
Cooking time: 30 minutes
Servings: 2

Ingredients:

Beef (sliced) – 1 lb.
Dill – 1 tbsp.
Onion powder – 1 tbsp.
Parsley – 1 cup
Paprika – 2 tbsp.

Garlic powder – 1 tbsp.
Lemon pepper – 1 tbsp.
Lemon juice – 2 tbsp.

Directions:

Add dill and onion powder into the pot.
Mix beef, parsley, paprika, garlic, lemon pepper and lemon juice.
Cook at 300 F for 30 minutes.
When ready, serve and enjoy!

Nutrition:

Calories: 90
Fat: 10g

Carbohydrates: 21g
Protein:95g

Pork with Honey Mix

Prep time: 6 minutes
Cooking time: 30 minutes
Servings: 2

Ingredients:

Red pepper – 1/2 tsp.
Ginger powder – 1/2 tsp.
Vegetable oil – 1/4 tsp.
Onions – 2

Garlic cloves – 2
Ketchup – 2 tbsp.
Soy sauce – 1 tbsp.
Cornstarch – 2 tbsp.
Honey – 1 tsp.
Pork (cubed) – 1 lb.

Directions:

Add ketchup and soy sauce into the air fryer pot.
Mix cornstarch, honey, red pepper, ginger powder, oil, onions, garlic and pork.
Cook at 300 F for 30 minutes.
When ready, serve and enjoy the meal!

Nutrition:

Calories: 100g
Fat: 10g

Carbohydrates: 8g
Protein: 110g

Beef with Soy Sauce

Prep time: 4 minutes
Cooking time: 20 minutes
Servings: 3

Ingredients:

Maple syrup – 1/2 cup
Soy sauce – 2 tbsp.
Garlic powder – 1 tbsp.

Salt and pepper to taste
Grounded beef – 1 lb.

Directions:

Add beef into the air fryer pot.
Mix maple syrup, soy sauce, garlic powder with salt and pepper.
Cook at 300 F for 20 minutes.
When ready, serve!

Nutrition:

Calories: 90
Fat: 8g

Carbohydrates: 20g
Protein: 25g

Pork with White Rice

Prep time: 6 minutes
Cooking time: 20 minutes
Servings: 2

Ingredients:

Pork (chopped) – 1 lb.
White rice – 2 cups
Cayenne powder – 1 tbsp.
Chili powder – 2 tbsp.
Salt and pepper to taste
Beef broth – 2 cups
Garlic cloves (minced) – 2

Directions:

Add pork and beef broth into the air fryer pot.
Mix white rice, cayenne powder, chili powder, garlic cloves with salt and pepper.
Cook at 300 F for 20 minutes.
When ready, serve and enjoy!

Nutrition:

Calories: 100g
Fat: 10g
Carbohydrates: 8g
Protein: 110g

Red Meat with Shrimps and Rice

Prep time: 4 minutes
Cooking time: 20 minutes
Servings: 2

Ingredients:

White rice – 2 cups
Red meat (cubed) – 1 lb.
Butter – 1 tbsp.
Garlic cloves (minced) – 2
Parsley – 1 cup
Salt and pepper to taste
Shrimps (cleaned) – 1 lb.

Directions:

Add red meat and garlic into the air fryer pot.
Mix white rice, butter, parsley, shrimps with salt and pepper.
Cook at 300 F for 20 minutes.
When ready, serve!

Nutrition:

Calories:100
Fat: 6g
Carbohydrates: 10g
Protein: 20g

Grounded Beef with Eggs

Prep time: 5 minutes
Cooking time: 20 minutes
Servings: 3

Ingredients:

Grounded beef – 1 lb.
Eggs – 2
Onion (chopped) – 2
Celery (chopped) – 2
Parsley (chopped) – 1 cup
Oil – 1 tbsp.
Salt and pepper to taste

Directions:

Add oil into the air fryer pot.
Mix eggs, onion, celery, parsley, grounded beef with salt and pepper.
Cook at 300 F for 20 minutes.
When ready, serve and enjoy!

Nutrition:

Calories: 155
Fat: 7g
Carbohydrates: 10g
Protein: 40g

Beef with Mushrooms and Onions

Prep time: 4 minutes
Cooking time: 20 minutes
Servings: 2

Ingredients:

Beef – 1 lb.
Potatoes (cubed) – 2
Onions (chopped) – 2
Butter – 1 tbsp.
Mushrooms – 1 cup
Salt and pepper to taste
Lemon juice – 1 tbsp.

Directions:

Add butter into the air fryer pot.
Mix beef, potatoes, onions, mushrooms, lemon juice with salt and pepper.
Cook at 300 F for 20 minutes.
When ready, serve and enjoy!

Nutrition:

Calories: 90
Fat: 8g
Carbohydrates: 20g
Protein: 25g

Shrimps and Red Meat Mix

Prep time: 6 minutes
Cooking time: 30 minutes
Servings: 2

Ingredients:

Shrimps – 1 lb.
Garlic cloves – 2
Oil – 2 tbsp.
Red meat (sliced) – 1 lb.
White rice (boiled) – 2 cups
Salt and pepper to taste
Parsley (chopped) – 1 cup

Directions:

Add oil into the air fryer pot.
Mix red meat, garlic, shrimps, parsley with salt and pepper.
Cook at 300 F for 20 minutes.
Add rice.
Cook for another 10 minutes.
When ready, serve and enjoy!

Nutrition:

Calories: 100
Fat: 20g
Carbohydrates: 8g
Protein:60g

Pork and Potatoes Recipe

Prep time: 5 minutes
Cooking time: 30 minutes
Servings: 3

Ingredients:

Salt and pepper to taste
Potatoes (cubed) – 2
White rice (boiled) – 2 cups
Grounded pork – 1 lb.
Lemon juice – 1 tbsp.

Directions:

Add white rice into the air fryer pot.
Mix potatoes, pork, lemon juice with salt and pepper.
Cook at 300 F for 30 minutes.
When ready, serve and enjoy!

Nutrition:

Calories:100
Fat: 6g
Carbohydrates: 10g
Protein: 20g

Beef loaf with Black Olives

Prep time: 4 minutes
Cooking time: 25 minutes
Servings: 2

Ingredients:

Beef loaf – 1 lb.
Oil – 2 tbsp.
Tomatoes (chopped) – 2
Peas – 1/2 cup
Basil (chopped) – 1 cup
Cheese (shredded) – 2 cups
Onion (chopped) – 1
Black olives – small pieces – ½ cup
Lemon Juice – 2 tbsp.
Salt and pepper to taste

Directions:

Add oil into the air fryer pot.
Mix tomatoes, peas, basil, cheese, onion, black olives, lemon juice with salt and pepper.
Add beef loaf.
Cook at 300 F for 25 minutes.
When ready, serve!

Nutrition:

Calories: 90
Fat: 8g
Carbohydrates: 20g
Protein: 25g

Red Meat Delight Recipe

Prep time: 6 minutes
Cooking time: 20 minutes
Servings: 2

Ingredients:

Red meat – 1 lb.
Lemon juice – 4 tbsp.
Butter – 2 tbsp.
Garlic cloves – 2
Parsley – ½ cup
Salt and pepper to taste

Directions:

Add butter into the air fryer pot.
Mix lemon juice, red met, garlic cloves, parsley with salt and pepper.
Cook at 400 F for 20 minutes.
When ready, serve and enjoy!

Nutrition:

Calories: 100g
Fat: 10g
Carbohydrates: 8g
Protein: 110g

Bacon Mixed Recipe

Prep time: 5 minutes
Cooking time: 20 minutes
Servings: 2

Ingredients:

Lemon juice – 3 tbsp.	Shrimp (pieces) – 1 lb.
Olive oil – 2 tbsp.	Bacon (slices) – 4
Cilantro (chopped) – ½ cup	Avocados (cubed) – 2
Salt and pepper to taste	Lettuce (chopped) – 4 cups
Cilantro – ½ cup	

Directions:

Add oil into the air fryer pot.
Mix lemon juice, cilantro, shrimps, bacon slices with salt and pepper.
Cook at 300 F for 20 minutes.
Meanwhile, mix avocados, lettuce and cilantro dressing.
When ready, serve and enjoy!

Nutrition:

Calories: 155	Carbohydrates: 10g
Fat: 7g	Protein: 40g

Pork with Shallots

Prep time: 5 minutes
Cooking time: 20 minutes
Servings: 3

Ingredients:

Pork (minced) – 1 lb.	Coconut milk – ½ cup
Carrots (sliced) – 2	Lemon juice – 1
Shallot (chopped) – 1	Chives to garnish
Butter – 2 tbsp.	

Directions:

Add butter into the air fryer pot.
Mix pork, carrots, shallot, coconut milk and lemon juice.
Cook at 300 F for 20 minutes.
When ready, garnish chives to serve!

Nutrition:

Calories: 100	Carbohydrates: 8g
Fat: 20g	Protein: 60g

Beef with Arugula

Prep time: 6 minutes
Cooking time: 30 minutes
Servings: 2

Ingredients:

Beef (chopped) – 1 lb.	Salt and pepper to taste
Parsley (chopped) – a bunch	Arugula – 2 cups
Dijon mustard – 1 tsp.	Lemon juice – 1
	White vinegar – 1 tsp.
	Olive oil – 1 tbsp.

Directions:

Add oil into the air fryer pot.
Mix beef, parsley, Dijon mustard, arugula, lemon juice, white vinegar with salt and pepper.
Cook at 300 F for 30 minutes.
When ready, serve and enjoy!

Nutrition:

Calories: 90	Carbohydrates: 21g
Fat: 10g	Protein:95g

Grounded Beef with Rice

Prep time: 5 minutes
Cooking time: 20 minutes
Servings: 2

Ingredients:

Shrimps – 3 cups	Salt and pepper to taste
Tomatoes – 2 chopped	White rice (boiled) – 2 cups
Olives – 2 cups chopped	Grounded beef – 1 lb.
Capers – 2 tbsp.	
Thyme – 1 cup chopped	

Directions:

Add tomatoes and shrimps into the air fryer pot.
Mix olives, capers, thyme, white rice with salt and pepper.
Add grounded beef.
Cook at 300 F for 20 minutes.
When ready, serve!

Nutrition:

Calories: 100g	Carbohydrates: 8g
Fat: 10g	Protein: 110g

Pork Cabbage Recipe

Prep time: 5 minutes
Cooking time: 20 minutes
Servings: 3

Ingredients:

Salt to taste
Lemon Juice – 1
Jalapeno
(chopped) – 1
Oregano – 1/2 tsp.
Cumin powder – 1/2
tsp.

Cayenne pepper –
1/2 tsp.
Oil – 2 tbsp.
Pork (cubed) – 1 lb.
Cabbage – 2 cups

Directions:

Add oil into the air fryer pot.
Mix lemon juice, jalapeno, oregano, cumin, pork and cabbage.
Cook at 300 F for 20 minutes.
When ready, serve and enjoy!

Nutrition:

Calories: 100
Fat: 20g

Carbohydrates: 8g
Protein:60g

Beef with Onion

Prep time: 4 minutes
Cooking time: 20 minutes
Servings: 3

Ingredients:

Beef (sliced) – 1 lb.
Tomatoes – 2 sliced
Lemon – 1 sliced
Onion – 1 sliced

Parsley – 1 cup
chopped
Olive oil – 2 tbsp.
Salt and pepper to
taste

Directions:

Add oil into the air fryer pot.
Mix tomatoes, lemon, onion, parsley, beef with salt and pepper.
Cook at 300 F for 20 minutes.
When ready, serve and enjoy!

Nutrition:

Calories:100
Fat: 6g

Carbohydrates: 10g
Protein: 20g

Shrimps with Honey and Beef

Prep time: 6 minutes
Cooking time: 20 minutes
Servings: 2

Ingredients:

Ketchup – 2 tbsp.
Soy sauce – 1 tbsp.
Cornstarch – 2 tbsp.
Honey – 1 tsp.
Red pepper – 1/2 tsp.
Ginger powder – 1/2
tsp.

Vegetable oil – 1/4
tsp.
Onions – 2
Garlic cloves – 2
Shrimps (tails
removed) – 1 lb.
Beef (cubed) – 1 lb.

Directions:

Add honey and ketchup into the air fryer pot.
Mix soy sauce, cornstarch, red pepper, ginger power, oil, garlic, onions and shrimps.
Add beef. Cook at 300 F for 20 minutes.
When ready, serve and enjoy!

Nutrition:

Calories: 100g
Fat: 10g

Carbohydrates: 8g
Protein: 110g

Broccoli With Pork Recipe

Prep time: 4 minutes
Cooking time: 10 minutes
Servings: 3

Ingredients:

Maple syrup – 1/2
cup
Soy sauce – 2 tbsp.
Garlic powder – 1
tbsp.

Salt and pepper to
taste
Grounded pork – 1
lb.
Broccoli – 2 cups

Directions:

Add maple syrup into the air fryer pot.
Mix soy sauce, garlic powder, grounded pork, broccoli with salt and pepper.
Cook at 400 F for 10 minutes.
When ready, serve and enjoy!

Nutrition:

Calories: 90
Fat: 8g

Carbohydrates: 20g
Protein: 25g

Amazing Beef Balls Recipe

Prep time: 4 minutes
Cooking time: 10 minutes
Servings: 2

Ingredients:

Beef balls (frozen) – 1 lb.
Dill – 1 tbsp.
Onion powder – 1 tbsp.
Parsley – 1 cup
Paprika – 2 tbsp.
Garlic powder – 1 tbsp.
Lemon pepper – 1 tbsp.
Lemon juice – 2 tbsp.

Directions:

Add onion powder and parsley into the air fryer.
Mix dill, paprika, garlic, lemon pepper and lemon juice.
Place the beef balls into the pot.
Cook at 300 F for 10 minutes.
When ready, serve and enjoy!

Nutrition:

Calories: 90
Fat: 10g
Carbohydrates: 21g
Protein:95g

Beef with Linguine Recipe

Prep time: 4 minutes
Cooking time: 20 minutes
Servings: 2

Ingredients:

Linguine – 1 pound
Butter – 1 tbsp.
White wine – ½ cup
Grounded beef – 1 lb.
Cheese (shredded) – 1 cu
Garlic cloves (minced) – 2
Parsley – 1 cup
Salt and pepper to taste
Shrimps (cleaned) – 1 lb.

Directions:

Add butter into the air fryer pot.
Mix linguine, white wine, grounded beef, cheese, garlic, parsley, shrimps with salt and pepper.
Cook at 300 F for 20 minutes.
When ready, serve and enjoy the meal!

Nutrition:

Calories:100
Fat: 6g
Carbohydrates: 10g
Protein: 20g

Beef Cooked Recipe

Prep time: 5 minutes
Cooking time: 20 minutes
Servings: 3

Ingredients:

Salmon (cooked) – mashed 1 lb.
Beef (pieces) – 1 lb.
Eggs – 2
Onions (chopped) – 2
Celery (chopped) – 2
Parsley (chopped) – 1 cup
Oil – 1 tbsp.
Salt and pepper to taste

Directions:

Add oil into the air fryer pot.
Mix salmon, beef, eggs, onion, celery parsley with salt and pepper.
Cook at 300 F for 20 minutes.
When ready, serve and enjoy!

Nutrition:

Calories: 155
Fat: 7g
Carbohydrates: 10g
Protein: 40g

Beef with Corn Kernels

Prep time: 6 minutes
Cooking time: 20 minutes
Servings: 2

Ingredients:

Corn kernels – 2 cups
Onions (chopped) – 2
Jicama – 1/2 cup
Bell pepper – 1/2 cup
Cilantro leaves – 1 cup
Lemon juice – 1/2 cup
Salt and pepper to taste
Beef – 1 lb.
Oil – 1 tbsp.
Corn tortillas – 5
Sour cream – 2 tbsp.

Directions:

Add Jicama and oil into the air fryer pot.
Mix corn kernels, onions, bell pepper, cilantro, lemon juice, sour cream and beef with salt and pepper.
Cook at 300 F for 20 minutes.
When ready, garnish corn tortillas to serve!

Nutrition:

Calories: 100g
Fat: 10g
Carbohydrates: 8g
Protein: 110g

Simply Beef and Shrimp Recipe

Prep time: 6 minutes
Cooking time: 20 minutes
Servings: 2

Ingredients:

Shrimps – 1 lb.	Red pepper as
Beef (sliced) – 1 lb.	needed
Garlic cloves – 2	Salt and pepper to
Oil – 2 tbsp.	taste
Butter – 1 tbsp.	Parsley (chopped) – 1 cup

Directions:

Add oil into the air fryer pot.
Mix garlic cloves, beef, shrimps, butter, red pepper, parsley with salt and pepper.
Cook at 300 F for 20 minutes.
When ready, serve and enjoy!

Nutrition:

Calories: 100	Carbohydrates: 8g
Fat: 20g	Protein:60g

Delicious Crab Beef Recipe

Prep time: 5 minutes
Cooking time: 14 minutes
Servings: 3

Ingredients:

Crab meat – 1 lb.	Salt and pepper to
Beef (cubed) – 1 lb.	taste
Cream cheese – 1/2	Lemon juice – 1 tbsp.
cup	Cheese (shredded) –
Mayonnaise – 2 tbsp.	1 cup
Sauce if needed	

Directions:

Add lemon juice into the air fryer pot.
Mix crab meat, beef, cream cheese, mayonnaise, sauce with salt and pepper.
Cook at 300 F for 14 minutes.
When ready, garnish cheese to serve!

Nutrition:

Calories:100	Carbohydrates: 10g
Fat: 6g	Protein: 20g

Pork with Black Olives

Prep time: 4 minutes
Cooking time: 15 minutes
Servings: 2

Ingredients:

Pork – 1lb.	Onion – chopped 1
Oil – 2 tbsp.	Black olives – small
Tomatoes – 2	pieces ½ cup
Peas – 1/2 cup	Lemon Juice – 2
Basil – chopped – 1	tbsp.
cup	Salt and pepper to
Cheese – shredded –	taste
2 cups	

Directions:

Add oil into the air fryer pot.
Mix pork with lemon juice.
Add tomatoes, peas, basil, onion, black olives with salt and pepper.
Cook at 300 F for 15 minutes.
When ready, serve!

Nutrition:

Calories: 90	Carbohydrates: 20g
Fat: 8g	Protein: 25g

Scallops with Beef Special Recipe

Prep time: 4 minutes
Cooking time: 20 minutes
Servings: 2

Ingredients:

Scallops – 1 lb.	Mushrooms – 1 cup
Beef – 1 lb.	Salt and pepper to
Onions (chopped) – 2	taste
Butter – 1 tbsp.	Lemon juice – 1 tbsp.

Directions:

Add beef and scallops into the air fryer pot.
Mix onions, butter, mushrooms, lemon juice with salt and pepper.
Cook at 300 F for 20 minutes.
When ready, serve!

Nutrition:

Calories: 90	Carbohydrates: 20g
Fat: 8g	Protein: 25g

Beef Steak Delight Recipe

Prep time: 6 minutes
Cooking time: 20 minutes
Servings: 2

Ingredients:

Beef steaks – 1 lb.   Parsley – ½ cup
Lemon juice – 4 tbsp.   Salt and pepper to
Butter – 2 tbsp.   taste
Garlic cloves – 2

Directions:

Add butter into the air fryer pot.
Mix lemon juice, garlic, parsley with salt and
pepper.
Add beef steaks.
Cook at 300 F for 20 minutes.
When ready, serve and enjoy!

Nutrition:

Calories: 100g   Carbohydrates: 8g
Fat: 10g   Protein: 110g

Shrimp and Beef with Lettuce

Prep time: 5 minutes
Cooking time: 20 minutes
Servings: 2

Ingredients:

Lemon juice – 3 tbsp.   Cilantro dressing – ½
Olive oil – 2 tbsp.   cup
Cilantro (chopped) –   Shrimp (pieces) – 1
½ cup   lb.
Beef – 1 lb.   Avocados – 2
Salt and pepper to   Lettuce – 4 cups
taste

Directions:

Add olive oil into the air fryer pot.
Mix shrimps with salt and pepper and lemon
juice.
Add beef.
Cook at 300 F for 20 minutes.
Meanwhile, mix avocados, lettuce and
cilantro into the bowl.
When ready, serve beef with avocado
mixture and cilantro

Nutrition:

Calories: 155   Carbohydrates: 10g
Fat: 7g   Protein: 40g

Vegetable Meals

Chicken Broth with Broccoli

Prep time: 6 minutes
Cooking time: 5 minutes
Servings: 3

Ingredients:

Butter – ½ cup
Onion (chopped) – 1
Broccoli (frozen) – 1 pack
Chicken broth – 2 cans

Garlic powder – 1 tbsp.
Cornstarch – 2/3 cup
Water – 1 cup

Directions:

Add butter into the air fryer pot.
Mix onion, broccoli, chicken broth, garlic powder and cornstarch.
Add water.
Cook at 300 F for 20 minutes.
When ready, serve and enjoy!

Nutrition:

Calories: 155
Fat: 7g

Carbohydrates: 10g
Protein: 40g

Pumpkin Taste Recipe

Prep time: 6 minutes
Cooking time: 10 minutes
Servings: 3

Ingredients:

Olive oil – 2 tbsp.
Onion (chopped) – 1
Carrots (chopped) – 1
Garlic (minced) – 2 cloves
Curry powder – 2 tsp.

Salt to taste
Vegetable broth – 4 cups
Pumpkin seeds – 2 tbsp.
Parsley to garnish

Directions:

Add oil into the air fryer pot.
Mix onion, carrots, garlic, curry powder, vegetable broth, pumpkin seeds and salt.
Cook at 300 F for 15 minutes.
When ready, garnish parsley to serve!

Nutrition:

Calories: 100g
Fat: 10g

Carbohydrates: 8g
Protein: 110g

Chicken and Mushroom Recipe

Prep time: 5 minutes
Cooking time: 10 minutes
Servings: 2

Ingredients:

Oil – ¼ cup
Bell pepper (chopped) – 1
Onion (chopped)- 1
Chicken (chopped, breast) – 2 cups

Mushrooms- 4.5 ounce
Tomatoes – diced – 2
Garlic cloves – 3
Salt and pepper to taste
Hot sauce – 3 drops

Directions:

Add oil into the air fryer pot.
Mix bell pepper, onion, chicken, mushrooms, tomatoes, garlic cloves with salt and pepper.
Cook at 300 F for 15 minutes.
When ready, add hot sauce and serve!

Nutrition:

Calories: 109g
Fat: 10g

Carbohydrates: 8g
Protein: 110g

Turkey Mixed Recipe

Prep time: 5 minutes
Cooking time: 15 minutes
Servings: 2

Ingredients:

Turkey (cubes) – 3 cups
Water – 2 cups
Celery – 3 stalks chopped
Garlic cloves – 2

Onion (chopped) – 2
Salt and pepper to taste
Green onion (chopped) – 2 cups

Directions:

Add water and turkey into the air fryer pot.
Cook at 300 F for 10 minutes.
Mix celery, garlic, onion, green onion with salt and pepper.
Cook for another 10 minutes.
When ready, serve!

Nutrition:

Calories: 155
Fat: 7g

Carbohydrates: 10g
Protein: 40g

Simple Chicken and Veg Soup

Prep time: 4 minutes
Cooking time: 10 minutes
Servings: 3

Ingredients:

Chicken breast (shredded) – 1 lb.	Peas (frozen) – 1 cup
Chicken stock – 2 cups	Sesame oil – 2 tbsp.
Ginger – 1 tbsp.	Salt to taste
	Green onions (chopped) – 3

Directions:

Add oil into the air fryer pot.
Mix chicken, stock, ginger, green onion, peas and salt.
Cook at 300 F for 20 minutes.
When ready, serve!

Nutrition:

Calories:95	Carbohydrates: 10g
Fat: 6g	Protein: 200g

Vegetable Broth with Veggies Soup

Prep time: 6 minutes
Cooking time: 14 minutes
Servings: 3

Ingredients:

Olive oil – 2 tbsp.	Thyme – 1 tsp.
Onion (chopped) – 1	Apple cider vinegar – 2 tbsp.
Vegetable broth – 2 cups	Carrots (sliced) – 2
Potatoes (diced) – 3	Parsley to garnish

Directions:

Add oil into the air fryer pot.
Mix onion, vegetable broth, potatoes, thyme, apple cider vinegar and carrots.
Cook at 300 F for 15 minutes.
When ready, garnish parsley to serve.

Nutrition:

Calories: 100g	Carbohydrates: 8g
Fat: 10g	Protein: 110g

Mushrooms Veggie Recipe

Prep time: 6 minutes
Cooking time: 10 minutes
Servings: 3

Ingredients:

Butter – 2 tbsp.	Thyme (chopped) – 2 cups
Onion (chopped) – 1	Flour – 2 tbsp.
Salt to taste	Chicken stock – 3 cups
Mushrooms (chopped) – 3 cups	Parmesan cheese (shredded) – 2 cups
Garlic cloves – 2	

Directions:

Add butter into the air fryer pot.
Mix onion, salt, mushrooms, garlic, thyme, flour and chicken stock.
Cook at 300 F for 20 minutes.
When ready, garnish cheese to serve!

Nutrition:

Calories: 90	Carbohydrates: 20g
Fat: 8g	Protein: 25g

Black Beans Mix Soup

Prep time: 6 minutes
Cooking time: 10 minutes
Servings: 2

Ingredients:

Black beans – 4 cups	Oregano – 1 tbsp.
Zucchini (chopped) – 2	Chili powder – 1 tbsp.
Onions (chopped) – 3	Green chilies – ½ cup
Olive oil – 2 tbsp.	Cilantro leaves to garnish
Salt to taste	

Directions:

Add oil into the air fryer pot.
Mix black beans, zucchini, onions, salt, oregano, chili powder, green chilies with salt.
Cook at 300 F for 20 minutes.
When ready, garnish cilantro to serve!

Nutrition:

Calories: 155	Carbohydrates: 10g
Fat: 7g	Protein: 40g

Corn and Potato Mix Soup

Prep time: 5 minutes
Cooking time: 10 minutes
Servings: 3

Ingredients:

Butter – 1 tbsp.
Chicken broth – 2 cups
Cornstarch – 2 tbsp.
Red pepper flakes – 2 tbsp.
Onion (chopped) – 1
Potatoes (cubes) – 2
Corn – 1 cup
Cooked bacon – 4 sliced chopped

Directions:

Add butter into the air fryer pot.
Mix chicken broth, cornstarch, red pepper flakes, onion, potatoes, corn and cooked bacon.
Cook at 300 F for 15 minutes.
When ready, serve and enjoy!

Nutrition:

Calories: 100g
Fat: 19g
Carbohydrates: 8g
Protein: 110g

Chicken Tomato Sauce Recipe

Prep time: 6 minutes
Cooking time: 10 minutes
Servings: 2

Ingredients:

Chicken broth – 2 cups
Chicken breast (chopped) – 1 lb.
Squash (chopped) – 2 cups
Salt to taste
Tomato sauce – 2 tbsp.
Beans – 2 cups
Cumin powder – 1 tbsp.

Directions:

Add chicken broth into the air fryer pot.
Mix chicken, squash, salt, tomato sauce, beans and cumin seeds.
Cook at 300 F for 14 minutes.
When ready, serve!

Nutrition:

Calories:95
Fat: 6g
Carbohydrates: 10g
Protein: 200g

Baby Spinach Recipe

Prep time: 4 minutes
Cooking time: 15 minutes
Servings: 3

Ingredients:

Ginger (minced) – 2 tbsp.
Garlic cloves (minced) – 4
Mustard seeds – 1 tbsp.
Vegetable oil – 1 tbsp.
Vegetable broth – 2 cups
Fenugreek – ½ tbsp.
Coriander powder – 1 tbsp.
Cumin powder – 1 tbsp.
Baby spinach – 4 cups

Directions:

Add oil into the air fryer pot.
Mix ginger, garlic, mustard seeds, vegetable broth, coriander powder and fenugreek.
Add spinach and cumin powder.
Cook at 300 F for 20 minutes.
When ready, serve!

Nutrition:

Calories: 100g
Fat: 10g
Carbohydrates: 8g
Protein: 110g

Bacon Vegetable Broth Recipe

Prep time: 5 minutes
Cooking time: 10 minutes
Servings: 3

Ingredients:

Corn – 2 cups
Onion (chopped) – 1
Cornstarch – 1 tbsp.
Bacon (sliced) – 4
Vegetable broth – 2 cups
Potato (sliced) – 1
Red pepper – ½ tsp.

Directions:

Add corn into the air fryer pot.
Mix onion, cornstarch, bacon, vegetable broth, potato and red pepper.
Cook at 300 F for 20 minutes.
When ready, serve!

Nutrition:

Calories: 90
Fat: 8g
Carbohydrates: 20g
Protein: 25g

Ham Hock with Spinach Recipe

Prep time: 4 minutes
Cooking time: 9 minutes
Servings: 3

Ingredients:

Ham hock – 2 lb.
Onion (chopped) – 1
Garlic cloves
(minced) – 2
Baby spinach – 2
cups
Bay leaves – 2
Chicken stock – 2
cups
Oregano powder – 2
tbsp.

Directions:

Add chicken stock into the air fryer pot.
Mix ham hock, onion, garlic, spinach, bay
leaves, chicken stock and oregano powder.
Cook at 300 F for 20 minutes.
When ready, serve!

Nutrition:

Calories:95
Fat: 6g
Carbohydrates: 10g
Protein: 200g

Broccoli Mix Recipe

Prep time: 6 minutes
Cooking time: 5 minutes
Servings: 2

Ingredients:

Vegetable broth – 2
cups
Broccoli – 3 cups
Cumin powder – 1
tbsp.
Cayenne powder – 1
tbsp.
Green onion – 3
Salt to taste

Directions:

Add vegetable broth into the air fryer pot.
Mix broccoli, cumin powder, cayenne
powder, green onion and salt.
Cook at 300 F for 20 minutes.
When ready, serve and enjoy!

Nutrition:

Calories: 100g
Fat: 10g
Carbohydrates: 8g
Protein: 110g

Chicken Noodle Soup Recipe

Prep time: 4 minutes
Cooking time: 15 minutes
Servings: 3

Ingredients:

Chicken breast
(cubes) – 1 lb.
Noodles (boiled) – 1
small pack
Bok choy – 1 lb.
Broccoli (chopped) –
2 cups
Celery stalks
(chopped) – 2
Salt to taste
Chicken stock – 4
cups

Directions:

Add chicken into the air fryer pot.
Mix noodles, Bok choy, broccoli, celery
stalks, chicken stock and salt.
Cook at 300 F for 20 minutes.
When ready, serve and enjoy the meal!

Nutrition:

Calories: 155
Fat: 7g
Carbohydrates: 10g
Protein: 40g

Beef Soup Recipe

Prep time: 4 minutes
Cooking time: 10 minutes
Servings: 3

Ingredients:

Grounded beef – 1
lb.
Oil – 2 tbsp.
Onion (diced) – 1
Garlic cloves
(minced) – 2
Beans (any) – 2 cups
Potato (cubes) –1
Tomatoes (cubes) – 2
Celery stalks
(chopped) – 2
Salt and pepper to
taste
Cumin powder – 2
tbsp.

Directions:

Add oil into the air fryer pot.
Mix beef, onion, garlic, beans, potato,
tomatoes, celery stalks, cumin powder with
salt and pepper.
Cook at 300 F for 20 minutes.
When ready, serve and enjoy!

Nutrition:

Calories:95
Fat: 6g
Carbohydrates: 10g
Protein: 200g

Sweet Potatoes and Corn Recipe

Prep time: 6 minutes
Cooking time: 10 minutes
Servings: 2

Ingredients:

Butter – 2 tbsp.
Onion – 1
Sweet potatoes – 2
Corn – 2 cups
Chicken broth – 2 cups

Salt and pepper to taste
Cornstarch – 1 tbsp.
Red pepper flakes – ½ tsp.

Directions:

Add butter into the air fryer pot.
Mix onion, sweet potatoes, corn, chicken broth, cornstarch, red pepper flakes with salt and pepper.
Cook at 300 F for 20 minutes.
When ready, serve!

Nutrition:

Calories: 90
Fat: 8g

Carbohydrates: 20g
Protein: 25g

Squash Soup Recipe

Prep time: 6 minutes
Cooking time: 10 minutes
Servings: 3

Ingredients:

Squash – 1 lb.
Butter – 2 tbsp.
Onion (chopped) – 1
Garlic cloves – 2 minced
Chicken broth – 3 cups

Nutmeg powder – 2 tbsp.
Half and half – ½ cup
Chicken breast (cubes) – 1 lb.

Directions:

Add butter into the air fryer pot.
Mix squash, onion, garlic, chicken broth, nutmeg powder, half and half with chicken.
Cook at 300 F for 20 minutes.
When ready, serve and enjoy!

Nutrition:

Calories: 100g
Fat: 10g

Carbohydrates: 8g
Protein: 110g

Kale and Chicken Mix Recipe

Prep time: 5 minutes
Cooking time: 8 minutes
Servings: 3

Ingredients:

Olive oil – 2 tbsp.
Chicken thighs (cubed) – 2 lb.
Chicken broth – 2 cups
Tomatoes (chopped) – 2

Potatoes (chopped) – 2
Salt and pepper
Kale (chopped) – 2 cups

Directions:

Add oil into the air fryer pot.
Mix chicken, chicken broth, tomatoes, potatoes, kale with salt and pepper.
Cook at 300 F for 20 minutes.
When ready, serve!

Nutrition:

Calories:95
Fat: 6g

Carbohydrates: 10g
Protein: 200g

Veggie Broth with Cauliflower Recipe

Prep time: 6 minutes
Cooking time: 10 minutes
Servings: 2

Ingredients:

Carrots (sliced) – 2
Vegetable broth – 2 cups
Salt to taste
Cauliflower florets – 4 cups

Garlic (minced) – 2 tbsp.
Thyme (dried) – 2 tbsp.
Celery stalks – 4
Cornstarch – 1 tbsp.

Directions:

Add vegetable broth into the air fryer pot.
Mix carrots, cauliflower, garlic, thyme, celery stalks, cornstarch and salt.
Cook at 300 F for 20 minutes.
When ready, serve and enjoy!

Nutrition:

Calories: 90
Fat: 8g

Carbohydrates: 20g
Protein: 25g

Black Beans with Lentils and Veggies

Prep time: 6 minutes
Cooking time: 10 minutes
Servings: 3

Ingredients:

Olive oil – 1 tbsp.
Red onion (chopped) – 1
Carrots (chopped) – 2
Oregano – 1 tbsp.
Garlic powder – 2 tbsp.

Tomatoes (chopped) – 2
Water – 1 cup
Lentils – 1 cup
Black beans – 4 cups
Salt to taste

Directions:

Add oil into the air fryer pot.
Mix red onion, carrots, oregano, garlic powder, tomatoes, water, lentils, black beans and salt.
Cook at 300 F for 20 minutes.
When ready, serve and enjoy!

Nutrition:

Calories: 155
Fat: 7g

Carbohydrates: 10g
Protein: 40g

Black Beans Chicken Mix Recipe

Prep time: 6 minutes
Cooking time: 15 minutes
Servings: 3

Ingredients:

Olive oil – 1 tbsp.
Chicken breast (cubes) – 2 cups
Green bell pepper – 1
Black beans – 3 cups
Cumin powder – 1 tbsp.

Cabbage leaves – 2 cups
Garlic powder – 1 tsp.
Cayenne powder – 1 tbsp.
Salt to taste

Directions:

Add oil into the air fryer pot.
Mix chicken, green bell pepper, black beans, cumin powder, cabbage leaves, garlic powder, cayenne powder and salt.
Cook at 300 F for 20 minutes.
When ready, serve!

Nutrition:

Calories: 100g
Fat: 10g

Carbohydrates: 8g
Protein: 110g

Black Eyed Peas Recipe

Prep time: 4 minutes
Cooking time: 10 minutes
Servings: 2

Ingredients:

Sweet potatoes (sliced) – 2
Coriander seeds – 1 tbsp.
Cumin seeds – 1 tbsp.

Black eyed peas – 4 cups
Salt to taste
Garlic cloves – 2
Tomato paste – 2 cups
Onion (chopped) – 1

Directions:

Add tomato paste into the air fryer pot.
Mix onion, garlic, salt, black eyes peas, cumin seeds and coriander seeds.
Add sweet potatoes.
Cook at 300 F for 10 minutes.
When ready, serve!

Nutrition:

Calories: 95
Fat: 6g

Carbohydrates: 10g
Protein: 200g

Rice Mixed Beans Recipe

Prep time: 5 minutes
Cooking time: 10 minutes
Servings: 3

Ingredients:

Onion (diced) – 1
Garlic cloves – 2
Brown rice (boiled) – 2 cups

Black beans – 2 cups
Water – 2 cups
Salt to taste
Avocado (cubes) – 1

Directions:

Add onion into the air fryer pot.
Mix garlic, brown rice, black beans, water, avocado and salt.
Cook at 300 F for 20 minutes.
When ready, serve!

Nutrition:

Calories: 155
Fat: 7g

Carbohydrates: 10g
Protein: 40g

Borlotti Beans with Tomato Sauce

Prep time: 6 minutes
Cooking time: 10 minutes
Servings: 3

Ingredients:

Tomato sauce – 2 cups
Oregano powder – 2 tbsp.
Red pepper flakes – 1 tbsp.
Carrot (sliced) – 1
Oil – 2 tbsp.
Garlic cloves – 2
Onion (chopped) – 1
Borlotti beans – 2 cups
Salt to taste

Directions:

Add oil into the air fryer pot.
Mix tomato sauce, oregano powder, red pepper flakes, carrot, garlic, onion, salt and Borlotti beans.
Cook at 300 F for 20 minutes.
When ready, serve and enjoy!

Nutrition:

Calories: 90
Fat: 8g
Carbohydrates: 20g
Protein: 25g

Spinach and Artichoke Recipe

Prep time: 4 minutes
Cooking time: 20 minutes
Servings: 2

Ingredients:

Spinach (chopped) – 2 cups
Artichoke hearts (chopped) – 1 cup
Cream cheese – 1 cup
Sour cream – S cup
Mayonnaise – S cup
Red pepper flakes – 1 tbsp.
Oil – 2 tbsp.
Salt and pepper to taste
Garlic powder – 1 tbsp.

Directions:

Add oil into the air fryer pot.
Mix spinach, artichoke, cream cheese, sour cream, mayonnaise, red pepper flakes, garlic powder with salt and pepper.
Cook at 300 F for 20 minutes.
When ready, serve and enjoy!

Nutrition:

Calories:70
Fat: 6g
Carbohydrates: 10g
Protein: 10g

Red Potatoes Recipe

Prep time: 3 minutes
Cooking time: 10 minutes
Servings: 3

Ingredients:

Red potatoes (mashed) – 3
Salt and pepper to taste
Garlic cloves (minced) – 2
Parsley (chopped) – 1 cup

Directions:

Add red potatoes into the air fryer pot.
Mix garlic, parsley with salt and pepper.
Cook at 300 F for 10 minutes.
When ready, serve and enjoy!

Nutrition:

Calories: 125
Fat: 7g
Carbohydrates: 10g
Protein: 40g

Cabbage Mixed Recipe

Prep time: 2 minutes
Cooking time: 10 minutes
Servings: 3

Ingredients:

Cabbage (shredded) – 1 cup
Mayonnaise – 1 cup
Oil – 2 tbsp.
White wine vinegar – 1 tbsp.
Celery seed – 2 tbsp.
Sugar – 1 tbsp.
Salt and pepper to taste

Directions:

Add oil into the air fryer pot.
Mix cabbage, mayonnaise, white wine vinegar, celery seed, sugar with salt and pepper.
Cook at 300 F for 10 minutes.
When ready, serve and enjoy!

Nutrition:

Calories: 105
Fat: 8g
Carbohydrates: 9g
Protein: 46g

Cabbage Mixed Noodles

Prep time: 4 minutes
Cooking time: 20 minutes
Servings: 2

Ingredients:

Noodles (boiled) – 2 lb.	Chicken broth – 2 cups
Cabbage (shredded) – 1 cup	Soy sauce – 2 tbsp.
Onion (sliced) – 1	Oil – 2 tbsp.
	Green onions (chopped) to garnish

Directions:

Add oil into the air fryer pot.
Mix cabbage, onion, chicken broth, soy sauce and noodles.
Cook at 300 F for 20 minutes.
When ready, garnish green onions to serve!

Nutrition:

Calories: 105	Carbohydrates: 9g
Fat: 8g	Protein: 46g

Potatoes with Chicken Stock

Prep time: 2 minutes
Cooking time: 20 minutes
Servings: 3

Ingredients:

Potatoes (boiled, diced) – 3	Dijon mustard – 2 tbsp.
White wine – 2 tbsp.	Oil – 2 tbsp.
Chicken stock – 2 cups	Salt and pepper to taste
Lemon juice – 2 tbsp.	Onion (diced) – 1
Garlic cloves (minced) – 2	Parsley (chopped) to garnish

Directions:

Add oil into the air fryer pot.
Mix potatoes, white wine, chicken stock, lemon juice, garlic, Dijon mustard, onion with salt and pepper.
Cook at 300 F for 20 minutes.
When ready, garnish parsley to serve!

Nutrition:

Calories:96	Carbohydrates: 10g
Fat: 9g	Protein: 35g

Easy Fried Recipe

Prep time: 4 minutes
Cooking time: 10 minutes
Servings: 3

Ingredients:

Potatoes (slice) – 2	Mayonnaise to serve
Salt to taste	Oil – 2 tbsp.

Directions:

Add oil into the air fryer pot.
Mix potatoes and salt.
Cook at 300 F for 10 minutes.
When ready, serve with mayonnaise to enjoy!

Nutrition:

Calories: 115	Carbohydrates: 9g
Fat: 7g	Protein: 40g

White Rice with Vegs

Prep time: 4 minutes
Cooking time: 20 minutes
Servings: 3

Ingredients:

White rice (boiled) – 2 cups	Ginger powder – 1 tbsp.
Chicken broth – 2 cups	Turmeric powder – S tbsp.
Shrimps – 1 lb.	Cumin powder – 1 tbsp.
Oil – 2 tbsp.	
Peas (frozen) – 1 cup	Salt and pepper to taste
Onion (sliced) – 1	
Garlic cloves (minced) – 2	

Directions:

Add oil into the air fryer pot.
Mix chicken broth, shrimps, peas, onion, garlic, ginger powder, turmeric powder, cumin powder with salt and pepper.
Add white rice.
Cook at 300 F for 20 minutes.
When ready, serve and enjoy!

Nutrition:

Calories: 105	Carbohydrates: 9g
Fat: 8g	Protein: 46g

Delicious Red Bell Pepper with Potatoes

Prep time: 2 minutes
Cooking time: 20 minutes
Servings: 2

Ingredients:

Potatoes (scrubbed) – 2	Salt and pepper to taste
Red bell pepper (cubed) – 2	Oil – 2 tbsp.
Green bell pepper (cubed) – 2	Chives (chopped) – 1 tbsp.
Onion (diced) – 1	Cilantro leaves (chopped) to garnish

Directions:

Add oil into the air fryer pot.
Mix potatoes, red bell pepper, green bell pepper, onion, chives with salt and pepper.
Cook at 300 F for 20 minutes.
When ready, garnish cilantro to serve!

Nutrition:

Calories: 125	Carbohydrates: 10g
Fat: 7g	Protein: 40g

Cauliflower with Potatoes

Prep time: 3 minutes
Cooking time: 20 minutes
Servings: 3

Ingredients:

Garlic paste – 2 tbsp.	Potatoes (chopped) – 2
Coriander powder – 2 tbsp.	Tomato (diced) – 2
Oil – 2 tbsp.	Onion (diced) – 2
Cauliflower head (chopped) – 2 cups	Water – 2 cups
	Cilantro leaves (chopped) to garnish

Directions:

Add oil into the air fryer pot.
Mix garlic paste, coriander powder, cauliflower head, potatoes, tomato, onion and water.
Cook at 300 F for 20 minutes.
When ready, garnish cilantro to serve!

Nutrition:

Calories:70	Carbohydrates: 10g
Fat: 6g	Protein: 10g

Fish and Potatoes Recipe

Prep time: 2 minutes
Cooking time: 10 minutes
Servings: 3

Ingredients:

Fish fillets – 1 lb.	Red pepper flakes – 2 tbsp.
Potatoes (diced) – 2	Oil – 2 tbsp.
Onion (diced) – 1	Parsley (chopped) – 2 tbsp.
Garlic cloves (minced) – 2	Olives (halves) – 2 cups
Ginger powder – 2 tbsp.	

Directions:

Add oil into the air fryer pot.
Mix fish fillets, potatoes, onion, garlic, ginger powder, red pepper flakes and parsley.
Cook at 300 F for 10 minutes.
When ready, serve and enjoy the meal!

Nutrition:

Calories: 105	Carbohydrates: 9g
Fat: 8g	Protein: 46g

Beans with Carrots

Prep time: 4 minutes
Cooking time: 20 minutes
Servings: 2

Ingredients:

Bacon (slices) – 4	Carrots (chopped) – 2
Oil – 2 tbsp.	Beet (chopped) – 1 cup
Dijon mustard – 2 tbsp.	Cucumber (sliced) – 1
Salt to taste	Beans – 1 small can
Lettuce (chopped) – 2 cups	

Directions:

Add oil into the air fryer pot.
Mix bacon, Dijon mustard, lettuce, carrot, beet, beans and salt.
Cook at 300 F for 20 minutes.
When ready, add cucumber to serve!

Nutrition:

Calories:96	Carbohydrates: 10g
Fat: 9g	Protein: 35g

Tomato Paste Recipe

Prep time: 3 minutes
Cooking time: 20 minutes
Servings: 2

Ingredients:

Onion (sliced) – 1
Butter – 2 tbsp.
Tomatoes (diced) – 2
Tomato paste – 2 tbsp.
Sugar – 1 tbsp.
Chicken (sliced) – 1 lb.
Salt and pepper to taste
Broccoli – 2 cups
Cream – 1 tbsp.
Oil – 1 tbsp.
Cilantro (leaves) to garnish

Directions:

Add oil into the air fryer.
Mix onion, butter, tomatoes, tomato paste, sugar, chicken with salt and pepper.
Add broccoli and cream.
Cook at 300 F for 20 minutes.
When ready, garnish cilantro to serve!

Nutrition:

Calories: 125
Fat: 7g
Carbohydrates: 10g
Protein: 40g

Simple Potatoes Recipe

Prep time: 4 minutes
Cooking time: 15 minutes
Servings: 2

Ingredients:

Potatoes (diced) – 2
Green bell pepper (chopped) – 2
Onion (sliced) – 1
Steak seasoning – 1 tbsp.
Sweet paprika – 2 tbsp.
Salt to taste
Oil – 2 tbsp.

Directions:

Add oil into the air fryer pot.

Mix green bell pepper, onion, steak seasoning, sweet paprika and salt.
Cook at 300 F for 15 minutes.
When ready, serve and enjoy!

Nutrition:

Calories: 115
Fat: 7g
Carbohydrates: 9g
Protein: 40g

Delicious Beef and Veg Recipe

Prep time: 4 minutes
Cooking time: 20 minutes
Servings: 3

Ingredients:

White sandwich bread – 4 slices
Milk – 2 cups
Grounded beef – 1 lb.
Eggs – 2
Oregano – 2 tbsp.
Cheese – 2 cups
Onion (sliced) – 1
Tomatoes (diced) – 2
Nutmeg – 2 tbsp.
Parsley (chopped) – 1 cup
Red pepper flakes – 1 tbsp.
Oil – 2 tbsp.

Directions:

Add oil into the air fryer pot.
Mix milk, beef, eggs, oregano, cheese, onion, tomatoes, nutmeg, parsley and red pepper flakes.
Cook at 300 F for 20 minutes.
When ready, serve with bread to enjoy!

Nutrition:

Calories:96
Fat: 9g
Carbohydrates: 10g
Protein: 35g

Sweet Potatoes Dessert Recipe

Prep time: 4 minutes
Cooking time: 10 minutes
Servings: 3

Ingredients:

Butter – 2 tbsp.
Sweet potatoes (mashed) – 3
Milk – 1 cup
Brown sugar – 1 tbsp.
Vanilla extract – 2 tbsp.
Salt to taste
Egg – 1
Pecans (chopped) to garnish

Directions:

Add butter into the air fryer pot.
Mix sweet potatoes, milk, brown sugar, vanilla extract, egg and salt.
Cook at 300 F for 10 minutes.
When ready, garnish pecans to serve!

Nutrition:

Calories: 105
Fat: 8g
Carbohydrates: 9g
Protein: 46g

Cauliflower with Cheese

Prep time: 2 minutes
Cooking time: 20 minutes
Servings: 3

Ingredients:

Cauliflower head (chopped) – 2 cups	Salt and pepper to taste
Cheese (grated) – 1 cup	Egg – 2
Garlic cloves (minced) – 2	Marinara sauce – 2 tbsp.
	Basil leaves (chopped) to garnish

Directions:

Add marinara sauce into the air fryer pot.
Mix cauliflower head, cheese, garlic, egg with salt and pepper.
Cook at 300 F for 20 minutes.
When ready, garnish basil leaves to serve!

Nutrition:

Calories: 125	Carbohydrates: 10g
Fat: 7g	Protein: 40g

Rice with Broccoli

Prep time: 2 minutes
Cooking time: 20 minutes
Servings: 2

Ingredients:

Broccoli (chopped) – 2 cups	Cumin powder – 1 tbsp.
White rice (boiled) – 2 cups	Frozen peas – 2 cups
Chicken broth – 2 cups	Onion (sliced) – 1
Salt and pepper to taste	Garlic cloves (minced) – 2
	Oil – 2 tbsp.
	Basil leaves to garnish

Directions:

Add oil into the air fryer pot.
Mix broccoli, white rice, chicken broth, cumin powder, peas, onion, garlic with salt and pepper.
Cook at 300 F for 20 minutes.
When ready, garnish basil to serve!

Nutrition:

Calories:70	Carbohydrates: 10g
Fat: 6g	Protein: 10g

Rice with Peas

Prep time: 4 minutes
Cooking time: 20 minutes
Servings: 3

Ingredients:

Frozen peas – 2 cups	Onion (sliced) – 1
Oil – 1 tbsp.	Red pepper flakes – 2 tbsp.
Salt and pepper to taste	Salt and pepper to taste
White rice (boiled) – 2 cups	Cilantro (chopped) to garnish
Water – 3 cups	

Directions:

Add oil into the air fryer pot.
Mix peas, white rice, water, onion, red pepper flakes with salt and pepper.
Cook at 300 F for 20 minutes.
When ready, garnish cilantro to serve!

Nutrition:

Calories:70	Carbohydrates: 10g
Fat: 6g	Protein: 10g

Beet Recipe

Prep time: 2 minutes
Cooking time: 20 minutes
Servings: 3

Ingredients:

Beet (diced) – 2 cups	Spinach (boiled) – 2 cups
Vinegar – 1 tbsp.	Cheese (shredded) – 2 cups
Honey – 1 tbsp.	Walnuts (chopped) to garnish
Onions (sliced) – 2	
Dijon mustard – 2 tbsp.	

Directions:

Add beet into the air fryer pot.
Mix vinegar, honey, onions, Dijon mustard and spinach.
Cook at 300 F for 20 minutes.
When ready, garnish cheese and walnuts to serve!

Nutrition:

Calories:96	Carbohydrates: 10g
Fat: 9g	Protein: 35g

Chicken Noodles with Vegs

Prep time: 3 minutes
Cooking time: 20 minutes
Servings: 3

Ingredients:

Oil – 2 tbsp.
Chicken (sliced) – 1 lb.
Soy sauce – 2 tbsp.
Scallions (chopped) – 2 cups
Carrots (sliced) – 2 cups

Wine vinegar – 2 tbsp.
Edamame – 1 tbsp.
Salt and pepper to taste
Noodles (boiled) – 2 cups
Cilantro (chopped) to garnish

Directions:

Add oil into the air fryer pot.
Mix chicken, soy sauce, scallions, carrots, wine vinegar, edamame, noodles with salt and pepper.
Cook at 300 F for 20 minutes.
When ready, garnish cilantro to serve!

Nutrition:

Calories: 115
Fat: 7g

Carbohydrates: 9g
Protein: 40g

Eggplant Recipe

Prep time: 3 minutes
Cooking time: 20 minutes
Servings: 2

Ingredients:

Eggplants (mashed) – 2 cups
Onion (sliced) – 1
Garlic cloves (minced) – 2
Cayenne pepper – 2 tbsp.

Salt and pepper to taste
Oil – 2 tbsp.
Lemon juice – 2 tbsp.
Tahini – 2 tbsp.
Parsley (chopped) – 1 cup

Directions:

Add oil into the air fryer pot.
Mix onion, eggplant, garlic, cayenne pepper, lemon juice, tahini with salt and pepper.
Cook at 300 F for 20 minutes.
When ready, garnish parsley to serve!

Nutrition:

Calories: 115
Fat: 7g

Carbohydrates: 9g
Protein: 40g

Rigatoni with Vegs

Prep time: 2 minutes
Cooking time: 20 minutes
Servings: 2

Ingredients:

Rigatoni (boiled) – 1 lb.
Cream cheese – 2 cups
Milk – 1 cup
Garlic powder – 1 tbsp.
Onion powder – 2 tbsp.

Red pepper flakes – 2 tbsp.
Frozen spinach – 2 cups
Salt and pepper to taste
Parsley (chopped) to garnish

Directions:

Add cream cheese and rigatoni into the air fryer pot.
Mix milk, garlic powder, onion powder, red pepper flakes with salt and pepper.
Add spinach.
Cook at 300 F for 20 minutes.
When ready, garnish parsley to serve!

Nutrition:

Calories: 105
Fat: 8g

Carbohydrates: 9g
Protein: 46g

Beef with Tomatoes

Prep time: 4 minutes
Cooking time: 20 minutes
Servings: 2

Ingredients:

Oil – 2 tbsp.
Onion (chopped) – 1
Garlic cloves (minced) – 2
Celery stalk (chopped) – 2
Carrot (chopped) – 2 cups

Beef (diced) – 1 lb.
Tomatoes (crushed) – 2
Parsley (chopped) – 1 cup
Salt and pepper to taste

Directions:

Add oil into the air fryer pot.
Mix onion, garlic, celery stalk, carrot, beef, tomatoes with salt and pepper.
Cook at 300 F for 20 minutes.
When ready, garnish parsley to serve!

Nutrition:

Calories:90
Fat: 10g

Carbohydrates: 10g
Protein: 45g

Chicken with Vegetables

Prep time: 3 minutes
Cooking time: 10 minutes
Servings: 3

Ingredients:

Lime juice – 2 tbsp.	Garlic cloves
Soy sauce – 2 tbsp.	(minced) – 2
Brown sugar – 1	Lettuce (shredded) –
tbsp.	2 cups
Scallions (chopped) –	Carrots (shredded) –
1 cup	2 cups
Red jalapeno	Peanuts to garnish
(chopped) – 1 cup	Cilantro leaves
Chicken (shredded) –	(chopped) to garnish
1 lb.	

Directions:

Add lime juice and soy sauce into the air fryer pot.
Mix brown sugar, scallions, Red jalapeno, chicken and garlic cloves.
Cook at 300 F for 10 minutes.
When ready, mix lettuce and carrots.
Garnish peanuts with cilantro to serve!

Nutrition:

Calories: 125	Carbohydrates: 10g
Fat: 7g	Protein: 40g

Shrimps and Potato Mix

Prep time: 4 minutes
Cooking time: 14 minutes
Servings: 2

Ingredients:

Shrimps – 1 lb.	Oil – 2 tbsp.
Potatoes (diced) –	Salt and pepper to
Cherry tomatoes – 2	taste
cups	Lemon juice – 2 tbsp.

Directions:

Add oil into the air fryer pot.
Mix shrimps, potatoes, cherry tomatoes, lemon juice with salt and pepper.
Cook at 300 F for 14 minutes.
When ready, serve and enjoy!

Nutrition:

Calories:70	Carbohydrates: 10g
Fat: 6g	Protein: 10g

Desserts

Coconut Mix Dessert

Prep time: 2 minutes
Cooking time: 15 minutes
Servings: 2

Ingredients:

Butter – 2 tbsp.
Sugar – 2 cups
Eggs – 3
Vanilla extract – 2 tbsp.
Almond extract – 2 tbsp.
Frosting:
Cream – 2 cups
Butter – 2 tbsp.

Flour – 2 cups
Baking powder – 2 tbsp.
Salt – 1 pinch
Milk – 2 cups
Shredded coconut – 2 cups
Vanilla extract – 2 tbsp.
Sugar – 1 cup

Directions:

Add butter and sugar into the bowl.
Mix eggs, vanilla extract, almond extract, flour, baking powder, salt, milk and shredded coconut.
Pour the batter into the round baking tray.
Bake at 300 F for 15 minutes in the air fryer.
Prepare the frosting: mix cream, butter, vanilla extract and sugar into the bowl.
When the cake is ready, cover it with the frosting to serve!

Nutrition:

Calories: 125
Fat: 7g

Carbohydrates: 10g
Protein: 40g

Peanut Butter Dessert

Prep time: 2 minutes
Cooking time: 15 minutes
Servings: 3

Ingredients:

Butter – 2 tbsp.
Sugar – 1 cup
Creamy peanut butter – 2 cups
Salt – 1 pinch

Chocolate (melted) – 2 cups
Heavy cream – 2 cups
Graham cracker crumbs – 2 cups

Directions:

Add butter and sugar into the bowl.
Mix peanut butter, salt, chocolate, heavy cream with graham crackers.
Pour the batter into the round baking tray.
Bake at 300 F for 15 minutes in the air fryer.
When ready, serve!

Nutrition:

Calories: 96
Fat: 9g

Carbohydrates: 10g
Protein: 35g

Dulce de Leche Recipe

Prep time: 4 minutes
Cooking time: 15 minutes
Servings: 3

Ingredients:

Butter – 2 tbsp.
Cocoa powder – 1 cup
Sugar – 1 cup
Vanilla extract – 2 tbsp.

Eggs – 3
Flour – 2 cups
Dulce de Leche – S can (14 oz.)
Powdered sugar for dusting

Directions:

Add butter and sugar into the bowl.
Mix cocoa powder, vanilla extract, eggs, flour and dulce de leche.
Pour the batter into the round baking tray.
Bake at 300 F for 15 minutes in the air fryer.
When ready, dust sugar to serve!

Nutrition:

Calories: 76
Fat: 6g

Carbohydrates: 8g
Protein: 49g

Heavy Cream Dessert

Prep time: 3 minutes
Cooking time: 20 minutes
Servings: 3

Ingredients:

Flour – 2 cups
Baking powder – 2 tbsp.
Salt – 1 pinch
Eggs – 3
Topping:
Heavy cream – 2 cups
Condensed milk – 1 can (14 oz.)

Sugar – 1 cup
Milk – 2 cups
Vanilla extract – 2 tbsp.

Evaporated milk – 1 cup

Directions:

Add flour and baking powder into the bowl.
Mix eggs, sugar, milk, vanilla extract and salt.
Pour the batter into the round baking tray.
Bake at 300 F for 20 minutes in the air fryer.
Prepare the topping: mix heavy cream, condensed milk and evaporated milk into the bowl.
When the cake is ready, cover it with the topping to serve!

Nutrition:

Calories: 105
Fat: 8g

Carbohydrates: 9g
Protein: 46g

Blueberries Fill Recipe

Prep time: 3 minutes
Cooking time: 15 minutes
Servings: 3

Ingredients:

Crust:
Butter – 2 tbsp.
Sugar – 1 cup
Flour – 2 cups
Filling:
Egg – 1
Sugar – 2 tbsp.
Lemon juice – 2 tbsp.
Flour – 2 tbsp.
Cornstarch – 2 tbsp.

Cinnamon powder – 2 tbsp.
Salt – 1 pinch

Vanilla extract – 2 tbsp.
Cinnamon powder – 2 tbsp.
Blueberries – 2 cups

Directions:

Add butter and sugar into the bowl.
Mix flour, cinnamon powder and salt.
Pour the batter into the round baking tray.
Bake at 300 F for 15 minutes in the air fryer.
Prepare the filling: mix egg, sugar, lemon juice, vanilla extract, cinnamon powder and blue berries into the bowl.
When the crust is ready, pour the filling and serve!

Nutrition:

Calories: 115
Fat: 7g
Carbohydrates: 9g
Protein: 40g

Red Velvet Cake

Prep time: 2 minutes
Cooking time:
Servings: 2

Ingredients:

Flour – 2 cups
Sugar – 2 tbsp.
Baking soda – 1 tbsp.
Salt – 1 pinch
Cocoa powder – 2 tbsp.
Oil – 1 tbsp.
Buttermilk – 1 cup

Eggs – 2
Red food coloring
Vanilla extract – 2 tbsp.
Cream cheese for frosting
Pecans (chopped) – 1 cups

Directions:

Add flour and sugar into the bowl.
Mix baking soda, salt, cocoa powder, oil, buttermilk. Eggs, red food color and vanilla extract.
Pour the batter into the round baking tray.
Bake at 300 F for 15 minutes in the air fryer.
When ready, cover it with whipped cream.
Garnish pecans to serve!

Nutrition:

Calories: 105
Fat: 8g
Carbohydrates: 9g
Protein: 46g

Golden Apples Recipe

Prep time: 4 minutes
Cooking time: 15 minutes
Servings: 3

Ingredients:

Golden apples (sliced) – 2
Sugar – 2 tbsp.
Lemon juice – 1 tbsp.
Topping:
Pecans (chopped) – 1 cup
Flour – 2 cups
Rolled oats – 1 cup

Flour – 2 cups
Cinnamon powder – 2 tbsp.

Brown sugar – 2 tbsp.
Butter – 2 tbsp.
Vanilla extract – 2 tbsp.

Directions:

Add flour and sugar into the bowl.
Mix golden apples, lemon juice and cinnamon powder.
Pour the batter into the round baking tray.
Bake at 300 F for 15 minutes in the air fryer.
Prepare the topping: mix pecans, four, rolled oats, brown sugar, butter and vanilla extract.
When ready, pour the mixture on the cake to serve!

Nutrition:

Calories: 105
Fat: 8g
Carbohydrates: 9g
Protein: 46g

Pecans Filled Dessert Recipe

Prep time: 3 minutes
Cooking time: 15 minutes
Servings: 2

Ingredients:

Pie Crust:
Flour – 2 cups
Vegetable shortening – S cup
Butter – 2 tbsp.
Filling:
Sugar – 1 cup
Brown sugar – 1 cup
Corn syrup – 2 tbsp.
Vanilla extract – 2 tbsp.

Egg – 2
White vinegar – 2 tbsp.

Butter – 2 tbsp.
Pecans (chopped) – 1 cup

Directions:

Add flour and vegetable shortening into the bowl.
Mix butter, egg and white vinegar.
Pour the batter into the round baking tray.
Bake at 300 F for 15 minutes in the air fryer.
Prepare the filling: mix sugar, brown sugar, vanilla extract, butter and pecans into the bowl.
When the crust is ready, pour the filling to serve!

Nutrition:

Calories:70
Fat: 6g
Carbohydrates: 10g
Protein: 10g

Sweet Potato Dessert

Prep time: 3 minutes
Cooking time: 15 minutes
Servings: 2

Ingredients:

Sweet potatoes (mashed) – 3	Salt – 1 pinch
Sugar – 2 tbsp.	Evaporated milk – 2 cups
Eggs – 2	Pie crust – 1
Vanilla extract – 2 tbsp.	Whipped cream – 1 cup
Cinnamon powder – 2 tbsp.	Maple syrup – 2 tbsp.
	Sugar – 2 tbsp.

Directions:

Add sugar and eggs into the bowl.
Mix sweet potatoes, vanilla extract, cinnamon powder, salt and evaporated milk.
Place the pie crust into the round baking tray and pour the batter.
Bake at 300 F for 15 minutes in the air fryer.
Meanwhile, prepare the topping: mix whipped cream, maple syrup and sugar.
When the pie is ready, cover it with the topping to serve!

Nutrition:

Calories:70	Carbohydrates: 10g
Fat: 6g	Protein: 10g

Cinnamon Mix Recipe

Prep time: 4 minutes
Cooking time: 20 minutes
Servings: 2

Ingredients:

Flour – 2 cups	Nutmeg powder – 2 tbsp.
Baking powder – 2 tbsp.	Salt – 1 pinch
Sugar – S cup	Whole milk – 2 cups
Cinnamon powder – 2 tbsp.	Butter – 2 tbsp.
	Vanilla extract – 2 tbsp.

Topping:	
Butter – 2 tbsp.	Cinnamon powder – 1 tbsp.
Sugar – 1 cup	

Directions:

Add flour and baking powder into the bowl.
Mix sugar, cinnamon powder, nutmeg powder, salt, whole milk butter and vanilla extract.
Pour the batter into the round baking tray.
Bake at 300 F for 20 minutes in the air fryer.
Prepare the topping: mix butter, sugar and cinnamon powder.
When ready, pour the topping over it to serve!

Nutrition:

Calories: 125	Carbohydrates: 10g
Fat: 7g	Protein: 40g

Lemon Zest Recipe

Prep time: 2 minutes
Cooking time: 15 minutes
Servings: 3

Ingredients:

Flour – 2 cups	Sugar – 2 tbsp.
Baking powder – 2 tbsp.	Eggs – 2
Salt – 1 pinch	Lemon zest – 2 tbsp.
Whole milk yogurt – 1 cup	Vanilla extract – 2 tbsp.
Glaze:	Lemon juice – 2 tbsp.
Sugar – 1 cup	Lemon juice – S cup

Directions:

Add flour and baking powder into the bowl.
Mix salt, yogurt, sugar, eggs, lemon zest, vanilla extract and lemon juice.
Pour the batter into the round baking tray.
Bake at 300 F for 15 minutes in the air fryer.
Prepare the glaze: mix sugar and lemon juice into the bowl.
When ready, pour the glaze over it to serve!

Nutrition:

Calories:96	Carbohydrates: 10g
Fat: 9g	Protein: 35g

Shortbread Cookies with Raspberries

Prep time: 4 minutes
Cooking time: 15 minutes
Servings: 3

Ingredients:

Raspberries – 1 cup	Cream cheese – 2 cups
Lemon juice – 2 tbsp.	Vanilla extract – 2 tbsp.
Shortbread cookies – 1 pack (10oz.)	Powdered sugar for dusting
Butter – 2 tbsp.	
White chocolate chips – 1 cup	

Directions:

Add butter and shortbread cookies into the bowl.
Mix lemon juice, white chocolate chips, cream cheese, vanilla extract and raspberries.
Pour the batter into the round baking tray.
Bake at 300 F for 15 minutes in the air fryer.
When ready, dust sugar to serve!

Nutrition:

Calories:80	Carbohydrates: 10g
Fat: 6g	Protein: 29g

Simple Gelatin Recipe

Prep time: 4 minutes
Cooking time: 15 minutes
Servings: 3

Ingredients:

Gelatin – 3 packs	Powdered sugar for
Sugar – 2 tbsp.	dusting
Corn syrup – 2 tbsp.	Strawberries
Vanilla extract – 2 tbsp.	(sliced) – 2 cups

Directions:

Add gelatin and sugar into the bowl.
Mix corn syrup, vanilla extract, and strawberries.
Pour the batter into the round baking tray.
Bake at 300 F for 15 minutes in the air fryer.
When ready, dust sugar to serve!

Nutrition:

Calories: 125	Carbohydrates: 10g
Fat: 7g	Protein: 40g

Oats and Blueberries Mix

Prep time: 2 minutes
Cooking time: 15 minutes
Servings: 2

Ingredients:

Brown sugar – 2 tbsp.	Flour – 2 cups
Butter – 1 cup	Salt – 1 pinch
Vanilla extract – 1 tbsp.	Baking soda – 1 tbsp.
Eggs – 2	Oats – 3 cups
	Blueberries – 1 cup

Directions:

Add brown sugar and butter into the bowl.
Mix vanilla extract, eggs, flour, salt, baking soda and oats.
Add blueberries.
Pour the batter into the round baking tray.
Bake at 300 F for 15 minutes in the air fryer.
When ready, serve!

Nutrition:

Calories:70	Carbohydrates: 10g
Fat: 6g	Protein: 10g

Soft Rice Recipe

Prep time: 2 minutes
Cooking time: 15 minutes
Servings: 2

Ingredients:

White rice – 1 cup	Egg yolks (beaten) – 2
Whole milk – 1 cup	Vanilla extract – 2 tbsp.
Lemon juice – 1 tbsp.	Corn flour – 2 tbsp.
White sugar – 1 cup	

Directions:

Add white rice into the air fryer pot.
Mix whole milk, lemon juice, white sugar, egg yolks, vanilla extract and corn flour.
Cook at 300 F for 15 minutes.
When ready, serve and enjoy!

Nutrition:

Calories: 105	Carbohydrates: 9g
Fat: 8g	Protein: 46g

Pastry with Honey

Prep time: 4 minutes
Cooking time: 10 minutes
Servings: 3

Ingredients:

Phyllo pastry – 2 sheets	Walnuts (chopped) – 1 cup
Butter – 1 cup	Honey – ½ cup
Sugar – 1 cup	Water – 1 /2 cup
Cinnamon powder – 1 tbsp.	Lemon juice – 1 tbsp.

Directions:

Add butter and sugar into the bowl.
Mix cinnamon powder, honey, lemon juice and water.
Place the phyllo pastry into the round baking tray.
Pour the mixture over it.
Bake at 300 F for 10 minutes in the air fryer.
When ready, serve and enjoy!

Nutrition:

Calories: 105	Carbohydrates: 9g
Fat: 8g	Protein: 46g

Cherry Pie Filling

Prep time: 3 minutes
Cooking time: 15 minutes
Servings: 3

Ingredients:

Cherry pie filling – 1 can (21 oz.)

White cake mix – 2 cups
Butter – 2 cups

Topping:
Peaches (sliced) – 2 cups
Butter – 2 tbsp.

Whipped cream – 1 cup

Directions:

Mix cherry pie filling and white cake mix into the bowl.
Add butter.
Pour the batter into the round baking tray.
Bake at 300 F for 15 minutes in the air fryer.
Prepare the topping: mix peaches, butter and whipped cream into the bowl.
When the cake is ready, spread the topping and serve!

Nutrition:

Calories:96
Fat: 9g

Carbohydrates: 10g
Protein: 35g

Cocoa with Nuts

Prep time: 3 minutes
Cooking time: 15 minutes
Servings: 3

Ingredients:

Flour – 2 cups
Baking soda – 2 tbsp.
Butter – 2 cups
Sugar – 2 tbsp.
Brown sugar – 2 tbsp.
Vanilla extract – 2 tbsp.
Eggs – 2

Cocoa powder – 3 tbsp.
Walnuts (chopped) – 1 cup
Chocolate chips – 1 cup
Almond extract – 2 tbsp.

Directions:

Add butter and flour into the bowl.
Mix baking soda, sugar, brown sugar, vanilla extract, eggs, cocoa powder and chocolate chips with almond extract.
Pour the batter into the round baking tray.
Bake at 300 F for 15 minutes in the air fryer.
When ready, garnish walnuts to serve!

Nutrition:

Calories: 115
Fat: 7g

Carbohydrates: 9g
Protein: 40g

Kiwi and Strawberry Mix

Prep time: 2 minutes
Cooking time: 15 minutes
Servings: 2

Ingredients:

Flour – 2 cups
Baking powder – 2 tbsp.
Salt – 1 pinch
Sugar – 2 cups
Butter – 2 tbsp.
Vanilla extract – 2 tbsp.

Eggs – 2
Kiwi (sliced) – 2
Strawberries (sliced) – 2 cups
Whipped cream – 2 cups

Directions:

Add flour and baking powder into the bowl.
Mix salt, sugar, butter, vanilla extract and eggs.
Pour the batter into the round baking tray.
Bake at 300 F for 15 minutes in the air fryer.
When ready, spread whipped cream on the cake.
Place kiwi and strawberries to serve!

Nutrition:

Calories:70
Fat: 6g

Carbohydrates: 10g
Protein: 10g

Almond Flour Recipe

Prep time: 4 minutes
Cooking time: 15 minutes
Servings: 3

Ingredients:

Almond flour – 5 tbsp.
Cocoa powder – 3 tbsp.
Splenda sugar – 3 tbsp.
Baking powder – 1 tbsp.

Water – 3 tbsp.
Avocado oil – 2 tbsp.
Vanilla extract – ¼ tsp.
Chocolate chips (sugar-free) – 1 pack

Directions:

Add flour and cocoa powder into the bowl.
Mix sugar, baking powder, water, avocado oil and vanilla extract.
Add chocolate chips.
Pour the batter into the round baking tray.
Bake at 300 F for 15 minutes in the air fryer.
When ready, serve!

Nutrition:

Calories: 125
Fat: 7g

Carbohydrates: 10g
Protein: 40g

Brioche Bread Recipe

Prep time: 2 minutes
Cooking time: 20 minutes
Servings: 2

Ingredients:

Butter – 2 tbsp.
Brioche bread – 1
loaf (1 lb.)
Pecans (chopped) –
1 cup
Half and half – 1 cup
Whole milk – S cup
Eggs – 2

Brown sugar – 2
cups
Vanilla extract – 2
tbsp.
Cinnamon powder –
2 tbsp.
Salt – 1 pinch
Nutmeg powder – 1
tbsp.

Directions:

Place the bread into the round baking tray.
Add butter and whole milk into the bowl.
Mix half and half, eggs, brown sugar, vanilla
extract, cinnamon powder, salt and nutmeg
powder.
Bake at 300 F for 20 minutes in the air fryer.
When ready, garnish pecans to serve!

Nutrition:

Calories:70
Fat: 6g

Carbohydrates: 10g
Protein: 10g

Almond and Walnut Taste Recipe

Prep time: 4 minutes
Cooking time: 20 minutes
Servings: 3

Ingredients:

Butter – 2 cups
Flour – 2 cups
Sugar – 2 tbsp.
Eggs – 2
Sour cream – 3 tbsp.

Almond extract – 2
tbsp.
Walnuts (chopped) –
1 cup
Chocolate chips – 1
cup

Directions:

Add butter and flour into the bowl.
Mix sugar, eggs, sour cream, almond extract
and chocolate chips.
Pour the batter into the round baking tray.
Bake at 300 F for 20 minutes in the air fryer.
When ready, garnish walnuts to serve!

Nutrition:

Calories: 115
Fat: 7g

Carbohydrates: 9g
Protein: 40g

Chocolate Chips Recipe

Prep time: 4 minutes
Cooking time: 15 minutes
Servings: 2

Ingredients:

Egg yolks – 3
Sugar – 2 tbsp.
Milk – 1 cup
Flour – 2 cups
Cheese – 2 cups

Grounded coffee – 2
cups
Cocoa powder – 2
tbsp.
Chocolate chips – 1
cup

Directions:

Add flour and milk into the bowl.
Mix egg yolks, sugar, cheese, coffee, cocoa
powder and chocolate chips.
Pour the batter into the round baking tray.
Bake at 300 F for 15 minutes in the air fryer.
When ready, enjoy!

Nutrition:

Calories: 105
Fat: 8g

Carbohydrates: 9g
Protein: 46g

Quick Cake recipe

Prep time: 2 minutes
Cooking time: 15 minutes
Servings: 3

Ingredients:

Milk – 2 tbsp.
Sugar – 2 tbsp.
Chocolate
(chopped) – 2 cups

Egg yolks – 2
Egg whites – 2
Flour – 2 cups

Directions:

Add milk and sugar into the bowl.
Mix chocolate, egg yolk, egg whites and
flour.
Pour the batter into the round baking tray.
Bake at 300 F for 15 minutes in the air fryer.
When ready, serve and enjoy!

Nutrition:

Calories: 125
Fat: 7g

Carbohydrates: 10g
Protein: 40g

Caramel Mix Recipe

Prep time: 2 minutes
Cooking time: 15 minutes
Servings: 3

Ingredients:

Pecan (halves) – 1 cup
Pretzel twists – 1 cup
Caramel – 1 cup
Milk chocolate (any, melted) – 2 cups
Flour – 2 cups
Sugar – 2 tbsp.
Vanilla extract – 2 tbsp.

Directions:

Add flour and sugar into the bowl.
Mix pecans, pretzels, caramel, milk chocolate and vanilla extract.
Pour the batter into the round baking tray.
Bake at 300 F for 15 minutes in the air fryer.
When ready, serve and enjoy!

Nutrition:

Calories:70
Fat: 6g
Carbohydrates: 10g
Protein: 10g

Simple Sweet Sheets Recipe

Prep time: 3 minutes
Cooking time: 15 minutes
Servings: 2

Ingredients:

Butter – 2 cups
Sugar – 1 cup
Salt – ½ tsp.
Apples (chopped) – 3
Brandy (any) – ½ cup
Phyllo dough sheets – 3

Directions:

Add butter and sugar into the bowl.
Mix salt, apples and brandy.
Place the dough sheets into the round baking tray.
Pour the batter into the try. .
Bake at 300 F for 15 minutes in the air fryer.
When ready, serve and enjoy!

Nutrition:

Calories: 105
Fat: 8g
Carbohydrates: 9g
Protein: 46g

Raspberry Jam Delight

Prep time: 3 minutes
Cooking time: 15 minutes
Servings: 2

Ingredients:

Butter – 2 cups
Vanilla extract – 2 tbsp.
Flour – 2 cups
Salt – 1 pinch
Raspberry jam – 1 cup
Dried fruit (any) – 1 cup
Almonds (sliced) – 1 cup
Sugar – 1 cup

Directions:

Add butter and flour into the air fryer pot.
Mix vanilla extract, salt, dried fruit, almonds and sugar.
Pour the batter into the round baking tray.
Bake at 300 F for 15 minutes in the air fryer.
When ready, apply raspberry jam and garnish almonds to serve!

Nutrition:

Calories:96
Fat: 9g
Carbohydrates: 10g
Protein: 35g

Vermicelli Mix Recipe

Prep time: 3 minutes
Cooking time: 20 minutes
Servings: 2

Ingredients:

Vermicelli – 3 cups
Milk – 2 cups
Sugar – 1 cup
Cardamom powder – 1 tbsp.

Directions:

Add milk and Vermicelli into the air fryer pot.
Mix sugar and cardamom powder.
Cook at 300 F for 20 minutes.
When ready, serve and enjoy!

Nutrition:

Calories: 125
Fat: 7g
Carbohydrates: 10g
Protein: 40g

Cake with Pears

Prep time: 4 minutes
Cooking time: 20 minutes
Servings: 3

Ingredients:

Flour – 1 cup   Shortening – 2 tbsp.
Salt – ½ tbsp.
Filling:
Pears (halves) – 3   Sugar – ½ cup
cups   Butter – 2 tbsp.
Lemon juice – 1 tbsp.

Directions:

Add flour and shortening into the bowl.
Mix sugar.
Pour the batter into the round baking tray.
Bake at 300 F for 20 minutes in the air fryer.
Prepare the filling: mix pears, lemon juice,
sugar and butter into the bowl.
When the baking is done, pour the filling to
enjoy the dessert!

Nutrition:

Calories:96   Carbohydrates: 10g
Fat: 9g   Protein: 35g

Lemon Juice Dessert

Prep time: 2 minutes
Cooking time: 20 minutes
Servings: 3

Ingredients:

Butter – 2 tbsp.   Milk – 1 cup
Sugar – ½ cup   Lemon juice – 1 tbsp.
Flour – 2 cups   Powdered sugar to
Lemon zest – 2 tbsp.   garnish
Egg white – 1

Directions:

Add butter and sugar into the bowl.
Mix flour, lemon zest, egg white, lemon juice
and milk.
Pour the batter into the round baking tray.
Bake at 300 F for 20 minutes in the air fryer.
When ready, dust powdered sugar to serve!

Nutrition:

Calories: 115   Carbohydrates: 9g
Fat: 7g   Protein: 40g

Delicious Buttercream Recipe

Prep time: 4 minutes
Cooking time: 20 minutes
Servings: 2

Ingredients:

Sugar – 1 cup   Food color (any) – 2
Almond flour – 3   tbsp.
tbsp.   Buttercream for filling
Egg whites – 3   (any) – 4 cups
Granulated sugar – 4
tbsp.

Directions:

Add flour and sugar into the bowl.
Mix egg whites, sugar and food color.
Pour the batter into the round baking tray.
Bake at 300 F for 20 minutes in the air fryer.
When ready, pour buttercream over it to
serve!

Nutrition:

Calories: 105   Carbohydrates: 9g
Fat: 8g   Protein: 46g

Whipped Cream with Strawberries

Prep time: 4 minutes
Cooking time: 15 minutes
Servings: 3

Ingredients:

Butter – 2 tbsp.   Baking powder – 2
Brown sugar – 2   tbsp.
tbsp.   Baking soda – 1 tbsp.
Eggs – 2   Salt – 1 pinch
Vanilla extract – 2   Whipped cream – 1
tbsp.   cup
Chocolate chips   Strawberries
(chunks) – 2 cups   (sliced) – 1 cup
Flour – 2 cups

Directions:

Add butter and brown sugar into the bowl.
Mix eggs, vanilla extract, chocolate chips,
flour, baking powder, baking soda and salt.
Pour the batter into the round baking tray.
Bake at 300 F for 15 minutes in the air fryer.
When ready, cover the cake with whipped
cream.
Place strawberries on the cake to serve!

Nutrition:

Calories:70   Carbohydrates: 10g
Fat: 6g   Protein: 10g

Saltine Crackers Mix

Prep time: 2 minutes
Cooking time: 15 minutes
Servings: 2

Ingredients:

Oil – 1 tbsp.
Saltine crackers – 30
Butter – 1 cup

Brown sugar – 2 tbsp.
Chocolate chips – 1 cup

Directions:

Add oil and butter into the bowl.
Mix saltine crackers, brown sugar and chocolate chips.
Pour the batter into the round baking tray.
Bake at 300 F for 15 minutes in the air fryer.
When ready, enjoy!

Nutrition:

Calories:70
Fat: 6g

Carbohydrates: 10g
Protein: 10g

Apples Mix Dessert

Prep time: 4 minutes
Cooking time: 15 minutes
Servings: 2

Ingredients:

Apples (sliced) – 2 cups
Lemon juice – 2 tbsp.
Sugar – 2 tbsp.
Flour – 2 cups
Rolled oats – 2 tbsp.

Brown sugar – 2 tbsp.
Cinnamon powder – 2 tbsp.
Butter – 3 tbsp.
Nuts (chopped) – 1 cup

Directions:

Add flour and sugar into the bowl.
Mix lemon juice, rolled oats, brown sugar, cinnamon powder, butter and nuts.
Pour the batter into the round baking tray.
Bake at 300 F for 15 minutes in the air fryer.
When ready, place apples on the cake to serve!

Nutrition:

Calories: 105
Fat: 8g

Carbohydrates: 9g
Protein: 46g

Simple Chocolate Chips Cookies

Prep time: 3 minutes
Cooking time: 15 minutes
Servings: 3

Ingredients:

Flour – 2 cups
Baking soda – 2 tbsp.
Butter – 1 cup
Brown sugar – 1 tbsp.

Eggs –2
Vanilla extract – 2 tbsp.
Chocolate chips – 1 cup

Directions:

Add flour and baking soda into the bowl.
Mix butter, brown sugar, eggs and vanilla extract.
Add chocolate chips.
Pour spoonful from the batter with equal sizes into the air fryer pot.
Bake at 300 F for 15 minutes.
When ready, enjoy the cookies!

Nutrition:

Calories: 125
Fat: 7g

Carbohydrates: 10g
Protein: 40g

Orange Zest Recipe

Prep time: 4 minutes
Cooking time: 15 minutes
Servings: 3

Ingredients:

Butter – 1 cup
Flour – 2 cups
Vanilla bean – ½
Almonds – 1 cup
Sugar – 2 cups
Salt – ½ tsp.

Egg whites – 4
Orange zest – 2 tbsp.
Chocolate (chopped) – 2 cups
Heavy cream – ½ cup

Directions:

Add butter and flour into the bowl.
Mix vanilla bean, almonds, sugar, salt, egg whites, orange zest and chocolates.
Pour the batter into the round baking tray.
Bake at 300 F for 15 minutes in the air fryer.
When ready, cover with heavy cream to serve!

Nutrition:

Calories:96
Fat: 9g

Carbohydrates: 10g
Protein: 35g

Simple Cocoa Mix

Prep time: 3 minutes
Cooking time: 20 minutes
Servings: 3
Water (cold) – ½ cup   Butter – 2 cups
Salt – ½ tsp.   Cocoa powder – 3
Flour – 2 cups   tbsp.
Bread flour – 2 cups

Directions:

Add flour and water into the bowl.
Mix salt, bread flour, butter and cocoa
powder.
Make small balls out of the mixture.
Place the balls into the air fryer pot.
Bake at 300 F for 20 minutes.
When ready, serve and enjoy!

Nutrition:

Calories:70   Carbohydrates: 10g
Fat: 6g   Protein: 10g

Chocolate Mixed Cocoa

Prep time: 2 minutes
Cooking time: 15 minutes
Servings: 2

Ingredients:

Chocolate   Egg yolks – 2
(chopped) – 2 cups   Cocoa powder – 1
Butter – 1 ½ cup   cup
Salt – ½ tsp.

Directions:

Add chocolate and butter into the bowl.
Mix salt, egg yolks and cocoa powder.
Pour the batter into the round baking tray.
Bake at 300 F for 15 minutes in the air fryer.
When ready, serve and enjoy!

Nutrition:

Calories: 115   Carbohydrates: 9g
Fat: 7g   Protein: 40g

Cake with Strawberries

Prep time: 4 minutes
Cooking time: 15 minutes
Servings: 3

Ingredients:

Vanilla extract – 2   Heavy cream – 2
tbsp.   cups
Flour – 2 cups   Sugar – ½ cup
Honey – 2 tbsp.
For Strawberries
Sugar – 1 cup   Vanilla bean extract –
Corn syrup – 2 tbsp.   1 tbsp.
Red wine – ½ cup   Strawberries
Cinnamon powder –   (halves) – 3 cups
2 tbsp.

Directions:

Add flour and sugar into the bowl.
Mix honey, vanilla extract and heavy cream.
Pour the batter into the round baking tray.
Bake at 300 F for 15 minutes in the air fryer.
Mix sugar, corn syrup, red wine, cinnamon
powder, vanilla bean extract and
strawberries into the bowl.
When the baking is done, pour the mixture
over it to serve!

Nutrition:

Calories: 125   Carbohydrates: 10g
Fat: 7g   Protein: 40g

Puff Pastry Recipe

Prep time: 2 minutes
Cooking time: 15 minutes
Servings: 3

Ingredients:

Milk – 2 cups   Cornstarch – 2 tbsp.
Vanilla bean extract –   Butter – 3 tbsp.
1 tbsp.   Puff pastry – 2 sheets
Egg yolks – 3   Confectioners'
Sugar – 2 tbsp.   sugar – ½ cup

Directions:

Place puff pastry into the round baking tray.
Add milk and vanilla bean extract into the
bowl.
Mix egg yolks, sugar, cornstarch and butter.
Pour the mixture into the baking tray.
Bake at 300 F for 15 minutes in the air fryer.
When ready, powder confectioners' sugar to
serve!

Nutrition:

Calories: 105   Carbohydrates: 9g
Fat: 8g   Protein: 46g

Honey Cake Recipe

Prep time: 2 minutes
Cooking time: 10 minutes
Servings: 2

Ingredients:

Butter – 2 cups
Flour – 2 cups
Sugar – 2 tbsp.
Brown sugar – 1 tbsp.
Honey – 2 cups
Egg whites – 3

Baking powder – 1 tbsp.
Chopped pistachios – 1 cup
Chopped almonds – 1 cup

Directions:

Add butter and flour into the bowl.
Mix sugar, brown sugar, egg whites and baking powder.
Pour the mixture into the round baking tray.
Bake at 300 F for 10 minutes in the air fryer.
When ready, cover the cake with honey and garnish with pistachios.
Add almonds to serve and enjoy!

Nutrition:

Calories: 105
Fat: 8g

Carbohydrates: 9g
Protein: 46g

Chocolate Shavings Recipe

Prep time: 4 minutes
Cooking time: 10 minutes
Servings: 3

Ingredients:

Heavy cream – 1 cup
Vanilla extract – 2 tbsp.
Flour – 2 cups
Salt – ½ tbsp.
Egg whites – 3

Sugar – 1 cup
Chocolate (chopped) – 2 cups
Chocolate shavings to garnish

Directions:

Add flour and vanilla extract into the bowl.
Mix salt, egg whites, chocolate and salt.
Pour the mixture into the round baking tray.
Bake at 300 F for 10 minutes in the air fryer.
When ready, cover the cake with heavy cream and chocolate shavings to serve!

Nutrition:

Calories:96
Fat: 9g

Carbohydrates: 10g
Protein: 35g

Lemon Zest Cake

Prep time: 3 minutes
Cooking time: 20 minutes
Servings: 3

Ingredients:

Eggs – 2
Sugar – 2 tsp.
Salt – ¼ tbsp.
Lemon zest – 2 tbsp.

Heavy cream – 2 cups
Vanilla extract – 1 tbsp.
Flour – 2 cups

Directions:

Add eggs and sugar into the bowl.
Mix salt, lemon zest, heavy cream, vanilla extract and flour.
Pour the batter into the round baking tray.
Bake at 300 F for 20 minutes in the air fryer.
When ready, serve and enjoy!

Nutrition:

Calories:90
Fat: 4g

Carbohydrates: 10g
Protein: 30g

Black Cherries Dessert

Prep time: 2 minutes
Cooking time: 15 minutes
Servings: 2

Ingredients:

Butter – 2 tbsp.
Milk – 1 cup
Sugar – 2 tbsp.
Vanilla extract – 2 tbsp.
Eggs – 3

Salt – ¼ tbsp.
Flour – 2 cups
Black cherries – 2 cups
Powdered sugar for dusting

Directions:

Add butter and milk into the bowl.
Mix sugar, vanilla extract, eggs, salt and flour.
Pour the batter into the round baking tray.
Bake at 300 F for 15 minutes in the air fryer.
When ready, cover the cake with blueberries and powdered sugar to serve!

Nutrition:

Calories:70
Fat: 6g

Carbohydrates: 10g
Protein: 10g

Cocoa Powder Recipe

Prep time: 3 minutes
Cooking time: 20 minutes
Servings:

Ingredients:

Butter – 1 tbsp.	Cocoa powder – 3
Flour – 1 cup	tbsp.
Eggs – 3	Vanilla extract – 2
Sugar – 2 tbsp.	tbsp.
Brown sugar – 2	Salt – 1 pinch
tbsp.	

Directions:

Add butter and flour into the bowl.
Mix eggs, sugar, brown sugar, cocoa powder, vanilla extract and sugar.
Pour the batter into the round baking tray.
Bake at 300 F for 20 minutes in the air fryer.
When ready, serve and enjoy!

Nutrition:

Calories:70	Carbohydrates: 10g
Fat: 6g	Protein: 10g

Lemon Filled Recipe

Prep time: 2 minutes
Cooking time: 15 minutes
Servings: 3

Ingredients:

Butter – 2 tbsp.	Sugar – 2 tbsp.
Flour – 2 cups	
Filing:	
Sugar – 2 cups	Lemon juice – 3 tbsp.
Flour – S cup	Powdered sugar for
Eggs – 2	dusting

Directions:

Prepare the crust: mix butter, flour and sugar into the bowl.
Pour the mixture into the round baking tray.
Bake at 300 F for 15 minutes in the air fryer.
Prepare the filling: mix sugar, flour, eggs, lemon juice into the bowl.
When the crust is ready, pour the filling by covering the crust.
Dust powdered sugar to serve!

Nutrition:

Calories: 115	Carbohydrates: 9g
Fat: 7g	Protein: 40g

Chocolate Chips with Walnuts

Prep time: 4 minutes
Cooking time: 10 minutes
Servings: 3

Ingredients:

Butter – 2 tbsp.	Vanilla extract – 2
Chocolate chips – 1	tbsp.
lb.	Flour – 2 cups
Chocolate (any,	Baking powder – 2
pieces) – 1 cup	tbsp.
Eggs – 2 cups	Salt – 1 pinch
Coffee granules – 2	Walnuts (chopped) –
tbsp.	1 cup

Directions:

Add butter and eggs into the bowl.
Mix coffee granules, vanilla extract, salt, baking powder and flour with chocolate chips.
Make sure the batter is without lumps.
Pour the batter into the round baking tray.
Bake at 400 F for 10 minutes in the air fryer.
When ready, garnish walnuts and chocolate pieces to serve!

Nutrition:

Calories: 125	Carbohydrates: 10g
Fat: 7g	Protein: 40g

Italian Panetton Cake Recipe

Prep time: 3 minutes
Cooking time: 20 minutes
Servings: 3

Ingredients:

Italian panetton – 1	Vanilla extract – 2
lb.	tbsp.
Butter – 2 tbsp.	Almond extract – 2
Eggs – 2	tbsp.
Half and half – 2	Sugar – 1 cup
cups	Almonds (sliced) – ½
	cup

Directions:

Place Italian panetton into the round baking tray.
Mix butter, eggs, half and half, vanilla extract, almond extract and sugar into the bowl.
Pour the mixture into the baking tray.
Bake at 300 F for 20 minutes in the air fryer.
When ready, serve!

Nutrition:

Calories:70	Carbohydrates: 10g
Fat: 6g	Protein: 10g

White Chocolate Recipe

Prep time: 3 minutes
Cooking time: 15 minutes
Servings: 2

Ingredients:

Butter – 2 tbsp.
Sugar – 1 cup
Vanilla extract – 2 tbsp.
Flour – 2 cups
Salt – 1 pinch
White chocolate (melted) – 2 cups

Directions:

Add butter and sugar into the bowl.
Mix sugar, vanilla extract, salt, flour and white chocolate.
Pour the batter into the round baking tray.
Bake at 300 F for 15 minutes in the air fryer.
When ready, serve and enjoy!

Nutrition:

Calories: 115
Fat: 7g
Carbohydrates: 9g
Protein: 40g

Simple Cake Recipe

Prep time: 2 minutes
Cooking time: 15 minutes
Servings: 2

Ingredients:

Flour (all-purpose) – 1 cup
Baking powder – 1 tbsp.
Salt – 1 pinch
Sugar – 2 cups
Butter – 2 tbsp.
Vanilla extract – 2 tbsp.
Milk – 1 cup

Directions:

Add flour and baking powder into the bowl.
Mix salt, sugar, butter, vanilla extract and milk. Make sure there are no lumps in the batter.
Pour the batter into the round baking tray.
Bake at 300 F for 15 minutes in the air fryer.
When ready, serve and enjoy!

Nutrition:

Calories: 105
Fat: 8g
Carbohydrates: 9g
Protein: 46g

Conclusion

Keep your food well-cooked and your cooking – simple. This air fryer cookbook offers you fast and convenient recipes for your health and enjoyment. What draws us to the air frying is the variety of options it can give to any cook, even the beginner one. An effortless air frying without numerous pots and pans is the simplicity this kitchen appliance provides.

The evenly cooked meat, rich-tasting vegetables, hot and sweet desserts, easy baking – this is what you get when you make this air fryer cookbook your daily choice. Most recipes take not more than 30 minutes to prepare and give you the tastiest meals you will switch to 'must-repeat' ones. Frozen and precooked meals crisp well after the air fryer, but let's be fair – meals, homecooked from scratch, are better!

As you have noticed, air frying is all about simplicity and giving you a chance to cook something deliciously well. Do yourself a favor, switch to air frying from the deep-oil cooking and enjoy your healthy, beneficial, and delicious meals made easily from what you can get in the nearest grocery.

Printed in Great Britain
by Amazon

56822498R00088